THE NEW COMPLETE NEWFOUNDLAND

American, Canadian, Bermudian and Bahaman CH. NEWTON, whelped 11-6-58. Winner of 15 Bests in Show, 55 Group Firsts, 199 Bests of Breed and 8 Specialties. By Topsail's Captain Bob Bartlett ex Merry of Sparry, Newton was bred by the Hon. Harold MacPherson (Westerland Kennels, Canada) and owned by Melvin Sokolsky of New York City. Pictured here with his handler, Alan Levine. — *Photo by Mr. Sokolsky.*

THE NEW COMPLETE
Newfoundland

by

Margaret Booth Chern

Second Edition—Sixth Printing

1981

HOWELL BOOK HOUSE Inc.
230 Park Avenue
New York, N.Y. 10169

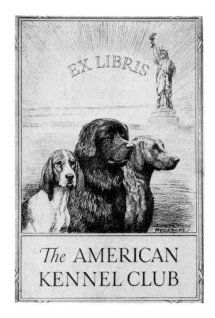

The AMERICAN
KENNEL CLUB

Bookplate of the American Kennel Club library, designed by Edwin Megargee in 1936.

Library of Congress Catalog Card No. 75-18266
ISBN 0-87605-217-0

Printed in U.S.A.

MARGARET BOOTH CHERN

(1905-1975)

Margaret Booth Chern was a person of remarkable capacities.

As a child, she astounded Oregon educators by working out an original solution to a theorem in Euclid geometry that was later incorporated into textbooks. Her aptitude for mathematics enabled her to originate various calculating devices, one of which was patented under the name of "Astro Query". She also held patents for improvements on typewriters.

A graduate of the University of Oregon, she had been an actress in a career that included leading roles on Broadway. When the Great Depression came, she turned to handling publicity for Hollywood stars including Glenda Farrell.

She devoted herself to many public interests. Daughter of an Oregon state senator, and niece of U. S. Senator Robert McNary (who ran as Vice-Presidential nominee with Wendell Willkie) she took to the hustings in the Republican presidential campaign of 1940 and proved herself an excellent and persuasive speaker. And at the end of World War II, when so many of the oppressed in Europe were left homeless, she worked with the Church World Service in underwriting trans-Atlantic passage, and in providing shelter, food, and jobs for over 100 families.

But the interest that was to dominate her life began in 1948 when she and her husband, Vadim, established Little Bear Kennels, dedicated to the preservation of the classic Newfoundland.

The record of Little Bear stands unchallenged in the breed—breeders of over 100 champions, and a successive line of nine generations of Best in Show and/or Group winners.

Mrs. Chern's widespread talents included writing, and she was author of a children's book based on Indian legends, and of many mystery stories and articles on dogs. In 1955, she wrote the first edition of *The Complete Newfoundland.*

The response was most enthusiastic. Jack Baird, writing in the NY World-Telegram and Sun stated: "It is not only the first book on Newfoundlands ever done in the English language, but is probably as fine a book on any breed that has come off the presses." Maxwell Riddle, in the *Cleveland Press*, wrote: "The writer knows her breed as very few do. It glitters with scholarship rarely found in dog books, particularly in those by breeders. She has marshalled her facts very well, and has not done outrage to what is known, as have others. As a result she has done a lot for her breed and as much for Labradors and Flat-Coated Retrievers."

In response to many requests, Mrs. Chern had undertaken preparing a new edition that would keep pace with developments in the breed. In this, as in all her interests in the Newfoundland, she worked in team with her husband. The manuscript was almost finished when Mrs. Chern died in January, 1975, and—with the wish that it stand as a memorial to her—Vadim stepped in and saw the work to completion.

The New Complete Newfoundland includes not only the best of the old but considerably expands its scope. The show story is brought up to date with the recognition of the "Newton" impact and the many important new breeders and dogs that have come upon the scene. The newest American, Canadian and English standards are presented and discussed (Mrs. Chern was a member of the Newfoundland Club of America's standard revision committee). The more than 200 illustrations include some real stunners, and the outstanding dogs of past and present are all here. And along with the show greats, there are stories of Newfs in the public eye including Bobby Kennedy's "Brumis" and the true-life dogs of the heart-warming best seller "To Love With Karen."

We think you'll find it an intriguing book. And together with Vadim, we hope it stands as a fitting testament to the great devotion that Margaret Chern had for the noble Newfoundland.

ELSWORTH S. HOWELL
Publisher

Contents

The Newfoundland—water dog and protector.

"The Lifeguard," from the painting by Edward Megargee.

Introduction

THE NEWFOUNDLAND has the distinction of being America's own dog. In the early days of white settlement in North America, his Homeric courage and loyalty made him a great help and source of much delight to his master. Few ships that sailed the western ocean left port without a Newfoundland pacing the quarter-deck. And as American clipper ships took their cargoes to all ports of the seven seas, America's own dog, the ever-present lifesaver, kept watch over his beloved skipper and the crew. Making landfall, he was the best hand on board for foretelling the proximity of land. Happily he would sniff the air and wag his tail, which would be the signal for sending a man aloft, for sure as the day is light, the shore would soon come into view. Or if misfortune came and his good ship foundered in a treacherous surf, the Newfoundland carried the life line ashore. And as the Yankee sails lay becalmed in the horse latitudes or faced the fury of the roaring forties, the skipper knew that his loved ones back in New England were well guarded by the family Newfoundland.

Thus the Newfoundland became a part of the American scene, a winning hero of countless sea sagas; in fact, his very name became synonymous with all the virtues of man's greatest friend, the dog. Little Johnny, bending over his lesson book in a Philadelphia school house, his fingers still numb from the icy blasts of the winter of 1799, glowed with pride as he read of a great rescue from a watery grave in faraway England by America's own dog, a Newfoundland like his own at home — the one that had guided his first footsteps and taught him to walk.

As the thirteen Colonies grew and the great western push carried the frontiers of the Republic to the very shores of the Pacific, we find Scannon, the ever-faithful Newfoundland, sharing all the hardships and giving every encouragement to the men of the Lewis and Clark expedition.

How the Newfoundland has come down to us from that time — and what manner of dog he has been and is — makes the story we have tried to tell here.

Headstudy of a working Newfoundland of the 1930s, owned by Mr. and Mrs. Hans Scherr-Thoss, of Litchfield, Conn.

The first edition of *The Complete Newfoundland* came into being through the wonderful cooperation of many truly devoted lovers of our noble breed. They contributed generously of their experience, knowledge, and records, and were enthusiastic in their encouragement. Our sincere thanks to them, and to those who have given further pictures, etchings and other Newfoundlandia for this, the second edition.

To the eminent anthropologist, Dr. William G. Haag, we are especially grateful for generous aid and for invaluable data that confirms the true origin of the breed. To Professor A. Heim, of Zurich, Switzerland, we must be always in debt for his scientific and forthright approach to origin and development in his book, *Der Newfundlanderhund.*

Last, we must not forget the innumerable friends of the breed from the dim past whose experiences, recorded in journals, diaries and personal letters, we have drawn upon to bring back to life the great dog of the past and to give evidence that the Newfoundland character transcends the barriers of centuries.

— MARGARET BOOTH CHERN

The beach patrol. Newfoundlands of Mr. and Mrs. Luke Wilson at Cape Cod.

Etching of "The Newfoundland Dog—Original Breed," with Newfoundland coast in background, from Macgilvray's *History of British Quadrupeds* (1790). Note triangular skull, strong level back, well-muscled running gear and scant feathering.

1

The Origin of
The Newfoundland

THE NEWFOUNDLAND, the great dog of the Algonquin and Sioux Indians, takes its name from the island of Newfoundland where the breed first became known to the British settlers. One of the few basic breeds existing today, the Newfoundland was domesticated directly from the wild by the Algonquin Indians. The giant black dog once roamed the central plains in great numbers and was found among the Indian tribes from the Eastern Seaboard to Montana, from the headwaters of Saskatchewan to the Gulf of Mexico.

Early writers on dogs were aware of the fact that the breed was indigenous to North America even though the dog had become vastly reduced on the continent after the introduction of the horse by the Spaniards. According to Professor Otis T. Mason in the *Handbook of American Indians*:

> In pre-Columbian times, the (Newfoundland) dog was the most perfectly subdued animal of the North Americans, as much so as the llamas in West South America . . . Keeping (dogs) for their service . . . for retrieving game or catching fish . . . packing, sledding, hauling travois . . . pets for young and old . . . Among the Algonquinian and Siouan tribes of the great lakes and plains, this animal attained its best as a hunter and beast of burden and traction.
>
> The Querecho (Vaquero Apache) of Coronado in 1500-1502 had a great number of large Indian dogs which they obliged to carry their luggage when they moved from place to place . . . not more than 50 pounds to be borne by one dog, but twice that amount could be moved on a travois. The coming of the horse to the great plains was a boon to the Indian tribes, all of which at once adopted the new instrument of travel and transportation.

Obviously the dog was not a match for the horse with its speed and carrying power. The dog began to disappear, especially in the plains and gradually wherever the horse was practical. Thus, when the British came to the New World they only found the Newfoundland dog on the island of that name and the nearby Continent — rugged land of ice and snow much of the year.

It was many years before the dog's early presence throughout all of the eastern and most of the central parts of what is now the United States and Canada became generally known. The earliest writers on dogs in North America recognized that the breed was indigenous to this country although they only knew of its Newfoundland background. But many later writers even wandered from that fact. Some historians even questioned the dog's very existence until more than fifty years after it had become the principal export from the Island of Newfoundland and an exceedingly popular dog in the colonies.

But, by far, most naturalists are in firm agreement that the Newfoundland is indigenous to the New World. It has taken centuries, however, for the evidence of archaeology, anthropology, biology and ethnological records to reveal the true origin of the breed and the extent of its existence throughout nearly half of North America north of Mexico.

Tookey, in 1805, in the *Cabinet of Quadrupeds,* refers to the Newfoundland as the native of the island of his name. Scott, in his *Sportsman's Repository* (1820), described him as the largest of the arctic breeds, as almost amphibious — "no other of the canine race being able to endure the water so long, or swim with so great facility" — and "the most useful of the whole canine race as far as hitherto known upon the face of the earth." As far back as any living man could recall, he states, Newfoundlands were brought from the island to England and the Continent, and most probably the first Newfoundlands were brought to England soon after the first discovery of the island by Englishmen "from Newfoundland, to which and to the neighbouring Continent, they are indigenous."

Early naturalists, F. Cuvier and Desmarest, also claimed the breed to be of American origin. They divided all dogs into three basic categories, namely, *Matins, Spaniels,* and *Dogues,* plus a fourth group, the mongrels or dogs of the street. Among the Spaniels of American origin we find the Alpine Spaniel (St. Bernard) and the Newfoundland Dog. Also under this general classification, the "Shepherd Dog, the Esquimaux Dog, and the Wolf Dog." Spaniels are described as "dogs having the head very moderately elongated; the parietal bones do not approach each other above the temples but diverge and swell out so as to enlarge the forehead and cerebral cavity."

The original interpretation of the Spaniel classification differs widely from the popular concept. Later writers, including William Youatt (c. 1846), classify the Newfoundland as a Spaniel, with the correct interpretation in mind. As the term Spaniel became clouded in the minds of some and drifted into the concept of Spanish origin, casual writers on the breed became confused. Undoubtedly, the theory of Pyrenean origin of the Newfoundland stems from such misconception. It is significant that Youatt flatly states that he is a "native of the island of which he bears the name." The same view is held by Pardon (1857), Wood (1865), Huntington (1901) and many others.

The protagonists of the European origin theory of our noble breed go to great length to prove their point. A curious example is found in Angelo Vecchio's *Il Cane*: "The breed was brought to the island of Newfoundland by the Norwegian fishermen in about 1820," he solemnly states. 1820! Years after the breed had already become the most popular in North America!

Other efforts to prove that the Newfoundland is not indigenous to North America are equally questionable. Such evidence as lack of mention of the Newfoundland by Whitbourne, an early explorer, is cited as proof that the dog did not exist. Curiously enough, Whitbourne writes that the "*wolves and beasts*" of the country visited his fish flakes where he was busily engaged curing fish. These beasts made great commotion "so that at each time my mastiffe-dogge went unto them (as the like in that country hath not been seen) the one began to fawn and play with the other, and so went together into the woods, and continued with them, every of these times, nine or ten days, and did return unto us without any hurt."

Anyone acquainted with the inborn animosity that exists between the dog, especially the "mastiffe-dogge," and the wolf must either dismiss the story as imaginary or examine it in an entirely different light.

It is significant that the Captain enumerated both *wolves* and *beasts*. Evidently he was not too sure in his own mind as to the exact nature of the quadrupeds that came to *play and gambol* with his Mastiffs. If we study the earliest drawings of the Newfoundland or the Great Labrador, it is not difficult to see how either could be taken for a wolf, especially from a distance.

The Black Wolf and the Newfoundland

The Black Wolf of America was once thought by some naturalists to be only a variety of the common wolf, but is now considered to be a distinct species, according to J. G. Wood in his *Illustrated Natural History* (1865). John Godman, M.D., had made the same claim earlier in his *American Natural History* (1836). Godman also referred to the earlier naturalist, Desmarest, as asserting that the North American Black Wolf was a new species.

In very early times the Black Wolf was most common in the great plains where the Newfoundland Dog was also most plentiful until the Spanish horse eased him out.

The early nineteenth century explorer, Mr. Say, wrote in *Long's Expedition to the Rocky Mountains* of the domesticability of the Black Wolf.

Whether or not the American Black Wolf was the immediate ancestor of the big black Algonquin dog now known as the Newfoundland, is somewhat open to conjecture. But is interesting to note what A. Pocock wrote on *Ancestors of the Dog* in the *Kennel Encyclopedia* (1907). "The Indians of Florida had a large Black Dog which only differed from the Wolves of that country in barking." This is an interesting difference to be observed inasmuch as a tamed wolf will learn to bark. Wolves in packs sing. So do Newfoundland dogs.

Mr. Pocock further states: "Since these American dogs were the property of uncivilized Indians, presumably without other breeds of dogs, it does not appear to be in the least likely that their resemblance to wolves can be assigned to anything but the fact of their being in reality tamed and slightly modified animals of that kind."

An interesting statement was made by the early nineteenth century British historian, MacGregor, who observed the Newfoundland in his natural wild state: "A Newfoundland Dog will, if properly domesticated and trained, defend his master, growl when another person speaks roughly to him and in no instance of danger leave him. This animal in a wild state hunts in packs, and is then ferocious, and in its habits similar to the wolf."

No creature is more susceptible to affection than the wolf, if captured while young and treated right. It will follow its master like a dog, obey orders readily, recognize him after a long absence, and in general conduct itself better than most domesticated dogs.

Many instances of this tamable disposition are well known. A kennel woman we once had working for us when our kennels were in Vermont showed me many photographs of herself with her wolf pets, which she had had in Yugoslavia. F. Cuvier, the naturalist, once had a tamed wolf that recognized him after an absence of three years.

Drawn by T. Landseer

The American Black Wolf appears to have been the most logical ancestor of the dog domesticated by the American Indians. According to early naturalists, its emotional makeup and behavior patterns were very similar to those of the Newfoundland. The American Black Wolf had the classical white spot in the center of its chest; prior to purebred registration, three white hairs on the chest of a black dog were looked for as proof of pure breeding.

A Mr. Grieff, a Norwegian, reared a pair of wolves. The female became especially tame, affectionate with him, licked his hands and would come when called. The male, although friendly with others, never forgave him for whipping him when he had seized a hen.

The Reverend Thomas Pearce, who under pseudonym of "Idestone" was author of *The Dog* (circa 1876), wrote of a Newfoundland he once owned. On one occasion, while playing, the dog was amusing himself with long-drawn-out howls and would not stop howling though ordered to do so by his master. At last, out of patience, Reverend Pearce took out his whip and calling his servant, said, "Give that dog a moderate thrashing!" The order was carried out and the Newfoundland hated the Reverend from that hour, though he never resented the servant who had whipped him. He became indifferent to his master and careless of his orders, though well-broken as a retriever and adept in recovering wounded game.

When tamed wolves and dogs are brought together, contrary to their age-old hatred in the wild, they develop a mutual attachment. The known cross-breeding of a wolf and a large Indian dog produced a half-breed animal more powerful and of greater courage than either parent. It pulled a sledge and was generally useful. On one occasion the half-breed animal saved the life of its master, a Mr. Palliser. On a hunting trip, Mr. Palliser was caught in sudden, sub-zero weather. With its long, warm fur, the wolf-dog lay close to his owner through the night and saved him from freezing to death.

The gestation period of the wolf is identical to that of the dog. Doctor Godman writes: "Between the dog and wolf there are striking external differences, yet they actually constitute but one *natural* group, of which the individuals should be regarded as *varieties* rather than *species*, because they may all be indiscriminately bred together, in such a manner as to result in new and prolific races, bearing but slight resemblance to the parent individuals, and exhibiting new modifications of external characters, of mental qualities, and of internal configuration."

Further, Godman is specific about frequent breeding between the Newfoundland dog and the wolf. And he finds strong resemblance between the large Indian dog, the Esquimaux dog and the wolf.

Professor Barton, of the late 17th century, held the opinion that the domesticated dog of the Indians more closely resembled the wolf than any other animal.

When one considers the unique character of the Newfoundland, it is interesting to note that Doctor Godman found that the Indians treated their big dogs better than many Europeans treated their children.

The entente that the Indians had not only with their dogs but also with the wolves, is mentioned by the early explorer, Hearne, in his *Journey to the Northern Ocean:* "Frequently the Indians take young wolves from their dens and play with them. They never hurt the young wolves, but always returned them to their dens. Sometimes they painted the faces of the young whelps with vermilion or red ochre.''

The difference in color of the American Black Wolf and other wolves is not the only difference. Also noted: position of eye, coat type and greater domesticability. The only divergence from pure, all black in the American Black Wolf was that the females had a white spot on the chest.

If the American Black Wolf is an ancestor of the Newfoundland Dog, it is to be noted that the white spot on the chest is no longer a sex-linked genetic factor. The white spot on the chest of an otherwise all black Newfoundland, today, is as frequent on the male as on the female. This white spot is considered quite characteristic of the Newfoundland.

The American Black Wolf is now extinct.

In *The Sportsman's Repository* (1820), Scott says that he thinks it even possible for the wolf and bear to have joined in contributing to the ancestry of the Newfoundland.

Probably the earliest reference to the breed as a *Newfoundland Dog* was made by Captain George Cartwright, in whose diary we find an entry under date of January 29, 1771, with an account of a faithful Newfoundland bitch. Before that date the dog had been known as the Bear Dog.

In 1732, ''A Person of Quality'' in his *Appendix on Dogs* writes: ''The Bear Dog is of a very large size commonly, sluggish in his looks but he is very watchful, he comes from *Newfoundland*, his Business is to guard a Court or House, and has a thundering Voice when Strangers come near him, and does well to turn a Water Wheel.''

The Indians and the Newfoundland

Another supposed substantiation to the theory of nonexistence of the Newfoundlands among the Indians is the bulkiness of the breed and its apparent inability to travel with an Indian in his canoe (although much of the bulkiness is latter-day development). The fact of the matter is that the dog did not travel in the Indian's canoe but customarily kept pace with him along the river banks. My husband, Vadim, who sailed on the Coast of Labrador when a very young man, came in close contact with the Indians. He tells me of having witnessed this very practice of the Indians and their dogs.

W. C. L. Martin in his *History of the Dog* states that the Newfoundland is not, in his opinion, an aboriginal of that island or of Labrador.

He considers it to be of European extraction, perhaps modified by a cross with an Eskimo or other American dog. Martin is the earliest authority to put forth the Viking theory of the dog's origin. He states:

> It is now well proven that Newfoundland was discovered by the Vikings in the year 1000 and that during the tenth and eleventh centuries Norsemen discovered and visited parts of North America. In 1497, Newfoundland was rediscovered by John Cabot. As early as 1500 the fisheries were operated by French, Portuguese, Basque, and other people. It is perhaps to the European settlers of the sixteenth and seventeenth centuries that the introduction of the original stock of the Newfoundland dog is owing, unless indeed we may venture to assign it to the Norsemen. Norwegian peasants possess at the present time (1845) dogs closely resembling the Newfoundland which they arm with collars set with iron spikes as means of protection against the wolves which attack and endeavor to seize them by the throat. It is remarkable that the bear usually retreats before these dogs.

One of the logical arguments against the post-Cabot European origin of the dog appears to be the short span of time between rediscovery of the island by John Cabot in 1497 and the presence both in England and the Colonies of the Newfoundland dog possessing all of his distinct characteristics.

Professor Heim lends authoritative and almost conclusive support to the indigenous claim. In reply to questions as to whence comes the black and brown Newfoundland, and were its ancestors brought from Europe to Newfoundland only after 1622, he answers that the old French butcher dog and old black Scotch shepherd dog, the Spanish alan and mastin, the Pyrenean dogs and Irish water dogs were brought to Newfoundland since 1500, and by bastardizing could theoretically have had a part in the development of the black and brown Newfoundland dogs, "None of these importations, however, could be proved," states Heim. "They were all surmised under a shade of possibility. These stories were believed and by doing so, *a biological impossibility was created.* One was of the opinion that the ancestors of *all* Newfoundland dogs were of European ancestry *solely* because Cabot *does not mention any native dogs.* But in spite of many variations, the black Newfoundland dog is physically, as well as psychologically, of a distinct type. Whether we take him from Newfoundland or from Canadian, German, Swiss or English pure stock, with or without blood addition, he always breaks through *with the very same type* which prevailed throughout with the native island dogs. Out of a constantly changing bastardizing mixture without any consequential breeding choice, as was the case here — and all this in only 200 years — *no such distinct type could have been created. There must be a definite ancient racial strain in our dogs.*

22

"The ever repeating *symmetrical* marking of the black dogs, and at times of dogs of other color as far as they originated from the black dogs, proves to us that these dogs could not be the result of bastardizing, as bastardizing of differently colored dogs always results in irregular spotting."

An adventurous Scotch explorer, Mr. Cormack, credited with being the first white man to cross the island from east to west (in 1822), upon reaching the interior of the island — in the vicinity of Indians' Crooked Lake, gives this pertinent account in his diary on the subject of Indians and their evident dependence upon the services of the Newfoundland dog: "The approach from the landing-place was by a mossy carpeted avenue, formed by the trees having been cut down in that direction for firewood. The sight of a fire not of our own kindling, of which we were to partake, seemed hospitality. It was occupied by his (the Indian's) wife, seated on a deer-skin, busy sewing together skins of the same kind to renew the outside of the canoe which we had found required it. A large Newfoundland dog, her only companion in her husband's absence, had welcomed us at the landing-place with signs of the greatest joy."

The Newfoundland was the only dog with these particular natives and, incidentally, this half-Micmac, half-Mountaineer Indian family was the only one Mr. Cormack came upon during his entire crossing of the interior. We can note with satisfaction that the larder was remarkably well stocked with five fat deer, beavers, and other delicacies of the forest, which speaks well for the Newfoundland as a hunting dog.

During his visits in the summer of 1932 with the Nascopie Indians in Labrador, my husband noted a close resemblance between the dogs of the Indians and our earliest known prints of the Newfoundland dogs. According to the lore of the Nascopies, these dogs had always been used for hunting on the frequent journeys of the tribe between Unguava Bay and the Coast of Labrador, their migratory custom since long before the coming of the white man. The Beothics, the Red Indians, the aborigines of the island, had a dog which early explorers noted and which bore even a stronger resemblance to the Newfoundland of today.

An argument used frequently against the Newfoundland being of American origin is that it is too majestic, intelligent, and beautiful a creature to have been bred by a savage. Inasmuch as the European, during two centuries of known close association with the breed, has in no way improved its original intelligence and benevolent instincts, and since no dog with greater capacity for sagacity and compassion has been bred on the Continent or in England, it is illogical to suppose the Newfoundland had to come from overseas.

The independent spirit of the dog, his ability to show initiative, plus other singular characteristics pertinent to this breed, and this breed alone, would indicate that a close partnership existed between the native dogs and the aborigines of the country. Uniting their strength and resources, they toiled together, wresting their living from a rocky and severe land where only a total effort on the part of both man and beast from the bravest and best could insure preservation of the species.

It was the white settler of the island who, having destroyed his Indian host, took over the dogs, and as Youatt aptly describes: "The carts used in the winter work are drawn by Newfoundlands, who are almost invariably urged and goaded on beyond their strength, fed only with putrid salt-fish, and an inadequate quantity even of that. A great many of them are worn out and die before the winter is over; and when the summer approaches, and the fishing season commences, many of them are quite abandoned, and uniting with their companions, prowl about preying on the neighboring flocks, or absolutely starving." How can anyone assume that a dog's life with the white man must always be superior to that with the Indian?

The Greenland Dog and the Newfoundland

Scott, writing in 1820 and quoting earlier sources, refers to the difficulties in differentiating between the Newfoundland and the Greenland dog, which at that time displayed greater physical similarity:

On discrimination between the two races, a Medical Gentleman, long resident on one of our Settlements in Hudson's Bay, offers the following remarks: "The Dog from Newfoundland may have reached the Arctic Regions, and vice versa — but the Arctic Dog is made truss and deep; the original one of Newfoundland loose and lengthy. The former has pricked ears, bushy tail, and deep russet coat, and without any extra cause of animation, looks always ready for a start. The latter has a fine lopped ear, and a very full tail, which, when erect and doubling over his back, boasts the richness of the most luxuriant Ostrich feathers. His colour is dingy black, or black and white, seldom russet, never liver-coloured; moreover, when not in action, the Newfoundland Dog is the most sleepy and most lazy of the canine species."

The two breeds agree generally, in regard to qualities, with some exceptions. Like the Bull Dog, they seldom or never bark, their vociferation being rather snarling and howling. On this point, the Rev. Mr. Asnach in his *History of Newfoundland*, has the following observations: "The Newfoundland Dog seldom barks, and only when strongly provoked; it then appears like an unnatural and painful exertion, which produces a noise between barking and howling, still strictly corresponding to the sounds expressed by the familiar words *bow wow;* and here he stops, unless it ends in a howl."

The Greenland Dog, identified by many naturalists as an early contributor to the ancestry of the Newfoundland.

The difference in coat color is really nonexistent. Greenland dogs, with black as well as white coats, were noted by Buffon as early as 1749. Bronze or rusty brown was once prevalent among Newfoundlands and exists to this day. The major physical difference appears to be between the pricked ear and the pendant ear of the present-day Newfoundland. However, in studying the early prints, we find that an 1800 engraving in Edward's *Cynographia Britannica* shows two Newfoundlands in which one had definitely pricked ears and a tail characteristic of the Greenland dog. This is the closest to the transitional type of any picture we know to be extant. Respected for his accuracy, Bewik, somewhat earlier, depicts the Newfoundland he knew as having a very small semi-pendant ear, which under stimulus of excitement could actually be pricked.

A very early drawing of an Esquimaux dog reappears in *Scott's Repository*, with the Greenland mountains backgrounded in, as the Greenland dog. Naturally, in that country, the dog belonged to the Eskimos. Hence, we can use the names interchangeably.

Godman describes the Esquimaux/Greenland dog as about equal to the Newfoundland in size, "but the nose (of the Newfoundland) is broad like that of the Mastiff. Both in the winter and summer the hair (of both Newfoundland and Esquimaux dogs) is very long, but there is a soft down undercovering in cold weather, which is not found in the warm season."

The Newfoundland was more thoroughly domesticated by his Indian masters than the Greenland dog, reflecting the Indian attitude of veneration and affection for the former as a hunting companion, whereas the lot of the Greenland relative was that of a beast of burden only.

Archaeological Tracings

Capping all of the above evidence of the Indian origin of the breed are the cold facts of archaeology. Note, too, that the date of *the domestication of the great Indian dog is placed one to two thousand years prior to the Vikings' visit to the Western Hemisphere.*

G. M. Allen, in his classic paper published in 1920, on the subject of prehistoric dogs but particularly on American dogs at the time of the advent of the white man, recognizes seventeen aboriginal types. One is Eskimo; eleven varieties are of the large Indian Dog; and five are varieties of the small Indian Dog. We can sum up his findings by dividing all dogs of the Northern Hemisphere into three major types:

(1) Eskimo
(2) Large Indian Dog
(3) Small Indian Dog

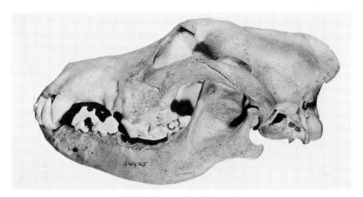

Skull of Greenland Dog.

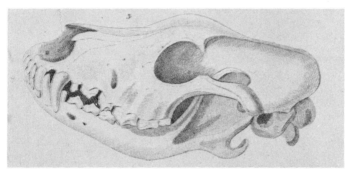

Skull of Newfoundland.—From *History of British Quadrupeds*.

Osteometric study of the aboriginal dog's remains is perhaps the most rewarding avenue into the past. Its cold and painstaking evaluations uphold the great arctic breed theory of the early naturalists and do much toward establishing the axioms of development.

Domestication of the dog in North America occurred about 1000-500 B.C. It is from the Archaic Period that dogs' remains are first found. Dogs were often placed in the graves with humans in the Archaic sites in New York, as well as in Alabama and Kentucky shell heaps.

This practice seemed to cease during the Woodland Period in Eastern North America, which started about 500 A. D. and marked the introduction of agriculture among the Indians. It is interesting to note that the skeletal remains of dogs are the earliest of domestic animals found with human remains. No cattle, sheep, or goats reached America in any numbers before 1492.

In arctic areas and among the Indians of the plains, dogs have always been the major source of transportation. Sledges were dog drawn, and we have evidence of the use of a dog sledge in 6000 B. C.

Osteometric measurements of the Alaskan, Siberian, and Greenland dogs indicate a great similarity. We must bear in mind, however, that the Siberian dog was much larger prior to its displacement by reindeer some five hundred years ago. The American dogs, however, demonstrated progressive increase in size; in fact, the date of a given archaeological site can often be determined by the size, small or large, of dog remains.

A comparative study of the cranial development of the Greenland dog with that of an 1800 Newfoundland is provided for by the illustrations on pages accompanying this text.

We may also refer to comparative anatomy for additional evidence in establishing the origin of our breed. Bewick, in 1779, in describing the Newfoundland, refers to him as being web-footed. We believe it to be the earliest recorded reference to the web-foot of the Newfoundland. Webbing between toes is a basic characteristic of our breed and other water dogs, most of which can be easily traced to a Newfoundland ancestor. Prior to the appearance of the Newfoundland in Europe, webbed feet are not recorded among other breeds. Introduction of Newfoundland genes into numerous European breeds produced a modified webbed foot in many.

Naturally, webbing is a relative matter except that the Newfoundland breed possesses it in its most extreme form. In fact, the Newfoundland is the only breed in which the fetus shows webbing as soon as the foot is formed. Other relatively web-footed breeds do not develop this characteristic until much later — in many breeds webbing is not developed until after birth. Students of biology will understand the sig-

28

nificance of such development in the fetus determining the antiquity of the Newfoundland breed.

Haag states that among the very few remains of larger aboriginal dogs in America found intact, "brindled blackish-brown coat" was characteristic. As we know, the dead coat on a living black Newfoundland turns rusty brown through dehydration. Therefore, the blackish-brown of the aboriginal we can assume to have been black on the living dog. The brindled black coat of the large Indian dog is not unlike the coat of the earliest Newfoundland recorded, which according to Harvey, was black with gray ticking and gray muzzle.

Haag expresses the strong belief that the aboriginal Greenland dog was a close ancestor or relative of the Newfoundland. Add to this that the Greenland dog either descended from, or from the same source, as the wolf. Then too, there is the American Black Wolf which must be given strong consideration as a direct contributor.

Certainly on the basis of osteometric analysis of aboriginal dogs, the supporting evidence of earliest authorities, explorers' findings including the Spaniards, as well as the ethnological records and biological observations, it is obvious that the Newfoundland is indigenous to the eastern and central parts of this continent. The only possible question is if, when and how much the Greenland/Esquimaux and the American Black Wolf contributed.

One fact is undeniable: *The Newfoundland is the American Indian's dog, a truly basic breed.*

Newfoundlands of the transitional period. At left, with semi-pendant ear—(from Cope's *Natural History*). At right, from a German print about 1800.

Transitional type Newfoundlands of the 18th century, as depicted in Sydenham Edwards' *Cynographia Brittanica* (1800). The original presentation in color shows that some of the transitional dogs carried the factor for yellow. Note the pricked ears and tail characteristic of the Greenland dog.

2

Development of
The Breed

THE FIRST MASTERS of the great dog, later to be known as the Newfoundland, were the Algonquin Indians, and later the Sioux. They developed the dog into the most versatile and useful of all breeds. Through long and close association, almost like that of a big brother, the Indians transmitted many of their unusual virtues to their dog. Among the tribesmen, clans were usually known by the name of an animal. If the family was named for the beaver, they emulated the industry and engineering skill of the beaver. If an eagle was the clan motif, pride, dignity and strength were their ideal.

With this innate respect for the virtues of the animals, their appreciation of the Newfoundland was profound. A Newfoundland tops one of their totem poles and he is referred to in legends as the gift of the gods.

Likewise, the great dog imitated the Algonquins. Their courage is formidable and their refusal to show that they feel pain, unique. Dignity is fixed and should always be honored. Sensitivity is of the highest. These characteristics and much more, the Newfoundland absorbed from the Indians.

The dog shared with the Indians and took over their portion of the work. When camp was to be moved for their nomadic masters, the dogs carried packs or pulled a loaded travois — a kind of sledge the Indians made with two tepee poles fastened onto the dog with a deerskin harness, over which was slung a deerskin tepee, like a hammock. On these travois all of the Indian supplies, cooking pots and gear were carried. Sometimes an old person or a child was carried on it. When a Newfoundland matron had young ones, the travois was covered with a round-topped cage woven with willow rods to protect them from the weather, and the puppies then became her complete load.

Retrieving game, diving for fish and care of children and the very old were responsibilities the dogs carried out enthusiastically and dependably for the Indians.

Thus the Indians developed a dog of greatest endurance, usefulness and versatility. Beauty came from a coordinated, muscular body, combined with dependability and eagerness to cooperate.

When the large Indian dogs joined the families of the early British settlers, it was for their usefulness that they were chosen and respected. No fads or fancy went into their breeding. They worked for their new masters as they had for the Indians, plus taking the job of lookout on board ship and as a rescuer for man-over-board or children ashore.

Necessity and the never ceasing battle with merciless elements shaped the breeding pattern for this resourceful helper of his hard-pressed masters. Functionability was his touchstone. A sturdy creature of grace and poise resulted.

Varieties of the Newfoundland

Before we begin to trace the development of the Newfoundland, let us consider the original varieties within the breed — each later to follow somewhat different paths and yet to mingle. First and foremost was the Newfoundland, also known as the Newfoundlander or the Great Newfoundland — a large, powerfully framed dog, straight-coated, black, brown, black and tan, or black-ticked. He was often referred to as the true breed. Then there was the Great Labrador, another very large variety, sometimes larger than the Newfoundland but with a more loosely knit frame, and either wavy or curly-coated, with considerable white. Also, there was the Lesser Newfoundland, or St. John's Newfoundland, a smaller, compact, well-built, relatively short-haired edition of the Great Newfoundland. And finally, the curly-coated type of the Lesser Newfoundland. All four of these showed the same great aquatic prowess, remarkable intelligence, and amenability to domestication.

The original Great Newfoundland Dog possessed all the admirable qualities which we esteem so much today. His change has been only superficial. In studying the earliest available records, we find him to be a formidable specimen with well-developed chest, strong neck, and very muscular shoulders. His forearms, though well-boned, lacked the feathers which we admire today but made up for the absence with rippling muscles. Magnificent pantaloons he did not sport. The head carriage has definitely undergone the most drastic change and one may venture to say that from the beginning of the nineteenth century up to

"Newfoundland Dog and Fox," etched from a drawing by Sir Abram Cooper, 1815. The dog represents the "long and lanky" type sometimes found in iron statues cast in that period.

Reinagle study of a Newfoundland of the 18th century, showing characteristic prominent super-orbital development of the skull, lean hard-muscled body, excellent reach and a typical cat's foot.—From Scott's *Sportsman's Repository*.

Left, statue in front of firehouse at Lafayette, Indiana, cast in 1800s, of short-bodied, curly-coated Newfoundland with "skunky" markings. Note differences of head with that of iron-casting at right, which dates from mid-1800s.

Iron-casting, now at Williamstown, Mass., of long-bodied Newfoundland of mid-1800s.

our present day, head carriage seems to date a dog as much as the formation of the head itself. Actually, it is the lengthening of the neck which is responsible for the elegant head carriage of the modern winning Newfoundland.

The early drawings of the breed distinctly follow the classic Spaniel pattern as delineated in the previous chapter of this book. The stop is almost imperceptible. The muzzle is elongated, the occiput bone development — though noticeable — is not paramount, and a flatness of dome is apparent. The body impresses the observer with the power of steely muscles sufficiently covered with dense coat yet short enough to be serviceable in the arctic snows. It appears that density rather than length was the distinctive characteristic of the dog's coat. Rather than the length of muzzle being decidedly different, it is the depth of the chop which differentiates the early dog from his modern progeny. The parietal bones seemed to diverge so as to enlarge the forehead and cerebral cavity to a greater degree than often found in the modern Newfoundland.

His ears, again following the classic Spaniel pattern, were somewhat pendulous. The straight top line and well sprung ribs in the Newfoundland of the past are very impressive; likewise, the well-bent stifle and strong pastern. As to depth of the chest, it does not appear to have been as deeply developed as it is now. However, individual dogs vary, and of course one must allow for the longer coat today which sometimes may conceal a shallow chest. Factual, naturalistic drawings depict the Newfoundland without any trace of dewclaws. The strenuous duties required of the dog in the rocky, mountainous, sea-girted terrain of the native island necessitated strong, well-developed legs, rather longer in proportion to depth of body than we find them at present. As one can readily see, it would be very difficult for a short-legged dog to ascend a slippery rock, washed by a powerful surf, or, on the other hand, to jump from a precipice far enough into the surf below to gain safe distance from the turbulence of wash around the rocks. The tail placement was as low as it is today, but its carriage has changed. It seems to have been customary for an early dog to carry his beautiful tail curled gracefully over his back in the manner of his Eskimo cousin. Gradually we see its carriage dropping until finally the gay tail was outlawed by the British Kennel Club in 1884. The general proportion of length and height, as among the best now, tended to be the same from shoulder to ground as from shoulder to base of tail, only there was an illusion of greater length in the earliest dogs which was the result of their having shallower bodies.

The *History of Quadrupeds* (1790) gives us dimensions of a Newfoundland that was considered to be a true and good specimen of the time. Overall body length from nose to end of tail was 6 feet, 2 inches; from one forefoot right over the shoulder to the other: 5 feet, 7 inches; girth behind the shoulder: 3 feet, 2 inches; around its head, over its ears: 2 feet; around the upper part of its foreleg: 9 ½ inches. Additional data on this Newfoundland includes mention of his webbed feet, swimming agility, love for raw trout — for which he usually fished on his own — as well as for little capelin, to which he helped himself right out of the nets.

Three Newfoundlands, approximately fitting the foregoing description, yoked together to a sledge were capable of drawing a load of 300 pounds for several miles with the greatest of ease. Any well-developed, mature Newfoundland of today can readily do as well. The remarkable thing, however, about the Newfoundlands of old was that they were capable of attending to their hauling duties without a driver in attendance. The order was given and the dogs carried out their tasks without further ado.

In discussing the Newfoundland and its development in England, where it underwent what might be termed scientific breeding, we cannot lose track of the fact that the English public in general was large-dog minded. Several authorities made significant statements that the demand in England for size in the Newfoundland was so great that dogs were exported to Nova Scotia from Newfoundland, bred up in size, and then shipped to the mother country.

The extraordinary intelligence and character of the Newfoundland had captivated the English public to the extent that the general demand for the breed was far in excess of the supply of dogs being brought from America, although nearly every ship from there docking at Pool quay, then the chief seat of the Newfoundland trade, brought a generous cargo of these glamorous lifesavers. In the effort to supply the demand, many instances are reported of matings with the large, black Mastiff then common in England. From the Mastiff genes can be traced the deeper muzzle with the pendulous upper lip, so prized today. Fortunately, however, these crossings were not repeated enough to affect the general character of the breed.

It may be worthwhile to know that the dogs that landed in England were truly multicolored and at that point had every color except gray on record; even a fine, purebred yellow Newfoundland is reported to have landed there. From this point on, a great deal of selective breeding occurred. It was very much a matter of fashion to improve on imported dogs once they reached England. It was assumed that it would be easier for a larger dog to perform as a lifesaver. The English likewise felt that a large dog by sheer weight of his body would make a better guard for the home. Last, but not least, they felt that size was very impressive.

An 1843 print depicting Newfoundland of elegance and power, with skull typical of that specified for the breed in the first breed standards composed by "Stonehenge" (Dr. J. H. Walsh), with ears square to top of skull. Note powerful back and beautiful angulation.

Parian ware reproduction of a Newfoundland, epitomizing the "Stonehenge" type. The accented super-orbital development of the skull gave the illusion of a stop. Curly coats were the "thermal wear" that provided insulation for dogs who swam in cold waters.

A great deal of thought has been given to such details as the neck, and we find that the English breeders favored a neck of fair length, holding that coupled with a great development of muscles, a longer neck would enable the dog to keep the object he was bringing ashore well out of water. Muzzle, too, was deemed to be best when neither too long nor too short, with mouth large and capacious, the bite level, giving the Newfoundland a facility to grasp and retain anything that was floating which he wanted to retrieve.

It is therefore safe to assume that what had been a pure breeding, protected by the geography of the home island, and well inbred basic stock, now entered on a wide arena of competitive living with other breeds. There were pitfalls and advantages in this situation. In an effort to create a showier dog, there was the ever-present danger of too much mingling with genes of other breeds. The basic stock, however, must have been sufficiently prepotent to stand all of this experimentation. For by accident or design, splendid specimens were evolved which combined all the stalwart virtues of the American dog with the elegance and grandeur of an English dandy.

Before us is a splendid example of this breeding, year 1840, caption, *Newfoundland Dog, Canis Familiaris, Var.* With his symmetrical white stockings and skunky head stripes as well as tip of tail, he could be a flashy winner today. For although rare, such markings are not disallowed in the breed standard.

Newfoundland Color

Sporting Magazine of 1819 reports that between the years of 1690 and 1798, the Newfoundlands in England, as a rule, were rough-coated, curly-haired, liver and white dogs. Prior to that, a large black and white shaggy or thick-coated dog was in favor, whereas a black dog was scarcely ever seen. Later, however, the trend was reversed. Whether it was a desire to go back to the original color of the breed, whether it was by chance, or perhaps the dominant black pressed for its inevitable victory in the battle of the coat colors — whatever the cause, this black trend continued strong both in England and on the Island of Newfoundland.

In fact, so strong was the trend that only the advent of Sir Edwin Landseer, the famous artist, saved the non-black Newfoundland from extinction. As a boy, Landseer had had a large black and white dog named Foam, and he lovingly blended his remembrance of him into his paintings of the Newfoundland.

Queen Victoria had acquired a large black and white Newfoundland and painted him under tutelage of Sir Edwin. With his talent and Her

"A Distinguished Member of the Humane Society" by Sir Edwin Henry Landseer (1802–1873). Sir Edwin's masterpieces were responsible for the rebirth in popularity of the variety that bears his name.

"Saved" by Sir Edwin Landseer.

Majesty's patronage, his paintings of giant white dogs with black markings became the overnight rage. Many Newfoundlands of the time, described by their owners as totally black, were painted by Landseer with artistic license as white and black. The variety, later to be called by the name of the painter, rather than being excluded from the ranks of the purebreds by the Newfoundland Club (England), suddenly came into favor with Newfoundland people in that country and was proudly accepted along with the blacks. On the island of Newfoundland, however, the preference has strongly been, and still is, for the all black dog.

In connection with the question of color in relation to the true breed, Hamilton, who has the distinction of having visited the island and is credited with being a capable observer, wrote on the breed in the *Naturalists' Library* (1840), describing the true Newfoundland as being black and tan. This he flatly calls the true old type and characterizes all others as crossbred dogs. Between the time of the publishing of his work and the year 1860, the tan markings were almost entirely bred out and the pure black (occasionally rusty black) became the prevailing color. Today the American Kennel Club standard does not allow black and tan.

In 1867, Stonehenge wrote that the purest specimens are of pure black color with the gloss on their coats so intense that it reflects light like a mirror. In the same vein, "Interloper," in a letter of July 10, 1869, which appears in the publication *Field*, states that dogs in Newfoundland are 24 inches in height and the purebreds are all black, and dogs with white (other than a few hairs on the chest) are considered impure. Further, in a letter of June 12th, appearing in the same publication, it is stated that no Newfoundland other than black is a true Newfoundland; also, the writer offers a twenty pound reward to anyone who can point out to him three Newfoundlands on the whole island taller than 25 inches at the shoulder.

Watson (1906), in noting this phenomenon, recognizes the nature of the native island as being an undeveloped land where dogs are not bred for points but are obliged to earn their living and mate as they like, hence this change from parti-color to solid black is of nature's own doing.

Youatt, in describing the varieties of Newfoundland, says: "The Large Labrador is a more loosely framed animal." Actually, Stonehenge, in his three successive editions of his book on the dog, illustrates the common confusion regarding the breed in the nineteenth century. In the first edition he does not even mention the black Newfoundland but divides the breed into two classes, the Large Newfoundland and the Lesser Labrador or Newfoundland, illustrating the former with a drawing. The same drawing is used in the succeeding editions, but in

Tibetan Mastiffs with characteristic fine bone, apple head, prominent eyes, abrupt stop, short muzzle and gay tail. The Tibetan Mastiff was used in England for an outcross—primarily to achieve massive head and giant size in the Newfoundland.

An 1886 illustration of participants in a dog show. The Landseer Newfoundland shown has a typical old-fashioned head, later modified by Tibetan outcrosses. Interestingly, a Tibetan dog is strategically placed to the right of the Newfoundland as if to provide visual comparison and to emphasize the ascendancy of its type.

the second edition it is titled "Large Labrador," and ultimately, in the third edition, the "Landseer." By this time he is speaking of the black Newfoundland as the true Newfoundland, and deplores the unsound tendencies in the Landseer.

Vero Shaw, an authority of the same period, illuminates further the question of parti-colored Newfoundlands. Although he considers them to be sprung from the true breed, he supports the native Newfoundland opinion in saying: "It is certainly true that in the island of Newfoundland itself many black-and-white dogs are to be found, but they apparently have no stronger claims to be considered pure Newfoundlands than any large-sized mongrel in this country has to be styled a Mastiff. Admirers of the black and white dog endeavour to believe that the colour of a Newfoundland is immaterial, and hence that their favourites are of the same variety as the black, but in doing so they neglect to notice several other points of distinction between the two breeds. In the first place the head of the Newfoundland generally is larger and more solid than that of his parti-coloured relation, whilst the latter is slacker in his loins, and the tendency to curl in his coat is more frequent."

As late as 1907, Bailey carries the poor estimate of the Landseers even further, for he states: "For many years the black variety has been the better in type; and in breeding. If blacks are desired, it will be safer as a general rule to insist upon the absence of white-and-black blood in any of the immediate ancestors of the sire and dam. But on the contrary, if white-and-black is desired, it is wise to make judicious crosses between the black-and-white and black varieties."

Miniatures of 19th century Newfoundlands from the outstanding collection of Mrs. Isabel Kurth.

Early retriever of the Newfoundland family.

Labrador Retriever.

3

The Great
Newfoundland Family

THE NEWFOUNDLAND family consisted in the past of two distinct types, namely, the Newfoundland Dog to which this book is devoted, and the Lesser Newfoundland. The Lesser Newfoundland, or St. John's Newfoundland, is considerably smaller than the Newfoundland proper, and the breed at one time flourished both in Newfoundland and Labrador. It is from Labrador that the Lesser Newfoundland derives its present name, which was not coined until 1870. The Labrador Retriever was officially recognized in England in 1903.

The Labrador Retriever

General W. N. Hutchinson, in his *Dog Breaking* (1876–6th Edition), gives this illuminating account of the breed:

> From education there are good retrievers of many breeds, but it is usually allowed that, as a general rule, the best land retrievers are bred from a cross between the Setter and the Newfoundland, or the strong Spaniel and the Newfoundland. I do not mean the heavy Labrador, whose weight and bulk is valued because it adds to his power of draught, nor the Newfoundland increased in size at Halifax and St. John's to suit the taste of the English purchaser; but the far slighter dog reared by the settlers on the coast, a dog that is quite as fond of water as of land and which in almost the severest part of North American winter will remain on the edge of a rock for hours, watching intently for anything the passing waves may carry near him. Such a dog is highly prized. Without his aid the

farmer would secure but a few of the many wild ducks he shoots at certain seasons of the year. The patience with which he waits for a shot on the top of a high cliff would be fruitless, did not his noble dog fearlessly plunge in from the greatest height, and successfully bring the slain ashore.

Colonel Hawker, in 1830, praised the St. John's Newfoundlands as being "by far the best of any kind for shooting." He describes the dog as being generally black and no bigger than a Pointer, with very good legs and short, smooth hair, an extremely quick runner, swimmer, and fighter. His sense of smell is almost incredible. In finding wounded game there is not a living equal in the canine race.

Comparing the Labrador Retriever, or St. John's Newfoundland, today with the present Newfoundland, we find an interesting example of two varieties of a single versatile breed embarking on two diverging paths, each excelling in its own field and crystallizing two different purposes and ideals.

The Chesapeake Bay Retriever

When an English brig was shipwrecked off the shore of Maryland in 1807, wily Poseidon presented the duck hunters of the Chesapeake Bay with a fabulous gift. Two Newfoundland puppies, on their way to England, were on board the ill-fated vessel and reached shore safely with the crew, as related in a letter dated January 7, 1845, from George Law, who was on board the *Canton.* He tells that the dog-pup Sailor was given to John Mercer, of West River, and the slut-pup, Canton, to Dr. James Stewart. "Both attained great reputation as water dogs. They were most sagacious in everything, particularly so in all duties connected with duck shooting. Governor Lloyd exchanged a Merino ram for the dog, at the time worth several hundred dollars." Sailor was destined to live on the Eastern Shore and Canton on the Western Shore. There is no record of any breeding between the two Newfoundlands.

On opposite shores, the dogs and their progeny were crossed and recrossed with local dogs, among them Water Spaniels, Coon Dogs or Hounds, and favorite local animals of less well-defined parentage. The mixtures contributed to the establishment of the combination of characteristics eventually resulting in the distinctive amphibian Retriever.

From the Newfoundland is believed to have come the Chesapeake Bay dog's good temper and faithfulness to man. Also from the Newfoundland comes the double coat, furry underneath, long and curly above. The varied colors of the miscellaneous crosses, the yellow and tan of the Hound, and the black and white of the Water Spaniel and

Sketch of various Retrievers born of cross-breeding: cross between Water Spaniel and Newfoundland, between Water Spaniel and Setter, and between Setter and Newfoundland.

Newfoundland, blended to produce the Chesapeake's characteristic liver color.

In 1877, some of the descendants of Sailor and Canton were brought together at the poultry and Fanciers' Show at Baltimore. Despite the hodgepodge breeding separately pursued on the two shores of the Chesapeake Bay, the Eastern and Western Shore dogs were found to be so alike in characteristics and conformation that they were together recognized as a distinct breed and named the Chesapeake Bay Ducking Dog, or Chesapeake Bay Retriever. They were divided into three classes: the Otter Dog, with wavy, almost kinky, short hair; the Curly Dog, with longer hair; and the Straight-haired Dog. All were reddish-brown in color, and generally had a white spot on the breast. With time, these distinctions tended to disappear, and the color of the dogs shaded to the color of dead grass.

Canton and Sailor were cast in iron in 1850 and their figures to the present day adorn the entrance of the Bartlett Hayward plant in Baltimore, whose founders were great devotees of the breed.

The Golden Retriever

Contrary to romantic speculations and claims that the Golden Retriever derived from a couple of glamorous Russian circus dogs, the facts of the breed's origin are well documented and were made public by the Earl of Ilchester in 1952. It was his great uncle, Lord Tweedmouth, who created the breed, beginning in 1864, with the aid of the fifth Earl of Ilchester.

A yellow strain was established with about 20 years of careful line breeding from a yellow retriever. Several black retrievers, two crosses to a tawny colored water-dog bitch, one cross to an Irish Setter and one to a sand-colored Bloodhound, along with numerous breedings to black Wavy-Coated Retrievers and Labradors, give us the genesis of the breed. Bear in mind that the retrievers, basic to the Goldens, were primarily of Newfoundland origin.

Golden Retrievers in England were entered in the Flatcoat Retriever register until 1913, when they gained recognition as a separate breed. Labradors had achieved Kennel Club recognition ten years earlier.

Other Retrievers

Sometimes the Newfoundland has been referred to as the Great Retriever, such a repository is he for the retrieving instinct. All of today's AKC-recognized Retrievers are of the Newfoundland family. The Cur-

48

Iron monuments (cast in 1850) of Sailor and Canton, the Newfoundland puppies credited (in separate breedings) with being the founding dogs of the Chesapeake Bay Retriever breed, that flank the doorway of the Bartlett Hayward plant in Baltimore. Some years ago the dogs were removed in the course of redesign of the building. Hard times followed, which some credited directly to absence of the dogs. They were placed anew at entrance to the plant, where they stand today in sign of the firm's continuing prosperity.

Retrievers of the great Newfoundland family—the Chesapeake Bay Retriever, Curly-Coated Retriever and Irish Water Spaniel.

Drawing of Newfoundland and St. Bernard from an 1884 issue of *Harper's Weekly*.

Cross between a Newfoundland and St. Bernard.

ly Coated Retriever comes from a cross with the St. John's Newfoundland and the Water Spaniel, and the Flat Coated Retriever from matings of the St. John's Newfoundland with Irish and Gordon Setters.

The Newfoundland in Other Crosses

According to Stonehenge, the original St. Bernard breed came nearly to an end at the Hospice due to losses from an avalanche in about 1830, and with general sterility due to poor breeding and disease, a cross from the Newfoundland was resorted to. In judges' critiques of St. Bernards at the dog shows shortly after the cross, numerous references emphasized the similarity of the St. Bernard to the Newfoundland.

The effect on unrelated breeds is indeed most illuminating. "Idestone" has this to say about it: "The unbounded intelligence of the Newfoundland dog has rendered him perhaps the greatest favorite, but apart from that mysterious sense which enables him to understand short sentences as well as words, he is, take him all in all, unsurpassed or perhaps unequalled as the companion of man for his fine formation, herculean strength, and grandeur of his carriage. The Newfoundland, and the Labrador or St. John's dog, have this peculiarity; they not only possess sagacity, but they disseminate it through any number of crosses or at least a great number of them. . . . Some of the best shepherds I have met with have told me that their favorite breed of sheep dog was descended from Labrador and Collie. I have been solicited by them, and never in vain, for services of my most intelligent Labrador Retrievers to put more sense into sheep dogs already showing distinctly the Newfoundland mixture. The Newfoundland's intelligence is retained in the absence of all approach to the shape of the progenitor, and the instincts of the Retriever, the love for water and the general gentleness and cordiality of the massive parent have discovered themselves more than twice in the insignificant little mongrels which were the produce of a Newfoundland and a Terrier."

Earl Dudley's Newfoundland "Bashaw, the faithful friend of man, trampling underfoot his most insidious enemy." This 1831 marble and bronze statue by Matthew Cotes Wyatt, now at the Victoria and Albert Museum, depicts the original breed type.

4

The Show
Newfoundland

THE DEVELOPMENT of the breed can be arbitrarily
subdivided into three distinct phases: first, their natural or wild state
east of the Rocky Mountains with their Indian masters, as well as their
subsequent life with the early settlers; second, their development outside of their native land in all countries of the world to which they had
been exported to be guards, companions, and lifesavers; and the third
period, which roughly began with the advent of the first large dog show
held in England, the Cremorne, held in Birmingham in 1864. At this
show we have a record of the breed winner, Mr. Robinson's Carlo,
who was said to measure at the shoulder, 30 inches; in length, 34
inches; girth at chest, 40 inches; girth at loin, 34 inches; around the
thigh, 29 inches; around the arm, 10½ inches; length of head, 14
inches; length of tail, 20½ inches; and length of ear, 7½ inches.

The Leonberg Dog

With the new era of shows, size, spirit, and type began to intrigue
the fanciers of the breed with a new impetus. The eager eye of the
breeder perceived the spectacular rise of the Leonberg dog which had
enjoyed a steady ascent since the day of Herr Essig's pioneering of
them in 1855. This larger, spirited dog was becoming a favorite among
European nobility. Three carefully selected puppies from the Essig establishment in Leonberg, Wurtemberg, Germany, were brought to the
island of Newfoundland. These puppies grew to the height of 33 to 36

inches and were reported to be over one hundred pounds in weight. In 1883, the Leonberg breed was reported to be multiplying on the island of Newfoundland, and it was even thought that in time they would supersede the smaller Newfoundland, or far worse, cross with the Newfoundland to the extent that the distinct characteristics of our breed might be submerged. This appeared to be a serious threat to the purity of the Newfoundland dog. Therefore, let us examine the background of the Leonberg.

Herr Essig owned both Newfoundlands and St. Bernards and interbred them. Pursing objectives of his own, it is claimed by Hubbard that Essig added crosses from Swiss Mountain Dogs, Wallis Sheepdogs, Kuvaszok, and either the Austrian Jagdgriffons or the Bayerischer Geburgsschweisshunde, or both. Harvey claims for the Leonberg only three progenitors — the Newfoundland, the St. Bernard, and the Wolf Dog of the Pyrenees. A more startling claim comes from H. C. Brooke that he owned a common European wolf bitch which mated freely with dogs and that he sold a number of these hybrid pups to a dog dealer in Leonberg. It has been further claimed that these powerful hybrids were successfully used in the creation of the Leonberg dog. Here let us consider the coat colors of the Leonberg dog. Although today blue-gray and fawn are prevalent, at one time black, black and white, and wolf-gray occurred frequently.

Whether or not any of the many Leonberg dogs on the island of Newfoundland were ever crossed with the pure Newfoundlands is unknown, though there has been some intimation that this occurred in some few cases. Perhaps it may also have occurred where the larger specimens were currently winning the shows and some English breeders were inclined to be less·conservative than the Newfoundlanders in their efforts to achieve a tall dog. *The phenomenon of the occasional so-called blue, actually wolf-gray Newfoundland could well be explained by the recessive gray from a Leonberg-wolf ancestor.* However, it should be kept in mind that the Leonberg dog was slighter in build than the Newfoundland, had a longer, shallower, and sharper muzzle, a narrower head and altogether had very little to contribute to the ideal Newfoundland. His importance to the development of the Newfoundland breed can be relegated primarily to the present existence of a blue Newfoundland, which, however, is not encouraged by the official Standard.

Carlo I, American-bred Newfoundland, from a photograph taken before 1888. Carlo was owned by Fred J. Hiker of Greenfield, N.H. Typical of the "Stonehenge" type, with ears square to top of skull and virtually no stop.

Charcoal drawing of Newfoundland, 1886, owned by the Williams family of Brattleboro, Vt.

Mr. Robinson's "Carlo," breed winner at the first large dog show held in England, the Cremorne at Birmingham in 1864. Carlo was said to measure 30 inches at the shoulder, and 34 inches in length.

Ch. Lord Nelson, well-known winner in England and on the continent in the late 1800s. Owner, Edwin Nichols.

Early Standouts

The closing decade of the nineteenth century presents the historian of the breed with rich material. From here on the whims of fashion, as well as the type and quality of the breed, could be gauged most accurately by following the careers and by studying a gallery of portraits of the breed's most illustrious winners. Perhaps these four English champions most closely approached the ideal of their day: Lord Nelson, his son Alderman, Leo, and Bruno.

One can be readily justified in questioning the report on development of the breed as having been confined to England and Newfoundland with no mention of the great ones in this country. Study of early American show records, when critiques were included in the official magazine of the American Kennel Club, *Purebred Dogs-American Kennel Gazette,* indicate without a shadow of a doubt that England was carrying the burden of the Newfoundland show breeding. This situation became apparent when English-bred stock made its debut in America.

The interesting thing, however, is that the show records in no way reflect the general popularity of the breed in the country as a whole. The Newfoundland was still a prime favorite of the American people, and although his name did not appear among the winners of the time, hardly a day passed without his remarkable character and heroism being subjects of current news.

In 1908, at the great Crufts show in London, a Newfoundland, Ch. Shelton Viking, won Best-in-Show, all breeds. The photograph of this dog gives evidence of how dog breeding has improved. Such a Newfoundland would be difficult to make into a champion today and probably impossible to make a top national winner. The picture shows a dog overly long in body, out of balance, slight of bone, and with a very poor rear. (Viking's measurements have been recorded as 29½" height, and 48" in length.)

Loosely line-bred from Viking was English Ch. Siki who became the model of his time and established through his progeny in England, the United States and Canada a type which was considered most beautiful. Dogs of this type began winning in competition with other breeds, and today there is probably no Newfoundland champion in the United States or Canada that cannot claim descent from Siki. Unfortunately Siki himself does not appear to have had a sound rear and there is no point in perpetuating the myth that Siki was a perfect Newfoundland. But the blending of his style with the strength and physical character of the old breed, has brought about the truly great ones of today.

"Leo," owned by S. W. Wildman, a foremost English winner of the late 1800s.

Ch. Shelton Viking, Best in Show all-breeds at Cruft's, England's largest dog show, in 1908. His great winning notwithstanding, in this picture Viking appears to have had a poor rear, and to have been cowhocked.

English Ch. Siki, "The Father of Champions," whose progeny, imported to America in the early 1930s, overwhelmed the American-bred Newfoundlands in the show rings and established the current type. Most of the major bloodlines in America today trace back to Siki.

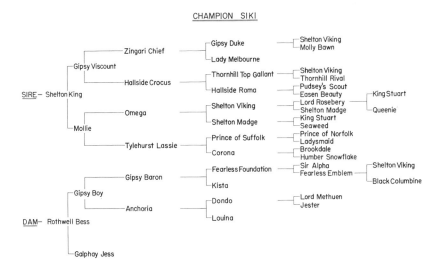

THE NEWFOUNDLAND IN
AMERICAN SHOW RINGS

The Adam of American Newfoundland champions was Sam, championed in 1883, and it was not until some thirty years later that the second United States champion was achieved by the breed in Major II, a Newfoundland of unknown pedigree, registered on his winnings. However, by the end of World War I, a Newfoundland was finished to championship every year or two.

The third U. S. champion, Graydon's New Jersey Big Boy, a Landseer, was the first imported Newfoundland to win the title and was of very important stock, both his sire and dam being grandchildren of the 1908 Crufts' Best in Show Newfoundland, English Champion Shelton Viking. The sixth U. S. Newfoundland champion was Biddie, who acquired the title in 1924 and had the added distinction of being the first champion by a champion sire out of a champion dam; her dam was the first bitch to win the title and her sire was an English import of distinguished lineage.

Decline

In 1926 there were sixteen Newfoundland entries at the Boston show. By 1928 there were only four and the overall registrations hit an all-time low, making it the least popular of all registered Working breeds. Newfoundlands were in real trouble, facing possible extinction. A small group of dedicated breeders and fanciers kept the breed alive and deserve all of the credit for its ultimate revival.

However, the native American stock did not survive this crisis. Generally speaking, the native dog was more in keeping with the original breed standard formulated by Stonehenge. For example, Stonehenge envisaged a much smaller dog, only 75 to 100 pounds for males and 50 to 75 pounds for females. Likewise, the head still followed Stonehenge's ideal in that it retained the flatness across the crown and the ears were set square with the top of the skull. The strongly developed occipital ridge was still a prominent feature and the muzzle was proportionately longer. It was a hard-muscled, sure-footed animal, somewhat rangy and inclined to be curly-coated, sometimes to the extreme. Overall, it looked like an oversized Labrador Retriever of today except for a heavy double coat.

What was lacking in massiveness of head and body was made up by superior intelligence, natural water prowess, sagacity, hardiness, and longevity.

Typical of the American-bred Newfoundlands at time of the importation of Siki offspring was Ch. Jonmunn Shakespeare II, bred by Dr. A. P. Munn. Note the triangular shaped skull, small size and curly coat. The American-breds of the time were inherently great swimmers.

Int. Ch. Seafarer, a Siki son out of a Siki daughter, imported by Miss Elizabeth Loring's (later Mrs. Powers) Waseeka Kennels in 1930. Seafarer, who stood 29½" at the shoulders and weighed 150 lbs., was an outstanding winner with 4 all-breed Bests in Show, many Groups, and win of the breed at Westminster in 1931 and 1932.

Array of champions at the Waseeka Kennels in Ashland, Mass. in the 1930s. From left to right: Ch. Seafarer, Ch. Waseeka's Sea King, Ch. Waseeka's Sailor Boy, Ch. Waseeka's Triton, Ch. Waseeka's Skipper and Ch. Waseeka's Pete the Pirate.

Ch. Harlingen Neptune of Waseeka, wh. 1929, an English-bred Siki son who became one of the most important producers. Sire of 10 champions including the first two Newfoundland American – breds to win Best in Show, and the first Obedience titlist of the breed.

Two Best in Show winning sons of Neptune, both owned by Waseeka Kennels. Left, Ch. Waseeka's Sailor Boy, whelped in 1931, and right, Ch. Waseeka's Sea King, whelped in 1930.

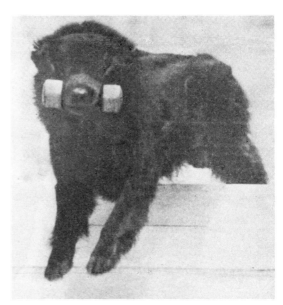

Ch. Mark Anthony of Waseeka, C.D., C.D.X., Obedience pioneer of the breed. Mark, whelped in 1933, was owned and trained by Mrs. A. B. Hilton's (later to become Mrs. B. Godsol) Coastwise Kennels.

Ch. Nerka of Denobie, whelped 1937, a handsome winner of his time. Owned by Denise O'Brien of Yonkers, N.Y.

Edwin Morris, the secretary of the North American Newfoundland Club and a great champion of the native Newfoundland once rhetorically asked me: "English imports look great in the ring, but can they swim?" The question was well justified — their natural water instinct *was* diluted.

By the same token, decades of indiscriminant back yard breeding took their toll. American Newfoundlands could no longer measure up in appearance to the better specimens of the past. Continuously defeated in the show ring, they vanished from the scene, vanquished by the giant English imports.

Revival

Nineteen hundred and twenty-nine was the crucial year in the history of the breed. Waseeka Kennels, owned by Miss Elizabeth Loring (later Mrs. Powers), made a grand entry into the Newfoundland ring with the famous English import, Ch. Seafarer (Best in Show at Middlesex in 1930, at Barnstable in 1930, and at Portland in 1932.) Seafarer was a son of Siki, "the father of champions", and his dam was Kaffi Girl. Other Siki-sired imports joined the kennel. They were: Seagrave Blackberry, Harlingen Neptune of Waseeka, and Harlingen Jess of Waseeka. An infusion of English Drummond bloodlines and other English imports followed, laying a solid foundation for an ambitious breeding program that soon carried Waseeka to the pinnacle of Newfoundland fame.

Ch. Waseeka Sea King went BIS at Ladies Dog Club, Brookline, Mass. in 1933 and Ch. Waseeka Sailor Boy followed suit at Canton, Ohio in 1936. Sea King and Seafarer scored another spectacular win — Best Brace all breeds at Westminster in 1933. The award was made by Mrs. M. Hartley Dodge, internationally famous breeder and judge. From 1929 and into the mid-1940s, Waseeka champions dominated the show ring and profoundly changed the Newfoundland type into their own image.

Competing against this formidable array of imports and later home grown champions were Edwin Morris and Q. Twachman. Their champion bitch Tanya must be mentioned at this point.

Campaigning at the same time was Dr. A. F. Munn, a prolific and successful breeder whose kennel carried the Jonmunn prefix. Champions Ready Money, Captain, Thunderer, Nakomis, Pluto, Wan-Ce-Na's Trixie, Wan-Ce-Na Rachel were the best of this kennel.

Ch. Oquaga's Sea Pirate, whelped 1945, a particularly outstanding Group winner, owned and shown by Seaward Kennels. This lovely head study shows Sea Pirate to have owned many of the virtues of the early Newfoundlands.

Ch. Coastwise Sailor Boy, bred by Mrs. Major Godsol.

J. S. Cameron's Kenmount Laddie and Elinor S. Ayers' Nigar of Camayer, bred by Mr. Cameron, were now in the show ring. This established the 1932 start of the Seaward Kennels, owned by Mrs. Ayers, which continues today as the longest-established kennel of the breed.

Among early breeders participating in "Operation Revival" was Oquaga Kennels, owned by Clifford F. Hartz. Their breeding may be identified by two phases. The first based on Canadian Shelton line made a decided mark on the breed. This stock was virtually wiped out by virus X which struck the kennel creating a major tragedy for the owner and the breed. This breeding survives in some strong lines of today.

The second breeding was based on Waseeka strain direct or Waseeka derivatives. Ch. Oquaga Sea Pirate (owned by Seaward Kennels) was perhaps best known for his Group wins and placings. An unsung heroine of Oquaga breeding was Queen Mary, a bitch that "could not be faulted" according to the judges and breeders of her time.

Left, Ch. Stubbart's Greetings O'Lady, wh. 1945, and right Ch. Little Bear's Avalon O'Lady, wh. 1951, owned by the Midway Kennels of Mr. and Mrs. Fred Stubbart.

Ch. Mill Creek Manitou's Dark Angel, wh. 1943, bred by John J. Patterson.

Coastwise Kennel played a vital role in breed revival on the West Coast. Owned by Mr. and Mrs. A. B. Hilton, (she was later to become Mrs. Major B. Godsol, and a distinguished all-round judge) it was based primarily on Waseeka stock and the Newfoundland cause was greatly enhanced by their efforts. Bing Crosby used Coastwise Newfoundlands for his breeding. Among the important Coastwise champions found in pedigrees of today's winners are: Mark Antony of Waseeka, Plum Duff, Steamboat Bill and Nantucket (Dreamy).

Midway Kennels, owned by Mr. and Mrs. Fred Stubbart, joined in a concerted effort during the World War II years. Their first champion, Mermaid Queen Gipsy, was bred by D. R. Oliver. It was followed by Mill Creek Seafarer of Manitou, bred by John Patterson. Both dogs were descendants of Siki offspring imported to Canada. Entire litters from all over the world were brought in and the best specimens kept for breeding stock. After much thinning, Canadian stock became their foundation. Line bred stock descending from two famous Siki offspring, Baron and Cabin Boy, was imported by Midway and combined in producing the best Newfoundland of his time, Can. and Am. Ch. Midway Black Ledge Sea Raider.

Black Ledge, a Nova Scotian kennel was owned by Zatha Hockridge, co-breeder of Raider. Raider won his first show at 15 months old: a Canadian Best in Show at Halifax, Nova Scotia. He was BIS in the United States at Long Island Kennel Club in May of 1953 under judge Thomas Carruthers III, and Reserve BIS in Toronto, Canada under Mrs. Geraldine Dodge. From 1941 to 1953 his show record included 12 Group wins and placings.

Among the important Midway champions were Ch. Stubbart's Greetings O'Lady, the dam of Little Bear's Big Chance; Midway Sea Queen; Midway Sea Raider (BIS at Staten Island under Mrs. Sherman Hoyt); Midway Black Ace and Stubbart's Nelson.

Waseeka bloodlines were continued in the breeding of Dryad Kennels, owned by Mr. and Mrs. Maynard K. Drury of Saranac Lake, N.Y. Ch. Dryad Coastwise Showboat, daughter of Ch. Waseeka's Crusoe and Ch. Waseeka's Hesperus, was the first Newfoundland bitch to win Best in Show (Tucson, Arizona, 1949). (Showboat is the Newfoundland currently pictured in illustration of the breed in the AKC's *Complete Dog Book.)* Her show career continued until 1953 with many Group placements. Ch. Dryad's Conversation Piece, a Group First winner, followed in her footsteps.

Dryad's Can. and Am. Ch. Trademark O'Golly went BIS. The Dryad honor roll lists 52 champions and sixteen Group winners or placers.

Waseeka-Coastwise bloodlines were crossed with Dutch Zeepardje lines to produce Ch. Dryad's Sea Rover (Group Winner) and Dryad's Lord Nelson. Sea Rover is consequential in Shipshape breeding and was 1965 Specialty winner at Lowell, Mass.

Ch. Dryad's Sea Rose was owned and shown by Mr. and Mrs. Charles O. Webster.

Irwindyl Kennels, owned by Mrs. Geraldine Irwin of Pennsylvania, has been active in breeding and showing since the late forties. The bloodlines are Kenmount, Perivale, Midway and some Little Bear. By 1971, their honor roll contained 28 champions. Outstanding among them: Lady Belle Isolt, Little Bear's Isolt of Irwindyl CD, Sir Lil Abner, Lady Guenievere CD, Sir Aliking, Sir Aliduke, King Arthur and Sir Lionel.

Harobed Hill Kennels, active in breeding and showing since the early fifties, was strongly endowed with Waseeka and Dryad stock, and some outstanding champions resulted. Among home-bred champions are Harobed's Sheila Pike and Everloving Dino. Ch. Harobed's Nancy of Noralview was a bitch of great soundness.

Kwasind Kennels of Dr. and Mrs. John D. Thomson of Syracuse, New York became actively engaged in breeding and showing in 1952. Ch. Little Bear's Black Sambo, litter brother of James Thurber, was their foundation dog and gave the kennel a good start by winning the West Coast Specialty in 1956.

Ch. Dryad's Coastwise Showboat, wh. 1946, the first Newfoundland bitch to win Best in Show. Bred by Mr. and Mrs. Maynard K. Drury, she was owned for a while by the Coastwise Kennels of Mr. and Mrs. Major Godsol, but resold to Mrs. Drury when Mr. Godsol became an AKC field representative.

Ch. Bonnavista, wh. 1948, pictured winning the 1952 Specialty under judge Mrs. M. Hartley Dodge. Bonnavista, owned by Little Bear Kennels, was dam of Ch. James Thurber.

Kwasind's outstanding Group winners include Ch. Little Bear's Tippo, Ch. Little Bear's Jiminy Cricket. Tippo's son, Little Bear's Royal Top Gallant, is responsible for starting a winning line in Denmark with a record number of BIS wins.

The best known Kwasind champions are Jennie Cake Jennie, Princess Starfire, Feather in Her Cap, and War Dance; Little Bear's Zulu Queen, St. Mary's O'Lady and Tao of Kwasind are also well known.

Black Mischief Kennels of Le Roy, Kansas is owned by Alice Weaver. Her foundation stock is based on Midway, Little Bear and Finnish bloodlines. An active breeder and exhibitor since the early 1950s, Black Mischief champions have been campaigned successfully in the Midwest and on the West Coast. Outstanding champions carrying the Black Mischief prefix are Christopher, Molly Brown and El Toro.

Roger Richards, a breeder and enthusiastic exhibitor of the '60s, left a definite mark on the breed with his BIS Ch. Little Bear's Thunder, U. D. and Specialty Winner. His other champions of note are Little Bear's Lightning, Harobed Hill's Magus, and Riley Roman.

Temanend Kennels, owned by Captain and Mrs. Henri Rice, contributed a great deal to the development of the breed. Among their best known champions we find Temanend Black Dolphin, Lady Nora, Prince Henry, Misty Dawn and Snow Flurry.

Amber Acres, owned by Mr. and Mrs. Ned Brower, were breeders of the outstanding Ch. Sinbad the Sailor. Their Newfoundlands, including five homebred champions, were prominent in Midwestern shows, chalking up an impressive record of wins.

Established in 1948, Little Bear Kennels (owned by the author and her husband, Vadim Chern) is actually a continuation of Midway and Black Ledge breeding. Can. and Am. Ch. Midway Black Ledge Sea Raider was Little Bear's foundation dog. In addition to winning BIS, he was also the sire of Am. and Can. Ch. Little Bear's James Thurber. James scored 8 Bests in Show — the record for the breed until it was broken in 1965 by Newton — and had 46 Group Firsts, and 70 Group placings.

There have been just two outcrosses in Little Bear breeding: the Perryhow bloodline was brought in during the '50s and the Newton strain, by way of Dryad's Compass Rose, in the late '60s.

The Little Bear Honor Roll contains a record number of champions — 104 as of this writing. Eighteen of the Little Bear champions have won a total of 75 groups. Six have won one or more Best in Show

Am. & Can. Ch. Midway Black Ledge Sea Raider, wh. 1948, winning Best in Show at Long Island KC, 1953, under judge T. H. Carruthers III. The foundation stud of Little Bear Kennels, Raider was the first of nine consecutive generations of Best in Show or Group winners at Little Bear.

Ch. Midway Sea Raider, son of Am. & Can. Ch. Midway Black Ledge Sea Raider, winning under Mrs. Sherman L. Hoyt at Staten Island, 1953. Owned by Dr. D. F. Coburn. Handler, E. J. Carver.

Am. & Can. Ch. Little Bear's James Thurber, whelped 1951. James' win of 8 Bests in Show was the record for his time. By Am. & Can. Ch. Midway's Black Ledge Sea Raider ex Ch. Bonnavista, he was bred by Little Bear Kennels, and owned and shown by Robert Dowling of New York City.

Am. & Berm. Ch. Little Bear's Black Thunder, all-breed Best in Show winner. Owned and shown by Mr. and Mrs. Charles Visich.

awards. Nine have been Specialty winners. Little Bear dogs who have won Best in Show include Am. Can. Ch. Little Bear's Thunder UD, and Little Bear's Eben. The most recent on the list of BIS winners is Am. & Ber. Ch. Little Bear's Black Thunder owned by Mr. and Mrs. Charles Visich. Black Thunder's show record also includes three Group wins, 17 other Group placings, and 88 Bests of Breed.

Additional outstanding Little Bear champions to win or place in the Working Group include Roaring Main, Hard Tack II, John Paul Jones, Big Chance, Canicula Campio, Sailing Free, Rebel Tug, Down Easter, John Smith, Tippo, Night Train, Three-Mile Limit, Grey Mug, Royal Top Gallant, Blockade Runner, Rig, Leopoldo, Bonnavista, Black Sambo, Commander Tucker, Beauregardless, Black Gallion, Broadside, Midway Black Ace, Gander, Drake's Drum, Jiminy Cricket, Emeer Boatswain, Gemini, Sailor Port O'Call, Dauntless, Commodore Perry and Midnight.

Little Bear's Eben was the first Newfoundland owned by Mel Sokolsky to win Best in Show, scoring all the way from the classes. But it was Mr. Sokolsky's Am. Can. Ber. & Bahamas Ch. Newton that was to rewrite the record books and inspire a tremendous revival of interest in the breed.

Newton completely shattered all marks with an awesome 15 Bests in Show, 55 Group Firsts, 138 other Group placements, 8 Bests in Specialty, and 199 Bests of Breed. His spectacular campaigning brought new attention and excitement to the historically glamorous breed, and at the height of his career it was common to hear Newfoundlands referred to as "Newtons".

When James Thurber had won his sixth Best in Show at Buffalo, a newspaper there had carried the headline "Black St. Bernard Wins Best in Show." But by 1968, after Newton had swept triumphantly across the breadth and width of North America, the populace at large was thoroughly acquainted with the image of a beautiful Newfoundland. His great show career did much to restore the breed to a warm place in the hearts of dog lovers.

The Newfoundland popularity explosion followed. Show entries tripled and quadrupled. The National Specialties continued to break their own numerical records: Lenox (1967) 117, Wallingford (1972) 254, Buffalo (1973) 185, Allentown (1974) 276. By 1974, there were more Newfoundland breeders listed by the Newfoundland Club of America than there had been actual club members in the early fifties.

In the period of revival it was relatively easy to name the Newfoundlands kings and queens of their day. These were Seafarer, Waseeka's great BIS, followed by Dryad's Coastwise Showboat, Black Ledge Sea Raider, James Thurber and finally, Newton.

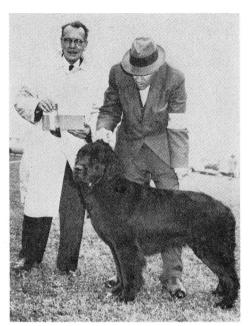

Am. & Can. Ch. Little Bear's Thunder, U.D., specialty and outstanding Obedience winner of the early 1960s. Owned by Roger E. Richards of Massapequa, N.Y.

Landseer bitch brace winning Best Brace in Show at Devon 1967 under judge Peter Knoop. Ch. Seaward's Frosty Morn and Ch. Maharanee, owned by Seaward Kennels, and handled by Betty Cummings.

Following Newton, it is no longer possible to pick a truly outstanding winner; rather, a multiplicity of winners exists. Newfoundland Group wins are no longer a rarity, perhaps due to tremendous breed entries which frequently surpass those of numerically stronger Working breeds.

Old kennel prefixes are still evident in the ring either directly, or through their derivatives.

The 1960s saw the beginnings of three New England Kennels that were to especially influence the type of Newfoundlands of the future.

Typical of the strong new blood in the ring is the Nashau-Auke (pronounced Nasha-Nook) kennels of Jane and Ron Thibault in Connecticut. All of the present day Nashau-Auke dogs descend directly from the kennel's original four.

In the early 1960s, Jane and Ronald acquired Little Bear's Black Cinderella, later to become a proficient Obedience dog as well as a producer of champions. Following Cinderella, Little Bear's Dauntless made his way to Nashau-Auke Kennels and finished at Farmington the same year. Soon after Dauntless, Ch. Shipshape Nana of Nashau-Auke and Little Bear's Cutty Hunk completed the foundation stock of Nashau-Auke. Nana bred to Dauntless produced Canadian and American Ch. Koki de Nashau-Auke, who is a Specialty Show winner and has placed in many Groups. Cutty Hunk, bred to Ch. Shipshape's Cutty Sark produced Ch. Tanda de Nashau-Auke, who is also a Specialty winner and has placed in Groups. Cutty Hunk was Top Producing Dam for 1972. When bred to Dauntless, Cutty Hunk produced Ch. Koki Winota de Nashau-Auke who was the Top Producing Dam for 1973. Other champions out of Cutty Hunk include Little Bear's Gemini, Keema de Nashau-Auke, Tasha de Nashau-Auke, Tanda de Nashau-Auke, and De Konya de Nashau-Auke.

Nana was also bred to Cutty Sark and produced Canadian and American Ch. Ki Nun Ka de Nashau-Auke and, from the same litter, Nena de Nashau-Auke, the first gray champijon in many years. Ch. Shipshape Nana of Nashau-Auke, bred to Ch. Indigo's Fritzacker, produced Ch. Canoochee de Nashau-Auke, a young legend. A consistent Group winner, Canoochee (The Gallant Brave), at Cape Cod in 1973 became the first Best in Show Newf in the East since Ch. Newton. In 1974, Canoochee was Best of Breed at Westminster and Best of Breed at the National Specialty Show. He has sired Winners Bitch and/or Best of Winners at Specialty Shows. The total number of Nashau-Auke champions at this writing is 30, with 23 Group placings including eight Group Firsts.

The Shipshape Kennels owned by Mr. and Mrs. Robert Lister of Massachusetts, also came to the forefront of showing activity in the mid-sixties. The kennel soon acquired Dryad's Sea Rover and Dryad's Compass Rose, sired by Newton out of Dryad's Christmas Holly. Both of these became champions and Group placers, and they were both Top Producers. Sea Rover was bred to Rose and produced Can. Am. Ch. Shipshape's Tugboat, Ch. Shipshape's Misty and Ch. Shipshape's Cutty Sark. Cutty Sark has been a Top Producing Sire for three years. Shipshape has produced many champions in the past decade and the impact of these will continue to be seen in future competition.

The Indigo prefix also came into prominence during the 1960s. The kennels are owned by Mr. and Mrs. Myron O'Neill. Indigo's Cape Elizabeth, bred to Isabel Kurth's Edenglen's Sovereign of the Sea produced Ch. Indigo's Fritzacker, Ch. Indigo's Bozo the Clown, and Ch. Indigo's Point Judith. Fritzacker and Bozo were each multiple Group placers and together won the Brace Class at the National Specialty show in 1971. Fritzacker was Best of Breed at the National Specialty in 1973, and all, including his competition, were delighted to see the bond of joy and love between the dog and his breeder-owner-handler. Fritzacker's untimely death just one year later deeply saddened Newfoundland breeders and exhibitors. In addition to Ch. Canoochee de Nashau-Auke, Fritzacker also sired Mrs. Malcolm Durgin's Ch. Silverbrook's Black Toro, a Group winner. Many of Fritzacker's progeny are only now beginning to be shown.

The Newfman kennel is owned by Mr. and Mrs. Guy Campbell. Starting in the early sixties, with Temanend's Prince Henry and Edenglen's Miss Muffett, they bred Can. Am. Ch. Newfman's Prince Danilo. Breeding Prince Danilo to Irwin-Dyl's Geneses produced a litter of eight puppies; of these, seven became Canadian and American champions.

The Kilyka kennels of Mr. and Mrs. George McDonnell owned Ch. Shipshape Sibyl U.D.T., the first champion U.D.T. bitch in the breed, and also Ch. Dryad's Lord Nelson U.D.T., the first male Newfoundland to hold both his bench and all Obedience degrees. Sibyl and Nelson have produced Ch. Kilyka's Black Bart, a BIS winner.

The Shipchandler kennel of Dr. and Mrs. Robert Chandler has produced a Group-winnning brace in Ch. Shipchandler's Sea Eagle and Ch. Shipchandler's Nanook. Sea Eagle has also placed in the Group and won BIS. Their foundation is Little Bear's Shipchandler Eno and Shipchandler Thunderoc Fluf.

Little Bear's Eben, all-breed Best in Show winner. Owned by Mel Sokolsky of New York City, and handled by Alan Levine. Pictured here in win under all-rounder judge Mrs. Bea Godsol (now retired), herself a noted Newfoundland breeder in the 1930s.

Int. Ch. Newton, all-time top winner of the breed. Owned by Mel Sokolsky and handled by Alan Levine to wins that included 15 Bests in Show.

Outstanding among latter day winners of the breed are Newton Ark Newfs, belonging to Alan and Janet Levine of Zionsville, Pa. To date they have some 40 champions on their honor roll, including three Group firsts and four Group placers.

Ch. Nashuma of Newton Ark, bred by Janet Levine and Ronni Farkas, and owned by Kurt and Kathi Sahner of Baldwin, N. Y., has become the top winning Newfoundland bitch of all time, surpassing Dryad's Showboat with a record that at this writing already includes 2 Bests in Show, 8 Group Firsts and 10 other Group placings.

Other Newton Ark champions of note are Knickerbocker, Sojowase's Shicksa and Am. and Can. Ch. Sleeper of Newton Ark.

Edenglen Kennels of Glenora, N.Y., owned by Willis and Helena Linn, is based primarily on Waseeka-Dryad bloodlines. Nationally prominent in the show ring for many years, Edenglen champions had a profound effect on the breed. Outstanding are Ch. Edenglen's Banner, Ch. Edenglen's Beau Geste and Edenglen's Sovereign of the Sea, owned by Isabel Kurth of North Andover, Mass.

Halirock Kennels owned by Dr. and Mrs. Roger Foster of Burlington, Vermont became seriously involved in breeding and showing in 1967. Their foundation bitches were Champions Dryad's Anthony's Penelope, Fronco-Cassandra and Little Bear's Chulavista. There are now 15 champions and 3 C.D.'s on the honor roll and many more on their way.

Seaward Kennels, already identified as having been established back in 1932, has for the past four decades primarily devoted itself to preservation and improvement of the Landseer variety. Many imports from abroad now include Samson of Fairwater (Landseer), Crufts BOB in 1973. Among the best known current Landseer champions are Aali Panda and Ermine Strom King. Noteworthy is Dryad's Strong Sea Pirate (black) out of Ch. Dryad's Dotty Que Que by Ch. Dryad's Tambaram of Cayuga.

Sojowase Kennels of Germansville, Pa. is owned by Mr. and Mrs. James Schmoyer. Active breeders and exhibitors, they have frequent winners in champions Sojowase Captain Ahab, Sojowase Ephraim and Sojowase Micah.

Benham Knoll kennels of Harwinton, Conn., owned by Mr. and Mrs. Philip Knowlton, started their breeding program in 1967. Active in the show ring, their champions are Mamacoke de Nashau-Auke and Benham Knoll's Baba Au Rhum. Many promising youngsters are on the way to their championship.

Tranquilus Kennels, owned by Capt. J. W. Bellows, USNR Ret. of Sterling, N. Y. has 16 champions and a record of top producing dam for 1968, 1970 and 1971.

Show dogs can be fun dogs, too. Int. Ch. Newton enjoying a relaxing moment with his handler, Alan Levine, in between triumphs at a Bermuda circuit of the 1960s.

Wildewood Kennels, owned by Sandra and Norman Beberman of Fitchburg, Mass., is presently active in the show ring. Their present stock is Little Bear and Shipshape.

Pouch Cove Newfoundlands (D. and Margaret Helming, Whitehouse Station, New Jersey), are the proud owners of Ch. Waldo of Pouch Cove, BOB at Westminster in 1972 and Specialty BOB in 1972.

New, but bearing promise for the breed is the Tuckamore Kennels owned by George and· Barbara Finch of Pennsylvania. Tuckamore started in 1972 with Edenglen's Wistful Wendy, who became their first champion and foundation bitch. In 1973, they bought Little Bear's Tim of Tuckamore, who soon became their second champion — and the 100th Little Bear to finish.

On the West Coast, Newfoundlands have been on the upswing since 1965. Starting the ball rolling in California was Ch. Little Bear's Night Train, owned by Bob and Fran Dibble, a Group and Regional Specialty BOB winner. Following in his footsteps was his kennelmate, Ch. Edenglen's Beau Geste, a multiple Group placement winner and also a Regional Specialty BOB winner.

To add a little femininity to the No. 1 Spot, Ch. Tranquilus Betty of Subira, owned by Penelope Freeman of Peppertree Kennels, started her show career with a Best of Breed at the National Specialty in 1969, the first held in California. She was also a Group placer, and finished her career by getting a leg toward her C.D. at the 1974 National Specialty in Pennsylvania.

In 1970, Northern California started to feel the vibrations of Ch. Edenglen's Jonathon, owned by Mr. and Mrs. Richard Guelich. Jonathon scored several Group placements and was a hard dog to beat at peak of his career. Late in 1971, Ch. Tranquilus Neptune, co-owned by Penelope Freeman and Capt. James Bellows, came on to win place as the West's top winning Newfoundland — and one of the Top Ten in the nation for three years — retiring in 1974 with 104 Bests of Breed and 13 Group placements including First.

Ch. Edenglen's Oscar, owned by Bob and Fran Dibble, and shown sparingly, also became a Group and Regional Specialty BOB winner. And in 1973, Ch. Brittania's Joshua Slocum, co-owned by William Tate and Kenneth Hulsey, copped a Group placing.

Among the kennels that came into prominence in California from 1965 to 1975 were:
Riptide Kennels, owned by Virginia and Grant Hoag. This kennel

Ch. Canoochee de Nashua-Auke, all-breed Best in Show winner. Bred and owned by Jane and Robert Thibault. Pictured here, handled by Gerlinde Hockla, winning the breed at Westminster 1974 under breeder-judge Mrs. Maynard Drury.

Ch. Kilyka's Black Bart, a 1974 all-breed Best in Show winner with many Group placements and Specialty wins to his credit. Owned by Elizabeth Keefer and Mrs. George McDonnell.

devoted itself to brown Newfoundlands, and in fact, produced the first bronze champion on the West Coast, plus several black champions. It is based primarily on Edenglo stock.

Peppertree Kennels is owned by Penelope Freeman. In 1967, Peppertree purchased a stud dog — Ch. Little Bear's Sergeant Pepper — and three bitches, Ch. Tranquilus Betty of Subira, Ch. Tranquilus Diamond Lil and Tranquilus Regina. From these came such champions as Peppertree's Sand Piper, Peppertree's Steamer Stan and Peppertree's Maggie Scannon. Two years later, in 1969, Ch. Tranquilus Neptune was added to the kennel. These dogs have all influenced the breed.

Brittania Kennels of Alana Manzer and William Tate produced several champions, including the Group-placing dog, Ch. Brittania's Joshua Slocum.

Pooh Bear Kennels, owned by Shelby Guelich and Julienne Crowl, started their breeding program with the stud dog Ch. Edenglen's Jonathon and two bitches: one from Oquaga Kennels, and the other from Nashua-Auke Kennels. They have produced several lovely champions.

Villade Kennels, of Garden Grove, California, is owned by Viki E. Palma. Best known of the Villade Newfs, based on Tranquilus breeding, is Ch. Tranquilus Tempting Tidbit ("Mr. Boggs").

For Newfoundlands on the West Coast, as with the breed elsewhere, prospects are bright.

The impressive show career of Ch. Carr's Black Sam of Bethward, owned by Paul and Betty Ramey, Bethward Kennels, Reg., in Lemont, Illinois, did much to focus attention on the Newfoundland breed in the Midwest. Sam was the winner of 56 Best of Breed awards, including the Best of Breed ribbon at the 1969 Midwest regional specialty show, and eighteen Group placements. Sam was the top-winning Newfoundland in the United States in 1968 and 1969.

The Rameys purchased their first Newfoundland in 1960 and established their kennel the following year. In 1965 the Rameys acquired the outstanding Black Sam, who completed his championship the next year. There are eleven champions among Sam's progeny. These include the Rameys' Ch. Dory-O's Sea Nymph of Bethward, Best of Opposite Sex at the 1972 NCA national specialty show; Jerald Kolls' Ch. Turtleridge's Cat Ballou, Best of Opposite Sex at the 1973 Midwest regional specialty show and the winner of a Group placement in Canada; and Norman O. Walk's Ch. English Valley's Sea Mist, Best of Opposite Sex at the 1974 Midwest regional specialty show.

Norman Walk's English Valley Kennels at South English, Iowa, includes Ch. harbour beem Rudder, winner of the 1971 Midwest region-

Ch. Nashuma of Newton-Ark, the all-time top winning Newfoundland bitch—a multiple Best in Show and Group winner. Bred by Janet Levine and Ronni Farkas, Nashuma is owned by Kurt and Kathi Sahner of Baldwin, N.Y., and handled by Alan Levine.

Ch. Shipchandler's Sea Eagle, an all-breed Best in Show winner at only two years of age. Finished for his championship in just four shows. Best of Breed at the 1975 National Specialty. Owned by Sandra L. Chandler, Redding, Conn.

al specialty show and a Group placement. Rudder is the sire of Ch. Dalma's English Valley Zero, co-owned by Mr. Walk and Virginia Halsema. Zero was the Best of Breed winner at the 1973 Midwest regional specialty show and topped the day by also winning the Working Group. Eight champions have been produced by English Valley Newfoundlands.

Ch. Semy Ye Gads Charlie, top-winning Newfoundland in the United States in 1972 and 1973, was bred by Mrs. Lu Ann Pingel of Sioux City, Iowa. Charlie's enviable record includes a Best in Show win, more than a dozen Group wins, and approximately one hundred Best of Breed wins. He is the sire of several champions. Charlie is currently owned by Mrs. Catherine Lundberg, The Riverhouse, Ochelata, Oklahoma. To date, seven champions bear the Semy kennel name. These include Ch. Semy Sebastian of Briarcreek, winner of several Group placements. He is owned by Susie Y. Schlienz, Solon, Iowa.

Other top-winning Newfoundlands in the Midwest in recent years are Ch. Little Bear's Three Mile Limit, winner of a Working Group in Canada and a Group placement in the United States, owned by Richard H. Lillie, Jr., Milwaukee, Wisconsin; Ch. Randybrook's A Big Clown, who boasts a Group placement and is owned by William and Gloria Bolton, Lake Zurich, Illinois; and Clown's son, Ch. Randybrook's Black Checkmate, who was the Best of Breed dog at the 1974 Midwest regional specialty show and climaxed the day with a Group placement. Checkmate is owned by Frank L. Grasso and James Bryan Meehan, Lake Zurich, Illinois. Ch. Bethward's Heimdahl of Ryann, C. D., owned by Phillip Snyder of Elkhart, Indiana, has a Group placement to his credit, and Sambo of Notalab, bred and owned by Thomas R. Robinson, Eagen, Minnesota, is the recent winner of a Working Group.

Robert M. Price, Jr., Edina, Minnesota, owns the only Newfoundlands in the Upper Midwest with championship and Obedience titles in both the United States and Canada. Am. & Can. Ch. Little Bear's Rebel Tug, Am. & Can. C. D., and Am. & Can. Ch. Little Bear's Tugboat Annie, Am. & Can. C. D., are among the Newfoundlands at Paddlewheel Kennels. Tug was Canada's top-winning Newfoundland in 1971 and 1972. He has won 55 Best of Breed awards and 18 Group placements, including Group First wins in both the United States and Canada. In addition, he earned better than 190 points in all Obedience trials entered. Mr. Price also owns Am. & Can. Ch. Little Bear's Shipshape Rig, winner of a Group placement in Canada and the sire of several champions and Group-placing Little Bear Sailor.

The Robert Quandts of Deerfield, Illinois, are the proud owners of two Newfoundlands with both companion dog and tracking dog titles.

Ch. Semy Ye Gads Charlie, Best in Show winner gaining friends for the Newfoundland in the Midwest. Owned by C. Lundberg.

Ch. Old Mole's Lucas, a multiple Best in Show winner in 1975. Bred by Michael Mole, Lucas is owned by James and Dail Corl of Pine Grove Mills, Pa., and handled by Tom Glassford.

They are Edenglen's Titanic and Edenglen's Chocolate Chip. Phillip Snyder, Ryann Kennels, has trained several of his Newfoundlands to Obedience titles. These include, in addition to the aforementioned Heimdahl, Ch. Ryann's Viking Rollo, C. D. X.

The Newfoundland breed in the Rocky Mountain states has experienced a marked increase in popularity in recent years. Denver, Colorado, is the present home of Dryad Kennels, Reg., originally established by Maynard and Kitty Drury in New York but now owned by the Drurys' daughter, Mrs. Jay M. Dewey. Nearby, in Greeley, Colorado, the Graniteledge Kennels, operated by Mr. and Mrs. James A. Ferguson. are the proud owners of Ch. Little Bear's Breakaway, C. D., Best of Breed winner at the 1973 Rocky Mountain regional specialty show. Several champion and Obedience-titled Newfoundlands have been produced by Graniteledge Kennels, including Ch. Graniteledge Chinook, a Group-placing bitch.

Ch. Black Bannon of Aspen, owned by John and Cynthia Callahan of Aspen, Colorado, claimed several Group placements and has four champion offspring to his credit. One son, Ch. Black Angus of Alta, has won Group placements. Angus was bred and is still owned by Larry and Joan Holder of Sandy, Utah. The Holders' Alta View Kennels were established in 1967. Their bitch, Ch. Barbara-Allen's Belle of Alta was Utah's first champion. To date, seven champions have been produced by Alta View Newfoundlands.

Some other kennels of note actively breeding and showing at this writing are: Beaupre, owned by Mr. and Mrs. E. E. Gleason: Ebonewf, owned by Mr. and Mrs. Roy Esiason; Tamiroka, owned by Mr. and Mrs. Henry Turek; Far Hills, owned by Mr. and Mrs. John White; Barbara-Allen Kennels of Bothell, Washington, owned by Mr. and Mrs. Allen A. Wolman; Timhurst, owned by Mrs. Jean Goodrich; Big Sky, owned by Mrs. Sharon Payne; Wanaka, owned by Dr. and Mrs. Robert Moesch; Bandom, owned by Mae Freeland; Hilvig, owned by Hilda Madsen; and Springfield, owned by Mrs. Robert V. Clark.

Ch. Dryad's Lord Nelson, U.D.T., foremost Obedience winning Newfoundland of 1968, 1969 and 1970, and winner of the Stud Dog Class at the 1974 National Specialty. Sire of 10 champions, including Specialty winners, two Westminster BOB winners and a BIS winner (Ch. Kilyka's Black Bart), and sire of 4 Obedience titlists. Owned by Mrs. George McDonnell.

Ch. Shipshape's Sibyl, U.D.T., Obedience star and dam of 7 champions and 6 Obedience titlists. Owned by Mrs. George McDonnell.

APPEARANCE: Large, heavy coated, deep bodied, well-muscled; appears square although slightly longer than tall; soft expression reflects benevolence, intelligence, dignity

EARS small, triangular with rounded tips; well set back, close to head

NECK strong; well set on shoulders

BACK broad, strong; level topline

TAIL set follows natural line of croup; bones reach to hocks; tail broad, strong at base; kink in tail objectionable

HINDQUARTERS powerful, well muscled, thighs fairly long, stifles well bent, hocks (rear view) perpendicular to ground

FEET proportionate to body, cat type, well rounded, tight; toes firm, arched, webbed; may be trimmed for neatness

SIZE:
Average adult height—males, 28''; bitches, 26''
Average adult weight—males, 130-150 lbs.
bitches, 100-120 lbs.

DISQUALIFICATIONS: Brindle, merle, tri-color; markings other than white on solid-colored dog; any color other than white on a black dog

HEAD broad, massive, strongly developed occipital bone; moderately sloped stop

EYES dark brown, relatively small, deep set, wide apart

MUZZLE broad, deep; clean-cut; covered with short, fine hair

CHEST full, deep, brisket reaches to elbows; shoulders well-muscled

FORELEGS well-muscled; straight, parallel (front view) with elbows pointing directly to rear; pasterns strong, slightly sloping

COAT: Water resistant, outer coat coarse, full, moderately long; straight, flat (slight wave permissible)

COLOR: Preferably black or white and black (Landseer); slight tinge of bronze in black coat acceptable; white on chin, chest, toes, tip of tail, acceptable on black dog; solid colors acceptable; excessive ticking on Landseer undesirable

5

Official Standard of The Newfoundland

(As revised by the Newfoundland Club of America, and approved by the American Kennel Club, May 8, 1979.)

GENERAL CHARACTERISTICS & APPEARANCE: The Newfoundland is a sweet-dispositioned dog that never acts either dull or ill tempered. His expression is soft and reflects the characteristics of the breed—benevolence, intelligence, and dignity. He is a multipurpose dog that is at home on land and in the water; he is capable of draft work and he possesses natural lifesaving instincts. He is a devoted companion to man and child.

He is large, heavy coated, well boned, strong, and appears to be square, although he is slightly longer than he is tall. He is balanced, deep bodied, and well muscled. A good specimen of the breed has dignity and proud head carriage. The dog's appearance is more massive throughout than the bitch's.

Head—The head is massive, with a broad skull, slightly arched crown, and strongly developed occipital bone. The slope of the stop is moderate but, because of well developed superciliary ridges, may appear abrupt in profile. The forehead and face are smooth and free of wrinkles. The muzzle is clean-cut and covered with short, fine hair. The muzzle is broad and deep; its length from the tip of the nose to the stop is less than that from the stop to the occiput. The top of the muzzle, when viewed from the front, is rounded. The bridge of the muzzle, when viewed from the side, is straight or only slightly arched. The nostrils are well developed.

The teeth meet in a scissors or level bite.

The eyes are dark brown, relatively small, deep-set and spaced wide apart. Eye color other than brown is very objectionable. The eyelids fit closely with no inversion.

The ears are relatively small and triangular with rounded tips. They are set well back on the skull, level with or slightly above, the superciliary ridges, and lie close to the head. When the ear is brought forward, it reaches to the inner corner of the eye on the same side.

Neck & Body—The neck is strong and well set on the shoulders. It is long enough for proud head carriage. The topline is level from the withers to the croup. The back is broad, strong, and well muscled from the shoulders through the croup. The chest is full and deep with the brisket reaching at least down to the elbows. The croup slopes at an angle of about 30 degrees. The tail set follows the natural line of the croup. The tail is broad at the base and strong. The tail bones reach to the hock. When the dog is standing relaxed, its tail hangs straight or with a slight curve at the end. When the dog is in motion or excited, the tail is carried straight out or slightly curved, but it never curls over the back. A tail with a kink is objectionable.

Forequarters—The forelegs are well muscled and well boned. When the standing dog is viewed from the front, the forelegs are straight and parallel from the shoulder point to the ground, with the elbows pointing directly to the rear. The shoulders are well muscled. The layback of the shoulder blade is about 45 degrees and the upper arm meets the shoulder blade at an angle of about 90 degrees. The pasterns are strong and slightly sloping.

Hindquarters—The rear assembly is powerful, well muscled, and well boned. The croup is broad. When the standing dog is viewed from the rear, the legs are straight and parallel. Viewed from the side, the thigh is fairly long, the stifle well bent and the line from the hock to the ground is perpendicular to the ground.

Feet—The feet are proportionate to the body in size, cat-foot in type, well-rounded and tight with firm, arched toes. Complete webbing is always present.

Coat—The adult Newfoundland has a water-resistant, double coat. The outer coat is coarse, moderately long and full. It is straight and flat, although it may have a slight wave. The coat, when rubbed the wrong way, tends to fall back in place. An open coat is objectionable. The undercoat, which is soft and dense, is often less dense during the summer months or in tropical climates. The hair on the face and muzzle is short and fine. Excess hair on the ears may be trimmed. The legs are feathered all the way down. Feet may be trimmed for neatness. The tail is covered with long, dense hair, but it does not form a flag.

Color—The Newfoundland colors to be preferred are black or white and black (Landseer). A slight tinge of bronze in a black coat is acceptable as is white on the chin, chest, toes, and tip of tail on a black dog. The Landseer is a white dog with black markings. Typical Landseer markings are a black head with white on the muzzle and/or white blaze (or a black head), and black central body markings and black on the rump extending on to the tail. Excessive ticking is undesirable. Beauty of markings should be taken into consideration, but never at the expense of type and soundness. Solid colors other than black are acceptable. The following colors are disqualified: Brindle; merle; tri-color; any color other than white on a solid colored dog; and any color other than black on a white dog.

Gait—The Newfoundland in motion has good reach, strong drive, and gives the impression of effortless power. Essential to good movement is the balance of correct front and rear assemblies. The forelegs and hindlegs travel straight forward and do not swing in an arc or move in and out in relation to the line of travel. As the dog's speed increases, the legs angle in from the shoulders and hips toward the center line of the body and tend toward single tracking. When moving, a slight roll of the skin is characteristic of the breed.

Size—The average height for adult dogs is 28 inches and for adult bitches, 26 inches. The approximate weight of adult dogs is 130 to 150 pounds, of adult bitches 100 to 120 pounds. Large size is desirable, but never at the expense of balance, structure and correct gait.

Structural and movement faults common to all working dogs are as undesirable in the Newfoundland as in any other breed, even though they are not specifically mentioned herein.

The foregoing description is that of the ideal Newfoundland. Any deviation from this ideal is to be penalized to the extent of the deviation.

DISQUALIFICATIONS:

The following colors are disqualified: Brindle; merle, tri-color; any color other than white on a solid colored dog; and any color other than black on a white dog.

Current Canadian Standard for the Newfoundland:

At their annual meeting of March 1978, the Board of Directors of The Canadian Kennel Club approved the following standard for the Newfoundland dog, to become effective January 1, 1979:

Origin and Purpose—The breed originated in Newfoundland from dogs indigenous to the island, and the big black bear dogs introduced by the Vikings in 1001 A.D. With the advent of European fishermen, a variety of new breeds helped to shape and re-invigorate the breed, but the essential characteristics of the Newfoundland dog remained. By the time colonization was permitted in 1610, the distinct physical characteristics and mental attributes had been established in the breed for all time.

The large size, heavy coat and webbed feet permit him to withstand the rigors of the extreme climate and sea while serving both as lifeguard and draught animal.

General Appearance—The Newfoundland is massive, deep bodied, well muscled and coordinated, projecting dignity in stance and head carriage. The appearance is square in that the length of the dog, from the top of the withers to the base of the tail is equal to the distance from the top of the withers to the ground. The distance from the top of the withers to the underside of the chest is greater than the distance from the underside of the chest to the ground. The body of the bitch may be slightly longer, and is less massive than that of the dog. A mature dog should never appear leggy or lacking substance. The Newfoundland is free moving with a slight roll perceptible. Substantial webbing between the toes is always present. Large size is desirable but never at the expense of gait symmetry and balance. Fine bone is to be faulted.

Temperament—The Newfoundland's expression is soft and reflects the character of the breed—benevolent, intelligent, dignified but capable of fun. He is known for his sterling gentleness and serenity. Any show of ill temper or timidity is to be severely faulted. Bad temperament is a disqualification.

Size—The average height for adult dogs is 28 inches, for adult bitches, 26 inches. The average weight for adult dogs is 150 pounds, for adult bitches, 120 pounds. Large size is desirable but it is not to be favored over correct gait, symmetry, soundness and structure.

Coat and Colour—The Newfoundland has a water resistant double coat. The outer coat is moderately long and straight with no curl. A slight wave is permissible. When rubbed the wrong way, the coat tends to fall back into place. The undercoat is soft and dense, but less dense during the summer months, but always found to some extent on the rump and chest. A completely open coat is to be faulted. The hair on the head, muzzle and ears is short and fine. The front and rear legs are feathered. The tail is completely covered with long dense hair, but does not form a flag. A short, flat, smooth coat, (Labrador Retriever type) is a disqualification. The traditional colour is black. A sunburned black is permissible. White markings on the chest, toes and or tip of tail are permissible. Markings of any colour other than white are

Canadian & American Ch. Hornblower's Long John Silver, Landseer Newfoundland, co-owned by Lynn Raymond, Stowaway Newfoundlands, Ottawa, Canada and Rosemary Carvallo of Elmont, L.I., NY. Long John was the top winning show dog in Canada (all breeds) for 1978 and at beginning of 1980 had a pace-setting record of 19 Bests in Show (including 16 all-breed), 53 Group Firsts and 158 Bests of Breed. Whelped 11-11-74, by Sailor of Hornblower ex Hornblower Storm Alert, he was bred by Dr. Gerald Neufeld.

most objectionable and the dog is to be disqualified. The Landseer New-foundland is white with black markings, and is of historical significance to the breed. The preferred pattern of markings for the Landseer is, black head with white blaze extending onto the muzzle, black saddle and black rump and upper tail. All remaining parts are to be white with a minimum of ticking. The symmetry of markings and beauty of pattern characterize the best marked Landseers. Landseers are to be shown in the same classes as blacks unless special classes are provided for them.

Head—The head is massive with a broad skull, slightly arched crown and strongly developed occipital bone. The forehead and face are smooth and free of wrinkles. The top is not abrupt. The muzzle is clean cut and covered with short fine hair. It is rather square, deep and moderately short. The nostrils are well developed. The bitch's head follows the same general conformation, but is feminine and less massive. A narrow head, snipey or long muzzle is to be faulted. Pronounced flews are not desirable. The eyes are dark brown, relatively small and deep set. They are spaced wide apart and show no haw. Round, protruding or yellow eyes are objectionable. The ears are relatively small and triangular with rounded tips. They are set well back on the side of the head and lie close. When the ear of the adult dog is brought forward, it reaches to the inner corner of the eye on the same side. The teeth meet in a scissors of level bite.

Neck—The neck is strong, muscular and well set on the shoulders. It is long enough to permit dignified head carriage, and should not show surplus dewlap.

93

Forequarters—When the dog is not in motion, the forelegs are straight and parallel, with the elbows close to the chest. The shoulders are well muscled and well laid back at an angle approaching 45 degrees. The pasterns are slightly sloping. Down in the pasterns is to be faulted. The feet are proportionate to the body in size, well rounded and tight, with firm compact toes. (cat foot type) Splayed toes are a fault. Toeing in or out is undesirable.

Body—The Newfoundland's chest is broad, full and deep, with the brisket reaching to the elbows. The back is broad, with good spread of rib, and the topline is level from the withers to croup, never roached, slack or swayed. The loins are strong and well muscled, and the croup is broad. The pelvis slopes at an angle of about 30 degrees. Viewed from the side of the body is deep, showing no discernible tuck-up. Bone structure is massive throughout but does not give sluggish appearance.

Hindquarters—Because driving power for swimming, pulling loads or covering ground efficiently is largely dependent upon the hindquarters, the rear structure of the Newfoundland is of prime importance. The hip assembly is broad, strong and well developed. The upper thighs are wide and muscular. The lower thighs are strong and fairly long. The stifles are well bent, but not so as to give a crouching appearance. The hocks are well let down, well apart and parallel to each other. They turn neither in nor out. The feet are firm and tight. Dewclaws if present should have been removed. Straight stifles, cow hocks, barrel legs, and pigeon toes are to be faulted.

Tail—The tail acts as a rudder when the Newfoundland is swimming, therefore it is strong and broad at the base. When the dog is standing the tail hangs straight down, possibly a little curved at the tip, reaching to or slightly below the hocks; when the dog is in motion or excited, the tail is carried straight out or with slight upward curve but never curled back over the back nor curved inward between the legs. A tail with a kink or curled at the end is very objectionable.

Gait—The Newfoundland has good reach and strong drive, giving the impression of effortless power. In motion, the legs move straight forward parallel to the line of travel. A slight roll is present. As the speed increases, the dog tends to single track, with the topline remaining level. Mincing, shuffling, crabbing, too close moving, weaving, crossing over in front, toeing out or distinctly toeing in front, hackney action and pacing are all faults.

Faults—legginess, narrow head, snipey or long muzzle, pronounced flews, short tail, long tail, tail with a kink, tail with a curled end, fine bone, any show of ill temper or timidity, open coat, eyes showing pronounced haw, round, protruding or yellow eyes, splayed feet, down pasterns, mincing, shuffling, crabbing, weaving, crossing over in front, toeing out or distinctly toeing in front, hackney action or pacing, straight stifles, cow hocks, barrel legs, roached, slack or sway back, lack of webbing between toes, overshot or under shot or wry mouth.

Disqualifications—Bad temperament, Short flat coat (Labrador Retriever type), markings of any other colour than white on a black dog, any colours other than the traditional black, or Landseer (white and black).

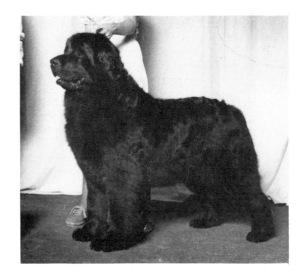

Can. & Am. Ch. Arval's Ocean Splendor, Canadian Group and Specialty (1975) winner. Bred by Arne Berg and owned by Margaret Brown.

Ch. Little Bear's HMS Challenger, sire of 20 champions. Owned by Barbara Ann Forth, Canada.

Can. Ch. Mariner's Happy Heidi, winner of 1979 Newfoundland Club of Canada Specialty. Bred and owned by Angie DeBruyn.

The current official English Standard for the Newfoundland:

CHARACTERISTICS.—A water dog, used for life-saving; he should have an exceptionally gentle and docile nature.

GENERAL APPEARANCE.—The dog should impress the eye with strength and great activity. He should move freely on his legs with the body swung loosely between them, so that a slight roll in gait should not be objectionable. Bone massive throughout, but not to give a heavy, inactive appearance.

Head and Skull.—Head should be broad and massive, the occipital bone well developed; there should be no decided stop; the muzzle should be short, clean cut and rather square in shape and covered with short, fine hair.

Eyes.—Should be small, of a dark brown colour; rather deeply set, but not showing any haw; should be set rather wide apart.

Ears.—Should be small, set well back, square with the skull, lie close to the head, and covered with short hair without a fringe.

Mouth.—Should be soft and well covered by the lips, should be neither undershot nor overshot but teeth should be level or scissor bite.

Neck.—Should be strong, well set on to shoulders and back.

Forequarters.—Legs should be perfectly straight, well covered with muscle, elbows in but well let down; feathered all down.

Body.—Should be well ribbed up with broad back and strong muscular loins. Chest should be deep and fairly broad; well covered with hair, but not to such an extent as to form a frill.

Hindquarters.—Should be very strong. The legs should have great freedom of action; slightly feathered. Slackness of loins and cow-hocks are a defect. Dew-claws are objectionable and should be removed.

Feet.—Should be large and well shaped. Splayed or turned out feet are objectionable.

Tail.—Should be of moderate length, reaching down a little below the hocks. It should be of fair thickness and well covered with hair, but not to form a flag. When the dog is standing still and not excited it should hang downwards with a slight curve at the end; but when the dog is in motion it should be carried up, and when he is excited straight out with only a slight curve at the end. Tails with a kink or curled over the back are very objectionable.

Coat.—Should be flat and dense, of a coarsish texture and oily nature, and capable of resisting water. If brushed the wrong way it should fall back into its place naturally.

Color.—Dull jet black. A slight tinge of bronze or splash of white on chest and toes is acceptable. Black dogs having only white toes and white chest and white tip of tail should be exhibited in classes provided for blacks.

Brown. Can be chocolate or bronze. Should in all other respects follow the black except in color. Splash of white on chest and toes is acceptable. Brown dogs to be exhibited in classes provided for blacks.

White with black markings only—Landseers. For preference black head with narrow blaze, even marked saddle and black rump extending on to tail. Beauty in markings to be taken greatly into consideration. Ticking is not desirable.

The above are the only permitted colors.

Weight and Size.—Size and weight are very desirable so long as symmetry is maintained. A fair average height at the shoulders is 28 inches for a dog and 26 inches for a bitch, and a fair average weight is, respectively: Dogs, 140 to 150 lbs. Bitches, 110 to 120 lbs.

Faults.—Weak or hollow back, slackness of the loins or cow-hocks. Dew-claws. Splayed or turned-out feet. Tails with a kink in them or curled over the back.

English breeder F. Cassidy (Little Creek Kennels) sets up one of his Newfoundlands for study by American breeders Mrs. Winthrop Wadleigh and author Margaret Booth Chern.

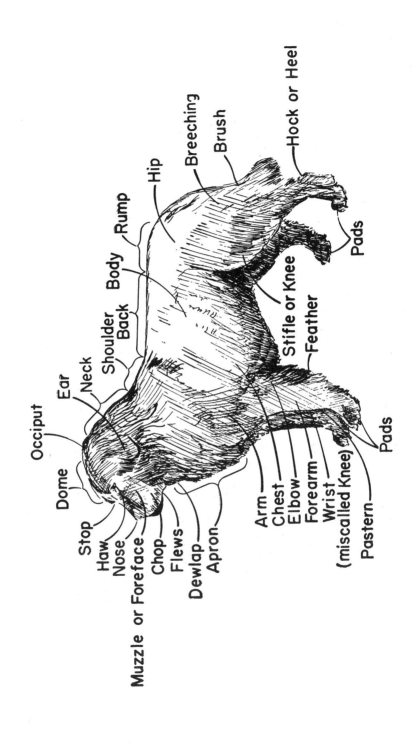

6

An In-Depth Look
At the Standard

THE OUTSTANDING characteristics of a true New-
foundland are his benevolent disposition and his lifesaving instinct.
Hence, these prime factors should manifest themselves in every expression of the dog's face and in his whole general demeanor. Everything about him must convey the feeling of kindness and friendliness.
All actions must indicate inquisitiveness, intelligence, and alertness.

Lack of any of the above qualities should be considered a cardinal
fault. Loyalty and obedience to his master, courage and resourcefulness in time of danger are more difficult to evaluate in the everyday
routine but in the last account represent the final test of a Newfoundland's excellence.

A dog dedicated to the heroic deeds of lifesaving, both on land and at
sea, must have a truly herculean frame to live up to the magnitude of
tasks imposed on him by a generous heart and unswerving obedience
to the call of duty. Soundness is an essential ingredient of type, for
without perfect framework, well-functioning running gear, coordination, and fine muscle tone, the Newfoundland could not accomplish his
purpose. Hence, soundness must ever be the foremost physical expression of the true Newfoundland type.

In lifesaving work the Newfoundland swims great distances through
the icy waters of a wintry ocean; to stand hours of submersion he requires a water-shedding outercoat and a thick, woolly undercoat resistant to water. To these add remarkable stamina, depth of chest to insure ample lung capacity, muscular, well-developed hindquarters, a
powerful neck, and a body well-padded with hard muscles.

In the more prosaic realm is the Newfoundland's role of helper to his
master in daily tasks (be it hauling wood, playing nurse, or guarding the

family children and property). Obedience and sweetness of disposition are paramount, and the desire to please is manifested by beneficent expression.

This summary gives us a basic understanding of the Newfoundland's nature, his reason for being, and his functional anatomy. In evolving a detailed "blueprint" based on our breed's Standard, at all points the true nature of the breed and its mechanics must be remembered. To evaluate the Newfoundland's characteristics and functions, compare them with the best examples that nature can provide and you have the criterion for excellence.

The purpose of any dog Standard is to describe specifically the qualities and character of the particular breed. Seek in nature for the best example of what you strive to comprehend. Thus, to understand a particular type of bite, analyze the porcupine, beaver, wolverine, deer, or moose — consider its purpose and the anatomic mechanics involved.

For speed, study the thoroughbred horse, the gazelle, or any of the fast movers. Every characteristic of an animal and its perfection can be evaluated for improvement by first determining the use of the animal and then, through study of the body, legs, etc., by seeing how nature has designed for the greatest efficiency.

Bear in mind that breeding is an art of putting the desired characteristics together in harmony and with effectiveness. A breed comes about by natural selection, by design of the originators of the breed, or by accident. Perfection, however, is not the result of an accident, but is directly achieved through sound knowledge of functional anatomy as incorporated in the breed Standard. There is no question that the early originators of the Newfoundland Standard had both thorough and broad concepts of functional anatomy and the proof lies in the Standard itself. Stonehenge can be given credit for formulating its basic principles.

Symmetry and General Appearance

First of all, look for a well-proportioned, closely knit body with a proud head carriage. The total effect of strength and symmetry could only be achieved by apparent perfection of head, body, legs, and properly placed and suspended tail in correct relation and proportion.

Movement should be well coordinated with strong forward thrust. Halting movement or unsteadiness is most undesirable. Although a slight roll may be considered characteristic, too much roll indicates looseness and reveals a too shallow hip socket. In spite of his size, clumsiness is not excusable in a Newfoundland, as it is contrary to the concept of an active and powerful dog. Being an aquatic dog does not

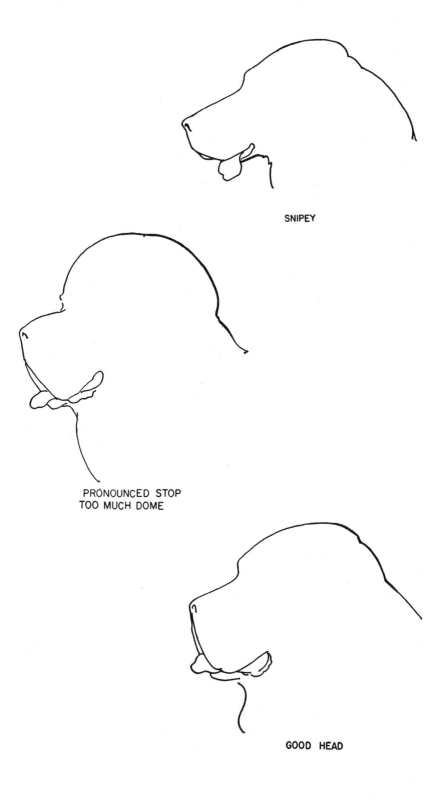

SNIPEY

PRONOUNCED STOP
TOO MUCH DOME

GOOD HEAD

absolve him from efficiency of movement on land. His basic lifesaving purpose requires him to possess great agility ashore as well as in the sea, for how otherwise would he ever reach the drowning man? Though water prowess is one of his great virtues, the Newfoundland has always been an all-purpose dog ashore, able to hunt, haul, and guard. Nothing short of complete coordination fits him for his very demanding roles.

The topline should be level. Sway or hollow back or roach back are to be guarded against. Loins must be muscular and broad.

Head

The head should be broad and massive, with the occipital bone well developed. The stop should be slight only. A decided stop, such as that found on a St. Bernard, is not good on a Newfoundland. A pronounced stop interferes with the sense of smell. Hunting breeds do not have it. Also undesirable is a head with no stop at all. As a water rescue dog the Newfoundland must have an easy slope of nasal passage — no abrupt stop — to allow quick intake of air to full lung capacity. Also this easy breathing facility makes the Newfoundland better able to adapt to hot weather and is a contributing factor to the remarkable vitality of the Newfoundland, its recuperative powers and longevity.

Being a creature of balance and harmony, the short muzzle is relative. The correct degree of shortness can be determined by the relationship of the length of head from stop to occiput as against the length from stop to tip of nose. The muzzle should be slightly shorter than the length of head. A too short muzzle should be guarded against because excessive shortness precludes a soft mouth. Bulldogs have short muzzles for their characteristic holding, death grip. The Newfoundland needs a soft mouth for retrieving or rescue work. Relationship of length to depth of muzzle should create the impression of squareness. A slight furrow runs down the middle of forehead to the stop. The muzzle should be straight or, very slightly convex, nearly straight. The Newfoundland should never be dish-faced nor snipey. A developed brow over the eye is one of the earliest distinguishing characteristics.

Teeth should be regular and strong. From a utilitarian standpoint, the Newfoundland must possess either a close scissors bite or a level bite to fulfill its tasks.

Eyes are dark, rather small, deep-set, wide apart. A large, round, protruding eye is subject to damage as well as an eye in which the haw is conspicuous. A structurally faulty eye is more vulnerable in extremely cold weather.

102

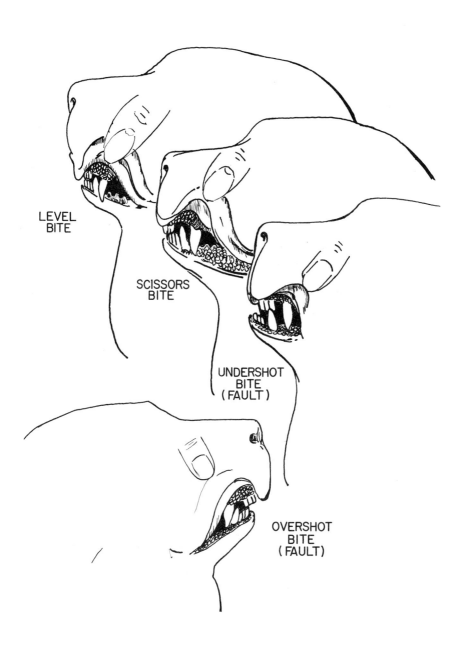

LEVEL
BITE

SCISSORS
BITE

UNDERSHOT
BITE
(FAULT)

OVERSHOT
BITE
(FAULT)

Ears are round-tipped, triangular, set a little below the top line of the skull. In a fully mature Newfoundland, when the flap is brought forward it can reach the inner corner of the adjacent eye. In a puppy the ear will be relatively longer because ears attain their growth in length long before the final width of head develops.

Coat

Correct body coat is important to the Newfoundland. Emphasis, however, should be on density rather than length. An overly long or shaggy coat would collect snow and ice and would not be serviceable in winter weather. In the winter, in northern climates, the body should be covered with a fine woolly undercoat. The outercoat should be coarse, straight and lie flat. If brushed the wrong way it should tend to fall back into place. A fluffy or woolly outercoat would not shed water and is strictly against the Standard. The ideal coat, although coarse, is not harsh to the touch; it has natural gloss and is much easier to keep groomed than the incorrect fluffy or woolly outercoat.

The muzzle should be covered with short, fine hair, the skull with dense, smooth hair. The ears should be covered with short, fine hair and if bushy looking or forming a fringe, should be trimmed.

Feet should not look like snow-shoes and its hair should be trimmed so as not to extend beyond the foot onto the floor. Forelegs should be feathered from elbow to foot. Hind legs should exhibit luxuriant pantaloons.

Body

The Newfoundland was described by a writer in 1802 as "the most majestic of all the canine variety." To live up to his regal reputation, the dog must be endowed with both elegance and strength. The body should be somewhat close-coupled with powerful rib spread, deep brisket, mighty chest, straight, wide back, broad loins with well-developed, hard muscles, and a gently sloping croup. Body depth should be measured through the section of the ninth rib and not just behind the elbows. Tuck-up should be confined to the abdominal area, otherwise space for essential organs will be insufficient for the speed and endurance required of the Newfoundland. From the tip of the sternum, at least a slight tuck-up is essential as indication of good muscle tone.

The center of gravity in the Newfoundland's body should be back toward the center, taking the weight off the forehand, and while swim-

Good topline—
Well bent stifle.

Roach back.

Sway back.

High rump—
Straight stifle.

ming, distributing it evenly over the submerged area. Power in the water is supplied by the rear legs; the front legs keep the body in the horizontal plane. A good swimmer requires the same leverage and power that make for a fast mover on land.

The croup slope should approximate 30° with change angle of 150°. This angulation is standard in good horses and deviation makes the croup flat or steep. For greatest agility, steepness is desirable. For greatest power in locomotion, flatness is preferred. The Newfoundland, being a creature of balance, should avoid both extremes.

Forelegs

The entire front assembly depends on the shoulder blade. To be efficient, there should be good length of shoulder blade. The layback should have a 45° slope. The legs should hang straight and parallel, with the long upper arm, or humerus, set at 90° to the blade, or as nearly at that angle as possible. When such is the case, the blade and humerus form a right-angle triangle. This assembly will act like a shock absorber and give reach and follow-through. Bend in pastern is required to keep the assembly in static balance. A sloping pastern should not be confused with a broken pastern. The slope should begin either above or below the joint, preferably above. Slope beginning at the joint will likely mean broken pastern. Knuckling over comes from a straight pastern; so does quivering. The only way to avoid these undesirable conditions is to have a bend in pastern to take the weight off dead center at the pastern joint.

Hindquarters and Legs

Since the driving power either on land or in the sea comes from the hindquarters, in the Newfoundland we cannot overestimate the importance of the rear assembly. Among large breeds, the all black Newfoundland has from earliest days been conspicuous for his powerful hindquarters, firmness of loin, muscular legs, and well-bent stifle. It is essential that serious breeders never lose this great heritage.

If the dog's hocks incline inward rather than point directly back, it is said to be cowhocked. This is a serious fault. In achieving the well-bent stifle which is essential, the thigh should be long, the hock joint wide, and the distance between hock joint and heel should be short.

Chest

If the angle of the humerus and shoulder blade is correct, there will be a protruding point in the chest. The proper depth of the chest is determined by the brisket in relation to the elbow, which the brisket must reach, or come slightly below. As the Newfoundland is in every way a dog of proportion, the deepest chest may not be a virtue in itself. Legs must be in correct proportion for the very deep chest, the upper arm necessarily being long in proportion to the lower. With a dog whose maximum allowable size is not subject to limitation, there is an ever-present danger of achieving a ponderous creature unable to attend to his tasks. The Standard takes full cognizance of this danger and the safeguard is most appropriate to insure the long-range, sound development of our breed. Within a breed, relative size of bone has a much greater effect on the individual dog than the layman may realize. Speed, endurance, pulling power, and even personality itself are affected by bone size. The lighter the bone, the greater is the agility, speed, and even endurance, but with these virtues comes undesirable nervousness and sometimes pugnaciousness. The heavier the bone, the greater the strength at the expense of endurance. A good example is the Newfoundland's sled-dog cousin, which retained greater endurance and speed along with smaller bone. With the large bone comes amiability, with a degree of laziness and even sloppiness in its extreme form.

Determination of bone size, just as is the case with all other components of the ideal Newfoundland, is a matter of seeking the golden mean. Giantism is an evil against which the breeders should be on guard. The favor sometimes shown in the ring to the large dog in preference to other considerations can very easily tempt the novice breeder to follow this seemingly easy path to glory. Oversize can rob the dog of the very qualities which made our breed famous. As long as the individual Newfoundland retains speed and stamina, the breeder has not reached the danger point of giantism, but when the Newfoundland becomes too heavy for strenuous activity and loses agility and coordination, the danger point has been reached.

Feet

A Newfoundland's feet must be webbed or impurity of lineage is revealed. The foot type should be the cat foot characterized by a shorter third digit. Without exception the early drawings emphasize the compact, large and powerful feet of the Newfoundland. Study the feet in pictures of the old breed, especially *Reinagle's Study of a Newfound-*

land and the Newfoundland from *Cope's Natural History* that are reproduced in this book. Such feet are built for endurance and resistance to injury.

Either a splayed foot or a thin-soled foot is an extremely serious fault. The splayed foot is subject to injuries. With the paper foot, with its too thin soles or pads, the entire foot usually breaks down. Too small a foot is uncharacteristic. The Newfoundland should neither toe in nor out.

Pasterns must bend and not stand rigid. But do not confuse a sloping pastern with a broken-down one. Slope should not start in the joint itself but either above or below it. Slope should be enough to bring the heel of the pad under center of gravity.

Dewclaws, or fifth toes, are liable to injury in the field. When found on rear legs of Newfoundlands, they should be removed. However, you will probably never encounter them, as they are rare. If needed, the operation for their removal is most easily performed before the puppy opens its eyes.

Nails should be strongly developed.

Tail

The set of the pelvis will determine the tail placement. Since for greatest efficiency the croup of the Newfoundland is neither flat nor steep, the tail set will also be moderate. It is broad at the base, long and alive all the way.

Height and Weight

The aim in size should be for the average indicated in the Standard or more. But in no case should proportion be lost. Size without balance and soundness is worthless.

Proportion

Proportion is everything in the search for the ideal Newfoundland. Never idolize any particular anatomical part or dimension, be it bone, head, depth or shortness of muzzle, or length of tail. No body part should be emphasized at the expense of general symmetry. It is only the complete image of the Newfoundland which counts. Inasmuch as it is an all-purpose dog, never seek any extreme. Magnify one part, or increase its size, and there is a relative decrease in other parts of the dog.

If the head and neck are enlarged, the trunk and extremities are reduced. Body length must be balanced by height, width of back and chest, and depth of chest.

The ideal animal must always be in proportion whereby all parts are rather normal. The champion should not be over-developed disproportionately or its title is undeserved. For perfection, avoid extremes. This is the law of nature, and nature's laws never change. There is always a great tolerance or survival would be more uncertain. As nature sets definite standards in the animal kingdom, each species develops with certain tolerances, the average of which produces the greatest health and usefulness. It is only through astute application of the law of compensation that a breeder can hope to improve the Newfoundland or even maintain its present qualities.

Color

Black is the classic color. White on chest, toes and tip of tail are not objectionable. Dogs with such white markings are considered all black for purposes of judging.

Other Than Black: Although recognizing the possibility of almost any color, the Standard discourages any colors other than black, bronze, or black and white. It is a disqualification for a Newfoundland to have a second color other than white.

The black and white is known as the Landseer, taking its name from the artist, Sir Edwin Landseer, whose paintings of black and white Newfoundlands made the variety popular.

In Landseers, evenness of markings is more than aesthetically desirable. Early historians of the breed did not believe the Landseer to be a true Newfoundland, but, as Professor Heim claims, primarily a development of the large black and white English mongrel dog, known as the butcher dog, with the addition of true Newfoundland, and Saint Bernard crosses. And inasmuch as the Newfoundland, according to Professor Heim, carries prepotently the factor of evenness in marking, unevenness in spotting shows too much retention of non-Newfoundland characteristics.

The early Landseer was larger than the true Newfoundland and possessed a larger, Saint Bernard head. When a Landseer is smaller in bone and size, and has a smaller head inclined toward snipiness, along with irregularity of markings, one may suspect that the parti-colored coat may have been obtained through infusion of Setter blood. Likewise, much ticking (black spots in white areas) is not desirable.

The future Ch. Little Bear's John Paul Jones as a 4-months old puppy.

Ch. LIttle Bear's John Paul Jones as a Group winning adult.

EVALUATING (AND PREPARING) YOUR NEWFOUNDLAND
FOR THE SHOW RING

For the benefit of a novice in the Newfoundland fancy, it may be necessary to give a graphic illustration as to how to apply the information gained from reading the Standard.

It is frequently desirable to be able to evaluate one's own dog without resorting to professional authority. It is, therefore, our aim to enable a fancier to forecast the chances of his loveable Newfoundland in the competitive show ring. There tends to be a sneaking feeling in everyone's heart that his growing Junior is destined to outshine and outwin the most glamorous ancestor in his pedigree, and that of course may be so.

On the other hand. . . . . .

Let us consider the facts. The first outdoor show premium list has just arrived. Junior has reached that delightful stage when he no longer consumes quantities of socks and bedroom slippers, but is seriously contemplating his life as a grownup yearling, no longer eligible for the puppy class.

He looks trustingly into your eyes and you begin to feel that you simply owe it to him to take him to that first spring show.

You also start taking judicious stock of the situation and find that Junior has signs of a deplorable fringe on his ears, whereas the Standard lamentably frowns on fringe.

Your glance follows the broad plane of his back as he stands plumb and true, foursquare, just as did his famous granddaddy, whose picture adorns the Standard in one of the magazines. You feel reassured. The coat, of course, lacks that lustre, that well groomed look with every hair in its place. Yet Junior has eaten well all winter and his body is well rounded out. His loins are muscular and hard from days of romping and playing in the snow with his two-legged companions.

There are many sterling virtues in this fellow — you think — but who on earth would recognize the diamond in the rough? Just to make matters more complicated, Junior forgets his new-found dignity and show stance, rolls flat on his back, and demands to be petted. Is that the way he plans to act in the ring?

A thorough combing and a shampoo are in order. Junior is cajoled into jumping on top of a thirty-six inch wooden crate. The slip chain collar, with the leash taut and fastened to a convenient eyebolt overhead, compels him to stand while he is being worked on.

Grooming

Using a metal wide-tooth comb, you seek out the matted hairs on his belly, and holding the mats firmly with one hand, you comb them out, making sure you are not hurting his tender skin. The comb gets tangled in the mats once in a while and you give it a sharp jerk to free it. It comes out all right, but you pull some hair with it. This must hurt Junior. Tears roll from his eyes. Yet he is duly impressed with the importance of the ceremony and takes it in the patient manner of a true Newfoundland. "Stoic, all right. A chip off the old block," and you give him an encouraging swish with the comb from down the spine. This he dearly loves, and, his pink tongue to the side of his mouth is curled up with pleasure.

You start down on his belly and work up his sides. You comb out the brisket, the feathers on the forelegs, the chest. Then you do the hocks, the pantaloons, and the under part of the tail, starting with the base and working outward, separating each hair as you go along. You hold the tail with one hand and comb away from the center, around and around until the tail is completed.

As the tedious task progresses, you begin to feel the pride of a sculptor, for Junior begins to emerge a living thing of elegance and beauty. Freed from the dead brownish hair which now litters the floor all around, Junior's coat, lustrous and alive, lies neater and hugs closer the rippling muscles of his body.

There is little work on his back except around the croup where a few matted thistles are complicating the matter.

Now you are ready to comb underneath his ears where the hair is of fine woolly texture; it's matted too, and it's a terrible mess. Junior has to use all of his true Newfoundland patience to stand the ordeal. Your comb slips again and Junior tries to tell you by gently grabbing your wrist with his teeth, "That's enough of a good thing."

The comb is put aside. You take a whalebone brush and start brushing hard against the hair, standing it up. This is a job which takes a great deal of "elbow grease," but using the whalebone brush on a Newfoundland is like simonizing your car — the more you rub, the glossier the result. Now that every hair has been electrified, you start brushing it down and it falls into place of its own accord, alive and lustrous.

You take a pair of scissors and snip off the luxurious whiskers and long hairs protruding from the eyebrows. This makes Junior's face look neater, just like shaving off your own mustache.

By now you begin really to feel that you owe that show to Junior and that Junior owes you a blue ribbon.

A carder brush is handy for keeping a 4-weeks-old puppy free of snarls and mud.

Rick and Diane Lillie prepare a dog for show.

But now that ear fringe. . . . You take the stripping knife which the local pet shop man persuaded you to buy, and with a great deal of prudence you carefully remove the excess fringe from the ear flaps, making the ears appear smaller — just what the Standard calls for.

There is no point in going halfway in grooming. The old idea that a Newfoundland can come into the ring full of mats and burrs and still win is as dead as a dodo. So you take stock to see if anything has been overlooked. Yes, a shampoo. A lanolin type shampoo three days before the show will make Junior's coat look its very best, though of course he will have to forego a little rough-housing in the mud between then and the red-letter day.

When Junior makes his debut at the show ring, he will, of course, be judged for conformation. In simple language, this is nothing more than the way with which the various parts of his body conform with one another and form a general picture as exemplified by the ideal dog of the Newfoundland breed, the description of which is the breed Standard.

Judging how closely Junior approaches the ideal, determines the honor which he brings home to his family. At the same time, he will be scrutinized not only for health, robustness, and spirit, but also for grooming and the cleanliness and health of the skin underneath the coat — factors just as important as luxurious, well-brushed-out pantaloons. And woe to the dog whose master has covered up a hot spot or eczema with a lot of fluff. The judge's experienced hand has an uncanny way of seeking out these innocent camouflages, and many a good dog has suffered ill consequences as a result.

A well-fed and well-brushed dog, of course, seldom falls prey to skin ailments. An occasional shampoo is essential in maintaining the skin in topnotch condition.

One of the really beneficial effects of showing is the stimulus it furnishes to an individual owner to keep his dog in its very best form.

Judging Your Dog
With the Standard

As you step back to admire your finished job, Junior wags his tail in a flourish of mutual admiration and bounds off the crate. He must realize that now you are going to attempt to apply your own understanding of the Standard to him. Obviously, he could not be far off in type, for with the most practical detachment possible for the unpracticed eye of the doting owner, you have decided that Junior looks mighty like some of the greatest champions in the book.

114

You snap a short lead onto his choke collar and lead him out to the terrace where you have a good, level, cement floor with plenty of room. Just as you have seen handlers do in the shows you have attended, you put a hand under Junior's chest and lift his front end slightly off the ground and let his legs fall naturally into place. Then, while talking quietly to him, explaining to him that he must hold his show pose, you position his rear legs one at a time, somewhat more than the width of his hips and a little back, so that the line from hock to heel is perpendicular to the ground and the legs are parallel. This you have to try several times before Junior gets the full idea of cooperation, and then you find that you cannot hold him in pose and get a good view of him at the same time, so you enlist the services of daughter Janie, who has been hinting all along to get in on the act. Of course Janie's participation is an immediate signal for Junior to bounce up and down and lick her ear and strike off for a roll in the freshly cut grass. After a quick brush off and time to recompose the central figure of all this effort, finally Junior is cajoled into holding the pose with Janie on the other end of the lead, and you step back and take inventory.

Junior glances at you so winsomely that you decide to start with the head. With one hand you measure the distance from stop to the protuberance at the top of the skull, called the occiput, against the distance from stop to end of muzzle and are reassured that the muzzle is not too long. It looks broad and deep to you, and the skull itself broad, too. So you tackle the job of examining the bite. Does the upper jaw protrude over the under jaw, or vice versa? No, you see that the teeth are regular and fit closely against each other, but you make a mental note that it would be a good idea to take a clean cloth, moisten it, and dip it into a mixture of table salt and baking soda and give the teeth a good scouring, with possibly a little scraping with a dentist's tool if that stain does not give way and proves to be a little tartar accumulation. You pat Junior on the head and tell him he has a good bite.

Could he be snipey? You look at his muzzle from all angles and decide that it is well developed, deep and broad. Fine. His skull is broad. His ears look neat and good to you now. His eyes are deep-set, you think, are dark enough, small and spaced apart well. You pat him admiringly on his sleek head, tell him you think he is beautiful, and he gives you the sweet, endearing look that only Junior knows how to give. "Look that way at the judge," you tell him, "and he'll give you extra consideration for benevolence."

OK, so you may have been a little prejudiced in saluting his head. Now you have the back, and *that* you can look at without personal feelings, you hope. It is broad—good! Does he have a sway back, a concave curve on any part or all of the back line? No, he is muscular and firm with no dip. Could he possibly be roach-backed, or wheel-backed, defined as starting at about the eleventh vertebrae and from that over the loin into the croup? No. Could he be high in the rear? You step back once more, and squinting your eye at his silhouette, decide that Junior possesses that wonder of wonders, a strong, straight top-line.

About this time Junior begins to fidget, and you help Janie to lead him around in a little circle and back to position and try to hurry up your critical deliberation, as you scrutinize the side rear view. Now the stifle, the joint between the upper and second thigh or gaskin in the back leg; you would call it the knee joint. You know that the stifle is a critical point in the mechanism of the Newfoundland. The truly best ones, back to the first records of the breed, had well-bent stifles. It is easy to see that Junior's stifle is right.

Why do they call it "cowhocks" when the hocks point inward toward each other in the back, Janie wonders. And you tell her too many cows are built that way, and while you explain to Janie that what may get by for a cow may not for a dog, you are noting that Junior's rear legs neither toe in nor out, that the hocks fit in perfectly in that straight line from hip to paw.

Your grin broadens as you go on to examine the side-view front. You know that Junior's pasterns should not be straight like a Terrier's, nor down, indicating weakness. Here you are frankly a little puzzled in trying to determine if that hinge in the mechanism which might be called a wrist or perhaps an ankle, in dog language called the pastern, is sufficiently flexible and a little down, but not too much down. This point, you think, will have to be determined by the judge. But you feel that at the worst Junior is not far off.

You pass around to the front and feel the deep chest; that lowest point called the brisket is well down to the knee joint, as it should be. You step back and observe the neat feet, you have so painstakingly trimmed; they point straight ahead, neither in nor out. No one in his most vivid imagination could call them splayed. The toes are certainly not spread wide apart. Nor is he flat-footed, observes Janie, pointing out the firm arch in Junior's foot. You feel the dog's elbows; they are neither in nor out. You feel his shoulders. You hope they are well laid back.

So far Junior is passing with flying colors. You are greatly relieved, thinking perhaps the judge will concur.

A dog may be set up in position and by careful manipulation and prodding even an unsound dog may be made to look like a paragon of doggy virtues. This does not hold true when the dog moves. For when he moves, all the hitherto hidden weaknesses come right out in the

Mr. and Mrs. Charles Visich evaluate a puppy for show.

open and glare into the eye of an experienced judge. Thus the actual test of whether the dog is sound, whether his running gear is correctly engineered, so to speak, comes only when the dog starts to move.

You remember that he is a Newfoundland, a working dog, and being one, his legs and feet are most important. To be worthy of his name he must, *first* and *last*, be *sound*.

Janie leads Junior out on the close-cut grass beside the terrace. You squat down and squint an eye, now semi-professional, all set not to miss a move. First Janie walks him around in a large circle. So far, so good, although he bites the lead a few times and jumps on Janie a time or two. That fellow will have to have more heeling exercises. A line is indicated for Janie and Junior to follow toward you and away from you. Back and forth they go, first slowly and then a little faster, until Junior begins to gait in earnest. As far as you can tell, there is no serious flaw. You think that his legs maintained a straight line from hip and shoulder to ground. You didn't see his pastern joint give way at any time nor observe any slump in his back.

Junior is a sound dog. He will not disgrace the family by going to the ring, where he will have a good chance to get that blue ribbon. So you take that entry blank, dig up the AKC registration certificate and begin filling out the form. You enclose the check for the entry fee and give Junior an extra helping of raw hamburger to keep that high spirit ship-shape. Junior feels very proud of himself. He gallops up to the bedroom and returns with a fiendish gleam in his eye carrying your brand new bedroom slippers. You call out, "Junior! You can't do that any more! Now you are a show dog."

The Newfoundland, officially proclaimed as the animal emblem of Newfoundland in 1972, had earlier been honored on postage stamps there. At top, the first issue—in 1887—featured a Landseer head. The 14-cent stamps, issued in 1931 (center) and 1937 (below) pictured Ch. Westerland Sieger, bred by the Hon. Harold MacPherson. In the latter issue, Sieger shared honor with the newly-coronated King George VI. Sieger was acquired by the Waseeka Kennels of Massachusetts in the early 1930s, and owner Miss Elizabeth Loring stated that it was quite a thrill to receive mail with stamps depicting one's own dog.

7

The Newfoundland
In Other Countries

ON OCTOBER 5, 1972, the Newfoundland dog was made the official animal emblem of Newfoundland by the government there.

The breed's debt to Canada is appreciable. Perhaps the Newfoundland even owes its survival to Canada. For when the Spaniards brought the horse to America, the great Indian dog was present in vast numbers throughout most of Eastern and Central North America. But in time the horse so effectively replaced the dog below the line of long winters and heavy snow, that when the British settlers came to the Eastern Coast of the New World there was no evidence to them that the breed had ever existed anywhere other than the island of Newfoundland, the coast of Labrador, and the shores of the Gulf of St. Lawrence.

In addition to helping in the preservation of the Newfoundland Dog, Canada must be given credit for generous contributions toward the breed. Very cooperative relations exist between breeders in Canada and the United States. Judges and show dogs cross the national line freely for the greater good of all.

Principal credit for the resurgence of the Newfoundland in its native heath must go to the late Hon. Harold MacPherson, at one time lieutenant governor of the province. Mr. MacPherson owned the famous Westerland Kennels.

Mr. MacPherson's keen interest in the breed dated back to 1901. In that year, the Duke and Duchess of Cornwall and York (later King George VI and Queen Mary) visited Newfoundland, and consented to accept a dog and cart for the children of the royal household. But the

The Hon. Harold MacPherson, one-time lieutenant governor of Newfoundland, with one of his favorites—Ch. Captain Bob Bartlett. More than any other figure, Mr. MacPherson helped save the Newfoundland from extinction in its native land, and his Westerland Kennels made important contributions to bloodlines throughout the world.

John J. Patterson, whose Mill Creek strain was an important one in Canada for decades.

Am. & Can. Ch. Topsail's Captain Cook, a mid-40s Best in Show winner of Mr. and Mrs. LeRoy Page's Topsail Kennels.

Newfoundlanders then found themselves embarrassed by the fact that good Newfoundlanders were scarce.

"We scoured the island to find the best available," recalled Harold MacPherson later. Just seventeen at the time, he had helped in the search. A dog was found and hastily trained to harness, and the Committee hoped it had something worthwhile to present. The man who trained the dog, however, had no such apprehensions. After the formal presentation of the Newfoundland and cart, Her Royal Highness went to pet and examine the dog. "Oh, isn't he a beauty!", she exclaimed. "Begobs, ma'am," the trainer replied (as the Committee gulped), "you won't find the likes of him nowhere!"

This incident inspired an ambition in Mr. MacPherson to do something to save the Newfoundland strain on the Great Island. How well he succeeded is seen in the considerable contribution that Westerland dogs have made to bloodlines throughout the world. Exemplary of this is the record-setting career of Int. Ch. Newton, the foremost winner in Newfoundland history, bred by Mr. MacPherson and imported to the United States by Mel Sokolsky.

As in America, Siki offspring played a prominent part in the development of Canadian lines. Montagu Wallace's Drumnod Kennels featured a Siki son—Ch. Shelton Cabin Boy, a three-time Best in Show winner almost upon importation. Important in the post-Siki development through the years were the Shelton Kennels of D. R. Oliver, John Patterson's Mill Creek Kennels, the Perivale Kennels of Mrs. Mercedes Gibson and the Topsail Kennels of Mr. and Mrs. Leroy Page.

Along with its designation of the Newfoundland dog as the official animal emblem, the Executive Council's proclamation of October 5, 1972, ordered that the account of the origin and the revised Standard that they attached, should apply for purposes of the order. This attached version of the origin read:

> The Newfoundland dog is indigenous to the island of Newfoundland. Documented proof shows that in 3000 B.C. the Maritime Archaic Indians in Newfoundland buried their dogs with their dead. It is also recorded that the Beothuck and Mountaineer Indians who inhabited Newfoundland before the white man, used native dogs as companions, guardians and beasts of burden.
>
> When Leif Ericson visited Newfoundland in 1001 A.D., he carried with him both family and animals. These big black bear dogs mated with and re-invigorated the native Newfoundland dogs. For another four hundred years, there were no visitors to the shores of this island home, and by the time the European fishermen started to arrive in the early sixteenth century, there was established a very definite breed of Newfoundland dog.
>
> By the time colonization was allowed in Newfoundland in 1610, the

Ch. Romy v.d. Schurz, a Canadian Best in Show winner. Owned by Mr. and Mrs. R. W. Nutbeem's harbour beem Kennels, of Harbour Grace, Newfoundland.

harbour beem Jack, at 9 mos of age.

Am. & Can. Ch. Little Bear's Rebel Tug, Can. & Am. C.D.X., top winning Newfoundland in Canada in 1971–72, and a Group winner in Canada and the U.S. Owned by the Robert Prices and W. D. Hesser of Minnesota.

distinct physical characteristics and mental attributes had been established in the Newfoundland for all time.

It is interesting to note that the earliest known dogs in Newfoundland were not as large as those of the present day. A larger and heavier dog became evident after the Viking expedition and size increased once again when white man arrived. The increase in size occurred not only from the infusion of foreign bloodlines, but as naturally as man's size increased. The Newfoundland is a natural pure-bred, and has developed because his natural geographical situation and the demands of his environment shaped him to be what he is and what he does.

The order then went on to offer the revised standard. This revision (with an added recapitulation of major and minor faults) was submitted to the Canadian Kennel Club by the Newfoundland Club of Canada, and laid the groundwork for the new standard that became effective January 1, 1979 (see Chapter 5). The general feeling of Canadian fanciers is to be much more strict on colors than prescribed by the AKC standard; this revision disqualifies all colors other than the traditional black or the white and black Landseers.

The revised Standard, as proposed by
The Newfoundland Club of Canada,
and submitted to the Canadian Kennel Club for approval:

Purpose: The Newfoundland is not a dog which was bred for a specific purpose. Rather he evolved over the years as an animal with inherent instincts. One of his greatest attributes is his life-saving ability which is instinctive. As a guardian, protector and companion he is renowned. His ability to act as radar on ships, before radar was invented, is legend. However his material value cannot be overlooked. As a beast of burden and sled dog he has been invaluable. His size and strength have often made the difference of his owner's survival in days of yore. He has been a benefactor to other breeds, by re-invigorating their strain and because of his loyalty and devotion has been a mascot for Navy, Army and Air Force in war-time. His modern purpose is to be the best, most useful all-round friend anyone ever had.

General Appearance: To fulfill his purposes, the Newfoundland is deep bodied, well muscled and well co-ordinated. A good specimen of the breed has dignity in stance and head carriage. He is square in that the length of the back from the top of the withers to the base of the tail, is equal to the distance from the ground to the top of the withers. A bitch, however, is not to be faulted if the length of her body is slightly greater than her height. The dog's appearance is more massive throughout than that of the bitch, the dog having a larger frame and heavier bone. The Newfoundland is free moving with loosely slung body. When moving, a slight roll is perceptible. Substantial webbing between the toes is always present. A grown dog should never appear leggy or lacking substance. His height is determined by depth of chest rather than length of leg. Large size is desirable but never at the expense of gait, symmetry, balance or conformation to the standard herein described. Fine bone is to be seriously faulted.

Temperament: The Newfoundland's expression is soft, and reflects the character of the breed — benevolent, intelligent, dignified but capable of fun, and of sweet disposition. He is known for his sterling gentleness and serenity. He has a noble bearing and a sense of strength and power. Any show of ill temper or timidity is not typical of the breed and is to be seriously faulted. Viciousness is a disqualification.

Size: The desirable height for adult dogs is 28 inches upward; for adult bitches is 26 inches upwards. Adult dogs under 28 inches and adult bitches under 26 inches are to be faulted. The average weight for adult dogs is 150 pounds, for adult bitches 120 pounds. Large size is desirable but is not to be favoured over correct gait, symmetry, soundness and structure.

Coat: The Newfoundland has a water-resistant double coat. The outer coat is moderately long and full but not shaggy. It is straight with no curl although it may have a slight wave. The coat, when rubbed the wrong way, tends to fall back into place. The undercoat, which is soft and dense, is often less dense during summer months or in tropical climates, but is always found to some extent on the rump and chest. An open coat is to be seriously faulted. The hair on the head, muzzle and ears is short and fine. The front legs are feathered from the elbows down. The hind legs have longer hair on the back of the thighs and from there down are feathered. The tail is covered with long dense hair but does not form a flag. A short flat smooth coat (Labrador Retriever type) is a disqualification.

Colour: The traditional colour of the Newfoundland is black. A sunburned black (reddish cast) is not objectionable. White markings on the chest and/or toes and tip of tail of a black dog are not objectionable. A white patch on the chest larger than the span of a hand is to be faulted. Markings of any colour other than white are most objectionable, and the dog is to be disqualified. The Landseer Newfoundland is white and black and is of historical significance to the breed. The proportions of

Ch. Coastguard Able Sea Mate, owned by Eva Gosby, Eastern Passage, Halifax, Nova Scotia.

Ch. Shipshape Tidal Bore, Group winner, owned by Robert and Ann Day's Cobequid Kennels of Nova Scotia.

Ch. Blackhalls Royal Punch, owned by Mr. and Mrs. R. C. Brown of Canada.

white and black should be two thirds white and one third black. The preferred pattern of markings for a Landseer is black head with white blaze extending onto the muzzle, black saddle and black rump and upper tail. All remaining parts are to be white. A minimum of ticking, the symmetry of markings and the beauty of pattern characterize the best marked Landseers. Landseers are to be shown in the same classes as blacks unless special classes are provided for them. As black and Landseer are traditional colours of the Newfoundland, any other colour is highly undesirable and therefore shall be disqualified.

Head: The head is massive with a broad skull, slightly arched crown and strongly developed occipital bone. The forehead and face are smooth and free of wrinkles. The stop is not abrupt. The muzzle is clean cut and covered with short fine hair. It is rather square, deep and fairly short. The length from stop to tip of nose is less than from stop to occipit, the ratio being 5 to 7. The nostrils are well developed. The bitch's head follows the same general conformation as that of the dog, but is feminine and less massive. A narrow head and a snipey or long muzzle are to be faulted. Pronounced flews are not desirable. The eyes are dark brown, relatively small and deep-set; they are spaced wide apart and have no haw showing. Round, protruding or yellow eyes are objectionable. The ears are relatively small and triangular with rounded tips. They are set well back at a median level on the side of the skull and lie close to the head. When the ear of the adult dog is brought forward, it reaches to the inner corner of the eye on the same side. The teeth meet in a scissors or level bite.

Neck: The neck is strong, stout, muscular and well set on the shoulders. It is long enough for dignified head carriage and should not show surplus dewlap.

Forequarters: When the dog is not in motion, the forelegs are straight and parallel with the elbows close to the chest. The layback of the shoulders is about 45 degrees and the upper arm meets the shoulder blade at an angle of about 90 degrees. The shoulders are well muscled. The pasterns are slightly sloping. Down in the pasterns is to be faulted. The feet are proportionate to the body in size, cat foot in type, well rounded and tight. The toes are firm and compact. Splayed feet are a fault. Toeing out or toeing in is undesirable.

Body: The Newfoundland's chest is broad, full, and deep with the brisket reaching at least down to the elbows. The back is broad and the topline is level from the withers to the croup, never roached, slack or swayed. He is broad at the croup, is well muscled, and has very strong loins. The pelvis slopes at an angle of about 30 degrees. Viewed from the side, he is deep in the body showing no discernible tuckup. Bone structure is massive throughout but does not give a heavy sluggish appearance.

Hindquarters: Because driving power for swimming, pulling loads or covering ground efficiently, is largely dependent upon the hindquarters, the rear structure of the Newfoundland is of prime importance. The hip assembly is broad, strong and well developed. The upper thighs are wide and muscular. The lower thighs are strong and fairly long: the stifles are well bent but not so as to give a crouching appearance. The hocks are well apart, well let down, and parallel to each other. They turn neither in nor out. There are no dewclaws on the rear legs. The feet are firm and close. Straight stifles, cow hocks, barrel legs and pigeon toes are serious faults.

Tail: The tail of the Newfoundland acts as a rudder when he is swimming. Therefore it is broad and strong at the base. The tail reaches down a little below the hocks. When the dog is standing the tail hangs straight down, possibly a little bent at the tip: when the dog is in motion or excited, the tail is carried straight out or slightly curved but never curled over the back nor carried curved inward between legs. The tail should not have a kink.

Gait: The Newfoundland in motion gives the impression of effortless power, has good reach and strong drive. A dog may appear symmetrical and well balanced when standing, but if he is not structurally sound, he will lose that symmetry and balance when moving. In motion, the legs move straight forward, they do not swing in an arc nor do the hocks move in or out in relation to the line of travel. A slight roll is present. As the dog's speed increases from walk to a trot, the feet move in under the center line of the body to maintain balance. Mincing, shuffling, crabbing, too close moving, weaving, crossing over in front, toeing out or distinctly toeing in in front, hackney action and pacing are all serious faults.

Minor Faults:
— doggy bitch, bitchy dog
— legginess
— adult dog under 28 inches
— adult bitch under 26 inches
— white patch on chest larger than the span of a hand
— narrow head, snipey or long muzzle
— pronounced flews
— short tail, long tail, tail with a kink
— slightly undershot or slightly overshot

Serious Faults:
— fine bone
— ill temper, timidity
— open coat
— eyes showing pronounced haw, round protruding or yellow eyes
— splayed feet, down pasterns
— toeing out or toeing in, in front when not in motion
— mincing, shuffling, crabbing, weaving, crossing over in front, toeing out or distinctly toeing in in front, hackney action and pacing
— straight stifles, cow hocks, barrel legs and pigeon toes on hind legs
— roached or swayed back
— lack of webbing between toes
— badly overshot or badly undershot bite, wry mouth
— tail carried curled over the back or curved inward between legs

Disqualifications:
— viciousness
— short flat coat (Labrador Retriever type)
— markings of any colour other than white as specified on a black dog
— any colours other than the traditional black or the white and black Landseers
— Monorchids
— Cryptorchids

Other Countries

There are many imports from Scandinavia and Finland being shown in the United States. At the same time, American stock is being exported to England, Denmark and France.

The European Newfoundland of today is a smaller dog, with a less impressive headpiece, but one that bears greater resemblance to the original breed. Infusion of American stock into Denmark seems to run parallel with the Siki saga here, and several Best in Show Newfoundland wins are now on record.

The two-way traffic may modify both the American and European stock and bring about a greater uniformity in size and style of a winning Newfoundland.

Eng. Ch. Mossie of Little Creek, a Best of Breed winner at Cruft's.

Ch. Eaglebay Domino, an English import, pictured after winning the breed at Westchester show (NY) in 1968. Domino, owned by Seaward Kennels, earned his American title in just 5 shows, only the second male Landseer champion in the United States.

Int. and Danish Ch. Cora von Ostzeestrand, Bundes Seigerin 1973, Brabo Winner 1973. Best in Show at Leuwarden, 1974, the first Newfoundland to go Best in Show in Europe since 1953. Bred in East Germany and owned by Birgitte Goshen, Denmark.

Ch. Bosun's Mate, a son of Newton, bred by Mrs. Gerard Fitzpatrick of Whitehouse Station, N.J., and shown in Brazil where his wins include an all-breed Best in Show.

Ch. Little Bear's Royal Top Gallant ("Toppo"), a Group winner and prolific sire in Denmark, owned by Fleming Uziel.

Ch. Caniz Major Skipper, son of Little Bear's Royal Top Gallant, pictured at 20 months. Skipper, at 2 years of age, went Best in Show in Denmark in May 1974, only the second Newf to win BIS in Europe since 1953. Bred by F. Uziel, and owned by K. Kumler, Denmark.

Scandinavian Ch. Bjornegaards Tom, pictured at 4 years. Bred by N. Strarup, Denmark, and owned by F. Uziel.

Breed judging at a Danish show.

Int. Ch. La Bellas Faust, owned by Leif Poulsen of Birkegarden, Denmark. Note that head type is close to that of original "Stonehenge" concept.

Am. & Can. Ch. Birkegarden Brave Boatswain, Danish import, owned by the Barbara-Allen Kennels of Bothell, Wash.

Marun Kille, a Finnish import of the mid-60s, owned by Alice Weaver, Black Mischief Kennels, Kansas.

With their Newfoundland mascot "Scannon" at the prow, the Lewis-Clark expedition is depicted returning to St. Louis in September 1806, after their historic journey of two years, four months, and nine days.

"Scannon" as recreated by Ch. Little Bear's Hardtack II for the television documentary of the expedition.

8

The Newfoundland In History

HISTORICALLY minded fanciers of the breed may be reminded that the course of world history may have been changed through Napoleon's rescue from drowning by a Newfoundland. While exiled on the island of Elba, Napoleon was making his last bid for return to power, which resulted in the famous One Hundred Days. His devoted followers arranged for a ship to take the Emperor to France where veteran soldiers of his many campaigns waited to win back the throne for him.

In secrecy, in the dead of night, Napoleon was smuggled to the Elban shore where a small boat waited to take him to the rescue ship. During his captivity he had grown fat and flabby. He was never a swimmer even in his younger days. In trying to reach the small boat, he slipped on a rock and fell into the dark sea. The drowning emperor thrashed about in the darkness and his panic-stricken escort sought frantically to help but could not even find him in the darkness.

A huge Newfoundland dog, belonging to one of the boatmen, sprang into the dark water, caught the sinking emperor by the coat collar and towed him to the boat. Otherwise, there might have been no triumphal return to France, no restoration to the throne, no crushing battle of Waterloo.

We know of a Newfoundland named Victor, who was mascot on board *H. M. S. Bellona*. During the Battle of Copenhagen, he kept the deck with such bravery that it endeared him to the hearts of the crew. After the Peace of Amiens, the ship was paid off. When the sailors had a parting dinner ashore, Victor was placed in a chair at the table and treated to roast beef and plum pudding. The menu for this banquet was made out in the canine hero's name.

In a gallant naval engagement between the *Nymph* and the *Cleopatra*, the former's mascot, a large Newfoundland, refused to be kept below deck but sallied out with his men in a state of violent rage. The mascot was among the first to board the enemy ship. He proudly paced the deck of the struck vessel, knowing full well who had won the battle.

During World War II,,Newfoundlands were used as water and supply carriers by the army. They were trained to lay telephone lines by carrying on their backs the reels from which the wires were unrolled. Their ability as pack animals was greatly prized, as the burden a Newfoundland could carry would have taxed a small burro. Consequently, they were relied upon to transport small ammunition to the outposts, as well as pigeon cases and dry socks, and to ford water with telephone sets and even machine gun parts.

In the memorable siege of Hong Kong by the Japanese in December 1941, Westerland Champion, bred by the Hon. Harold MacPherson of St. John's, and attached to Canada's Royal Victoria Rifles, became another hero. A Japanese hand grenade was tossed into the trench among a company of men. The company mascot seized the grenade in his jaws and darted away. The explosion blew the Newfoundland to pieces, but he saved the lives of twenty of his soldier friends.

Kenneth Roberts in his *Trending into Maine* tells of the men who left Maine to fight in the Civil War and of the Newfoundland the men of the Tenth Maine Regiment took with them. When they were setting out for the South, a large black Newfoundland suddenly appeared in the railway coach occupied by Company H. Tail wagging, the general appearance of belonging, and his stalwart mien, caused the men to adopt him. They gave him the name of Major. The dog remained with Company H for nearly two years.

Major had a strong sense of belonging to his own regiment and did not on his own make friends with any other soldiers. The exception was when captured by the Confederates during the retreat from Winchester. Then he did deign to recognize a Tenth Maine, Company F prisoner of war, who helped the dog to escape and reunite with his own company.

At the battles of Antietam and Cedar Mountain, Major went into action with the first wave of troops. The Newfoundland so identified himself with his company that he fought the Confederates with his best weapon, his teeth. He *bit* all he could.

When his own regiment was mustered out, May 8, 1863, Major re-enlisted with many of his compatriots of the Tenth, who joined the

Twenty-ninth Maine. On April 8, 1864 Major went into the Battle of Mansfield, in Louisiana. He fought with all his strength and cunning until killed on the field of battle with a musket ball through his head.

"Scannon" of the
Lewis and Clark Expedition

Probably the greatest Continental exploration of North America within what is now the United States was the Lewis and Clark Expedition (1804-1806). Young army captains Meriwether Lewis and William Clark had been commissioned by President Thomas Jefferson (and financed by Congress with $2,500) "to explore the river Missouri from its mouth to its source . . . and seek the best water communication lines to the Pacific Ocean."

By keel boat, canoe and overland trek went the courageous crew. With them as mascot and working member of the party journeyed the Newfoundland dog, Scannon — all the way to the Pacific, to Fort Clatsop at the mouth of the Columbia River. Today, Scannon's name is recorded at Fort Clatsop on a bronze plaque as one of the party to make the entire journey.

Early in the expedition, a respectable looking Shawnee offered Captain Lewis three beaver skins for the dog, but Lewis politely declined the offer. He wrote: "I prized him much for his docility and qualifications generally for my journey and, of course, there was no bargain."

The dog delighted his master by bounding into the river to retrieve geese shot by the soldiers.

Scannon was highly valuable as a guard against predatory wild animals. We find in the journal: "The white bears have now become exceedingly troublesome; they constantly infest our camp during the night, though they have not attacked us, as our dog who patrols all night gives us notice of the approach."

The dog pulled or carried loads. He was quick, resourceful, and in countless ways made himself useful. But to Meriwether Lewis, Scannon's greatest virtue was his loyalty. Captain Lewis wrote in his journal that although equipment for his Corps of Discovery was important, the most critical factor was personnel. At the start of winter, he stated that other than Clark and himself, *he was sure only of one member of the expedition — the big Newfoundland, Scannon.*

The winter of 1805–1806 was exceedingly difficult. The misery of continuing cold rain in the Columbia River valley made it impossible for the men to get dry. The unending dampness and the diminishing supplies were both physically and from the standpoint of morale debilitating to the crew.

The Chinook Indians estimated the situation and harassed the party quite openly. They threw stones at two soldiers. And Shields, who in more cheerful times the year before, had had a tributary creek of the Missouri named for him by Lewis, was pushed off the trail by the Chinooks.

But the last straw for Lewis was when the natives tried to steal Scannon. A friendly Indian told him that the Newfoundland had been kidnapped. Captain Lewis dispatched three men in hot pursuit to fire on the rustlers if they offered the least resistance. The Chinooks abandoned Scannon and fled.

In 1964, the National Broadcasting Company made a faithful documentary of this great venture and naturally a Newfoundland had to be a member of the cast. Ch. Little Bear's Hard Tack II played the role of Scannon.

One day I had a call from Ted Yates, considered by some the greatest documentary film producer of our time. Bobby Kennedy had suggested that he phone me, that Little Bear could surely provide a good Newfoundland for the production. I agreed and began ticking off in my mind which dog would be most suitable. Hard Tack seemed the likeliest candidate to me.

Mr. Yates was asking questions and I was answering yes. Just as a man must be considered innocent until proven guilty, I am inclined to feel that a Newfoundland Dog should be considered capable until proven otherwise. So while Mr. Yates was asking if the dog could sit upright in a canoe while shooting the rapids, I knew Hard Tack had never failed in such an effort for the good dog had never seen a canoe, much less a rapids. But Hard Tack was smart and cooperative, and I felt if Scannon had been able to do it, so could our boy.

Of course, I visualized time to train and for one of us from the kennels going along to care for and direct the dog. But Mr. Yates' plans were different. The dog was to go without any of us. And what was more he was to be in Washington only four days hence, in order to fly with the production company to location which was to be the exact route of the great exploration.

Well, we managed to get permission to use a canoe on a quiet lake at a nearby children's camp for the three days before the trip to Washington, but for seven minutes a day only.

The first day, my husband Vadim and I lifted the vastly heavy dog into the center of the canoe where he lay so still that scarcely a whisker moved, while we paddled three and a half minutes out and three and a half minutes back. Paddling back I suggested to Vadim that the next day we should teach Hard Tack to sit upright in the prow of the canoe.

138

The next morning, without a moment's hesitation and without instructions, Hard Tack jumped from the pier to the canoe alongside. His balance was superb. The canoe lay steady while the big dog nimbly took his place sitting upright in the prow.

We were so impressed that we scarcely spoke until the return to the pier. On the final training day Hard Tack demonstrated that he could do the same with a stranger in the canoe.

The next morning, bright and early, we set off from New Milford, Connecticut, for Washington, D.C., and delivered our dog to the Ted Yates company.

From here I would like to quote from that delightful radio and television columnist, Lawrence Laurent. In the *Washington Post* of April 3, 1965, he wrote:

Yates hired a dog. It was a valuable champion but accustomed to the easy indolence of a Connecticut kennel. Yates insured the dog for $5000.

"I like dogs," Yates continued, "but this one was over 4 feet high and weighed over 200 pounds. It had an enormous requirement for water and a daily diet that required about five pounds of meat." Yates brought the dog to his Washington home, "to make friends."

The thirsty animal promptly quenched his thirst by emptying all water out of toilet bowls.

"My kids," Yates added, "thought he was wonderful."

The next morning, the dog was missing. Yates called the police. A bored and sleepy desk sergeant said: "Okay, so you've lost a dog. Can you describe him?"

"Yes, sir," answered Yates. "He's a Newfoundland . . . about four feet high . . . weighs over 200 pounds . . ."

The sergeant's boredom vanished, but all he could yell was "What?!"

The dog was found quickly. Seems that he had grown thirsty about dawn and had set out to find water. He had gone to DuPont Circle, where two sleepy gardeners were watering the grass. At the sight of the dog — about the size and shape of a small bear — the men had thrown down their hoses and fled.

The dog had drunk his fill. He had rolled around in the cool water, getting his heavy coat soaked. By this time, people had gathered at the DuPont Circle bus stop and the friendly animal loped over to the crowd.

Then he shook himself dry. Someone called the cops.

When the party was camping, the dog preferred sleeping in a tent to outdoors. He shared sleeping quarters interchangeably with the producer, the unit manager and the assistant producer: Mr. Yates, Mr. White and Mr. Rogers. Hard Tack traveled principally by boat, car or truck. He was a good traveler and always the first one on board. During an overnight stop at a tavern at the Powell Ranger Station in Idaho, near the Lolo Trail, a traveler, not connected with the Lewis and Clark party, had left his car door open while taking out luggage and returned to find the mammoth Hard Tack sprawled out across the driver's seat. The man was terrified. He knew it was a bear!

One day the keel boat ran aground on a sand bar and the entire party was marooned until after midnight. Least disturbed of all was Hard Tack. One thing a Newfoundland can do when everything stops — a Newf can always sleep.

Hard Tack found the Western Indian dogs mystifying. He was amiable but distant — did not want to associate with them. The Western Indian tribes had a distinctly different breed of dog from the Algonquins' big hunting, fishing and working dog, now known as the Newfoundland. Once one of these Western dogs became too familiar with Hard Tack. The Newfoundland gave him one slap and the little one went away tumbling. Dignity was restored.

Ted Yates told me that Hard Tack was the most responsive and obedient actor of the group. His enthusiasm, eagerness and ability to do what he was told was incredible. The dog was all attention and seriousness while the film was being shot, and mostly eating and sleeping the rest of the time.

There were only two things Hard Tack flatly refused to do. At the Indian Museum in Oregon at the mouth of the Columbia, there is a room filled with scalps, skulls, tomahawks and other weapons. The dog bounced in with the men; then suddenly with tail between his legs and head down, slunk out of the room. Neither force nor persuasion would make the dog reenter the room.

The other refusal on the part of the dog was when on the trail, one of the men had shot a deer. The cameraman wanted to get a sequence of Scannon ripping into the carcass. Hard Tack flatly refused. The animal had to be butchered and portioned before Hard Tack would touch the meat, which when so served he ate with gusto and in quantity. I explained to Mr. Yates that the Indian training still persisted in the breed. The early conditions were so well similated that the old Indian protocol must have seemed closer. Surely, no one could imagine a well disciplined Algonquin dog grabbing ahead of his masters. I am sure it would have been strictly out of character for a well-fed Scannon to rip open the day's kill.

When the Newf actor returned to his home kennels his newly acquired dignity was tremendously impressive. Traveling had definitely broadened his already expansive personality. When we met him at Kennedy Airport, Vadim and I naturally wanted to interrogate him on his experiences.

So the questions began, "Hard Tack, did you enjoy your trip?" A tail thumping combined with serious expression indicated that it had been a satisfying experience but one that carried heavy responsibilities. "Did you like Captain Lewis?" brought no response nor "How about Captain Clark?" or mention of Meriwether Lewis. But, "Did you like Sacajawea?" brought the heartiest of tail thumpings and a quite rowdy smile.

Sacajawea, you will remember from American history, was the Shoshone wife of the worthless French-Canadian, Toussaint Charbonneau. Sacajawea, along with Scannon, was one of the most useful members of the expedition. Her husband had been engaged in order to get her. Even with the handicap of him and a newly born baby, which survived the entire expedition, the sturdy and resourceful Sacajawea was a triumph of personnel work.

A squaw with her papoose was reassuring to Indians fearful of an armed party and the threat of possible massacres was reduced.

When I was talking later with the producer, Ted Yates, I told him of our Hard Tack's reactions and asked if the actress playing Sacajawea was not quite a charming girl. At first Mr. Yates was perplexed. He said that four Hollywood stunt men played Sacajawea and that the only contact Hard Tack had with them was shooting the rapids.

An entire day was spent filming the rapids sequence. It was the aim to have the canoe stay upright through most of the rapids, then spill at a precise point. The canoe would either tip over too soon with man and dog swimming and scrambling over rocks and ledges to shore, or the canoe would make the entire run upright. Taking turns the four stunt men answering calls of "Sacajawea One!" Two, Three or Four, would try again from the head of the rapids. Always the Newfoundland responded first to the call of Sacajawea and was there sitting in the bow of the canoe ready for the dangerous descent. Apparently Hard Tack's greatest delight was shooting the rapids.

Hard Tack never failed to recognize Ted Yates' voice. Whenever he was on TV the Newfoundland would edge up close to the set, tilt his head slightly to one side, and lift his ears a little.

When we had news that Ted Yates while on news assignment was wounded by shrapnel in Jordan during the fighting between Israel and the Arab States, I went to Hard Tack and told him.

When we told him that Ted Yates had died, Hard Tack visibly grieved. Later, when the life story of Ted Yates was being shown over NBC, we called the dog in to watch it. I think it was a two hour show. In it Ted Yates stated that the Lewis and Clark was the favorite of his documentaries. When the TV story took up the account of that particular documentary, Hard Tack watched and listened for a while, then went to the kitchen porch. When the film was over, I went out to pet the dog. He licked my hand. His eyes were filled with tears.

The Newfoundland—serene on land or in water.

9

The Character of
The Newfoundland

"A man is not a good *man* to me because he will feed me if I
should be starving, or warm me if I should be freezing, or pull
me out of a ditch if I should ever fall into one. I can find you a
Newfoundland dog that will do as much."

—*Walden*, Thoreau

THE NEWFOUNDLAND'S strength of character is
beyond the point of easy comprehension and can only be understood in
the light of the heroic tradition of the breed. It seems that though many
changes have taken place in the Newfoundland's appearance through
the generations, his basic make-up remains constant. Before us is an
old diary of Captain George Cartwright from which two entries speak
simply but eloquently of a Newfoundland:

> *Tuesday, January 29, 1771.* . . . Guy pursued the track to the mouth of
> Niger Sound, and upon the North end of Round Island he found the un-
> fortunate Mr. Jones frozen to death, with his faithful Newfoundland
> bitch by his side! He gave the poor creature what bread he had about him
> but could not prevail on her to leave her master. . .
>
> *Thursday, January 31, 1771.* The Chateau men went off for Seal Island
> early this morning; from which place my man returned today, accompa-
> nied by those whom I sent from Chateau; also another party from the
> same place, joined them upon the road. These people brought me what
> things they found in Mr. Jones' pockets, and informed me that they had
> covered the corpse with snow and boughs of trees; but they could not
> prevail on the Newfoundland bitch to leave her deceased master.

From the early tales of the everyday intelligence of the breed, the
story of a Harbour Grace Newfoundland, who lived in the early part of

Ch. Little Bear's Big Chance, Group winning son of Can. & Am. Ch. Midway Black Ledge Sea Raider.

Ch. Little Bear's Roaring Main, Group winning son of Ch. Little Bear's Big Chance.

Ch. Little Bear's John Smith, Group winning son of Ch. Little Bear's Roaring Main.

the nineteenth century, stands out as a delightful example of traits we all enjoy finding in our dogs today:

"One of the magistrates of Harbour Grace had an animal of this kind, which was in the habit of carrying a lantern before his master at night, as steadily as the most attentive servant could do; stopping short when he made a stop, and proceeding when he saw him disposed to follow. If his owner were from home, as soon as the lantern was fixed in his mouth, and the command given, 'Go fetch thy master' he would immediately set off, and proceed directly to the town, which lay at the distance of more than a mile from his place of residence. When there, he stopped at the door of every house, which he knew his master was in the habit of frequenting, and laying down his lantern would growl and beat at the door, making all the noise in his power, until it was opened. If his owner was not there, he would proceed farther in the same manner until he found him. If he had accompanied him only once to a house, this was sufficient to induce him to take that house in his round."

At about the same time, across the seas from his native island, a Newfoundland in Scotland named Dandie left this charming paw print for posterity:

A number of gentlemen, well-acquainted with Dandie, are daily in the habit of giving him a penny, which he takes to a baker's shop and purchases a roll. One of these gentlemen was accosted by the Dog in expectation of his usual present. Mr. T. said, 'I have not a penny with me today, but I have one at home.' On his return to his house, he heard a noise at the door which was opened by the servant, when in sprang Dandie to receive his penny. In a frolic, Mr. T. gave him a bad one, which he, as usual, carried to the baker, but was refused his bread. He immediately returned to Mr. T.'s, knocked at the door, and when the servant opened it, laid the penny at his feet, and walked off seemingly with the greatest contempt.

Although Dandie, in general, makes an immediate purchase of bread with the money he receives, yet the following circumstances clearly demonstrated that he possesses more prudent foresight than many who are reckoned rational beings. One Sunday, when it was very unlikely that he could have received a present of money, Dandie was observed to bring home a loaf. Mr. M'Intyre, the owner, being somewhat surprised at this, desired the servant to search the room to see if any money could be found. While she was engaged in this task, the Dog seemed quite unconcerned till she approached the bed, when he ran to her, and gently drew her back from it. Mr. M'Intyre then secured the Dog which kept struggling and growling, while the servant went under the bed where she found seven hapence, under a bit of cloth; after this he was frequently observed to hide his money in a corner of a saw pit, under the dust.

Ch. Carr's Black Sam of Bethward, the top winning Newfoundland of 1968 and 1969. Owned by Paul and Betty Ramey, Lemont, Ill.

Ch. Little Bear Canicula Campio, Group winner and twice BOB at the National Specialty in early 1960s. Owned by Little Bear.

Ch. Little Bear's Three-Mile Limit, a Group winner of the early 1960s, owned by the Richard Lillies of Milwaukee.

Ch. Dryad's Sea Rover, Group winner, owned by the Shipshape Kennels of Mr. and Mrs. Robert Lister. Pictured being shown to win under the late Miss Alva McColl by his breeder, Mrs. Maynard Drury.

Ch. Little Bear's Tippo, Group winning son of Canicula Campio. Owned and shown by Dr. and Mrs. John Thomson's Kwasind Kennels.

Ch. Scipio of Shipmates, a 1967 Group winner, owned by John MacCauley.

Ch. Sarja's Sir Lional of Irwindyl, winner of over 70 BOBs and many Group placements in the '50s. One of many champions and Obedience titlists produced at the Irwindyl Kennels of Mrs. Geraldine Y. Irwin.

Am. Can. & Berm. Ch. Dryad's Yoga Bear, C.D., a Group-winning Newton son. Owned by Newton-Ark Kennels.

One of Dandie's favorite parlor games was to single out a specifically called-for card from a deck that his master had scattered about the room. Another way of amusing his master and the guests of the house was for him to find a comb which had been hidden, sometimes as high as the top of the mantelpiece. To make the game more interesting, Mr. M'Intyre would scatter several personal things about the room, but when Dandie was readmitted and ordered to seek the comb, he would quickly pass over the unrelated objects and bring to his master the comb he had been asked to fetch. It is interesting that in this case, since Mr. M'Intyre had touched all the objects, Dandie was obviously not depending on his power of scent but understood the words. Whenever Dandie wanted to come inside from outdoors, he would pull the bell rope and wait patiently for a servant to open a door. Likewise, inside the house, whenever he wanted to be admitted into another room, if there was a hand bell available, he would take it in his mouth and shake it until a door was opened for him.

As might be expected, Mr. M'Intyre's drawing room was always filled with friends eager to be entertained by the intriguing pet. On a well-remembered evening, one of the callers had dropped a shilling on the floor, which after diligent search could not be found. Mr. M'Intyre, seeing his dog sitting in the corner and looking quite unconscious of what was transpiring, said, "Dandie, find us the shilling and you shall have a biscuit." The dog promptly jumped up on the table and laid down the shilling, which he had previously picked up without having been perceived.

One morning Mrs. C. A. Richardson, of Lowell, Massachusetts, a sister-in-law of President Grant's Secretary of the Treasury, took some of her children and her fine big Newfoundland, Caesar, to a daguerreotypist for a group picture. For nearly an hour she tried to pose the dog. As soon as she could get all of the children and the dog posed, and get herself back in the group, the dog would get up, shake his huge body, and of course spoil the picture.

Finally out of patience, Mrs. Richardson opened the door and in a stern voice said to Caesar, "Go home, sir! You have displeased me very much: you shall not stay with us any longer." Whereupon poor Caesar slunk away with a crestfallen look. Mrs. Richardson made no further attempt to get him in the picture.

The next day, much to her surprise, Caesar came home with a box tied around his neck. The Newfoundland seemed greatly pleased, and wagged his tail expressively while waiting for Mrs. Richardson to open the box.

His mistress was vastly surprised when she found that it contained a fine daguerreotype of Caesar himself. She found out that the dog had returned to the studio shortly after the Richardsons had left, knocked on the door and by his actions persuaded the daguerreotypist to take his picture.

A Newfoundland Dog doorman for a tavern in High Street, Glasgow, is written about by Edward Jesse in his *Anecdotes of Dogs* (1858). When anyone came to the tavern the Newfoundland would trot before him, ring the bell, then resume his station at the door.

Recognition and hospitality are qualities of the Newfoundland borne out by a story related by Mrs. Clara Ramsey, who had lived on a rather isolated farm in New Hampshire when a young woman. Mrs. Ramsey had been startled by a voice at the kitchen door singing out, "Merry Christmas!" She was alone and was not a little shocked to see a dirty and unshaven stranger who bore signs of long cross-country walking.

It was the day before Christmas and her husband had taken the children along to town in the farm wagon for the ride. Tramps did not often reach the backwoods farms in that part of New Hampshire and the farmer's wife would have been frightened but for Neptune, the 150-pound Newfoundland at her side. She was turning away the stranger when, to her utter astonishment, Neptune snatched a freshly baked, still-warm loaf of bread from the table and wagging his tail in the friendliest manner, delivered it to the hungry man.

"We had a Newfoundland big as him on our ship," said the beggar, patting the dog. It turned out he was from a coasting schooner that had been wrecked off Cape Porpoise and he was hiking his way back to the family farm in northern Vermont hoping to get there for Christmas.

The dog's friendly recognition of a man who meant no harm, gave Mrs. Ramsey confidence and she was suddenly apologetic for her inhospitality at Christmas time. She invited the hungry, frost-bitten sailor into the warm kitchen and fed him generously with good things she had been preparing for the holiday. In the midst of the eating, Neptune was suddenly taken with a fit of barking and scratching at the kitchen door.

"That Newfoundland means business!" said the sailor rushing to open the door. The dog ran out, the sailor and Mrs. Ramsey close behind. A tremendous shower of fireworks was leaping high and shooting burning cinders everywhere. There had been no snow and the roof was dry.

The sailor took charge. Well accustomed to climbing the rigging of a sailing vessel, in moments he had thrown a ladder against the house and was up on the roof putting out the fire with buckets of water.

The chimney fire was out before Mr. Ramsey returned. He related

Ch. Little Bear's Princess Teeka, early 1960s winner owned by Isabel Kurth.

Ch. Little Bear's Sailing Free, Group winner owned by Mrs. Kurth.

Ch. Little Bear's Gander, a Group winner with over 100 BOBs in the 1950s. Owned by James A. Herrington.

this story not so long ago, about 65 years after the happening. "I had a home to come back to," he said. "If it had not been for Neptune and his sailor friend, there would have been no Christmas for us. And, you know, that Neptune was the best guard dog we ever had. Funny how a Newfoundland knows an honest man."

Sometimes non-Newfoundland people feel that the fanciers of the breed use a heavy hand in endowing the object of their affection with human intelligence. But in a 1957 issue of the magazine, *Yankee*, A. B. Stockbridge went one step further and credited the Newfoundland with extra-sensory perception.

According to his delightful account, titled *The Psychic Dog*, a Newfoundland was picked up by a homeward bound Gloucester schooner about 50 years before the time of Mr. Stockbridge's writing. The dog was found swimming 300 miles from the nearest point of land, with not another vessel in sight. He was taken on board and brought back to the home port where his mysterious appearance became a never ceasing cause of speculation. The dog became a great favorite and the fishing schooner that rescued him never sailed without him. No matter how she was fitted out nor who the skipper, over many years she was always among the high-liners and the dog was believed responsible for her good luck.

Then one season, as the day for her sailing approached, the dog began to show signs of restlessness. When the day arrived, his agitation was apparent to everyone. No amount of coaxing could get him aboard; he showed his disapproval by loud barking which was very unusual for him. One of the crew shrugged his shoulders and said they would have a broker if the dog would not go. But his refusal had more significance than that. They sailed without him—the vessel rounded Eastern Point, disappeared into the offing and has not been seen nor heard tell of since.

Nearly ten years ago Mr. H. E. E. Reimer, of Sydney, Australia, wrote me of the Newfoundland of his childhood, Pup (1902–1916). Despite his juvenile name, Pup was of heroic build and great dignity.

Of course his dignity was a thing like that of any Newf, something one could wear or take off as the occasion might demand. Pup was always ready for a game. Hide-and-seek was a favorite. Not only would he be search and search, indoors and out, until he found you, but he would also hide himself so that you would have to find him.

Pup was not trained at all in the proper sense. He would of course carry things, fetch papers, etc. But there was one special incident. Mr.

Ch. Little Bear Sailor Port O'Call, a mid-1960s winner, owned by Marvin Frank and handled by Wm. J. Trainor.

Ch. Berwick Sitting Bull, owned by the Berwick Foundation, and handled by Philip L. Marsman.

Ch. Little Bear's Compass Rose, a mid-50s winner, handled by Ed Carver.

Ch. Niote of Newton-Ark, BOS at the 1971 National Specialty. Owned by Janet Levine and Mel Sokolsky's Newton-Ark Kennels.

Ch. Molly B of Newton-Ark, an Eben daughter, dam of many champions. Owned by Newton-Ark Kennels.

Ch. Hanah of Newton-Ark, Winners Bitch at Westminster, 1970. Owned by Newton-Ark Kennels.

Ch. Tranquilus Neptune, wh. 1968, Group winner with over 100 BOBs, and consistently placing in Top Ten. Bred by Capt. James Bellows, and co-owned by him and Penelope Buell. Handled by Wm. Buell.

Am. & Can. Ch. Tranquilus Tempting Tidbit, wh. 1971, currently registering strong on the West Coast. Bred by Capt. James Bellows (Tranquilus Kennels, Reg.) and co-owned by him and Villade Kennels, Reg. Handled by Peter Miller.

Reimer was then a lad of five or six, attending a small suburban primary school, about a quarter of a mile from home. Pup had never been to school. It had been a fine day when young Reimer had started to school, but suddenly the weather changed and heavy rain fell making the roads and paths muddy. As the boy had but recently recovered from a severe cold or influenza, his mother was concerned that his feet would get wet. All that the boy was aware of was that of a sudden Pup marched into the school room with a pair of galoshes in his mouth. The dog walked between the desks of the other children until he came to the one of his young master, dropped the galoshes at his side, gave him a kindly greeting and promptly walked out of school again. On the boy's return home his mother told him that she had wanted him to have the galoshes and more as a matter of joke she had given them to Pup and bade him take them to school. To her surprise and amazement Pup took them and promptly walked out of the house in the direction of the school, shortly afterwards returning home minus the galoshes. Pup had never been to the school before, nor did he ever visit it again.

These stories out of the past would scarcely seem credible were it not for many instances within our own experience. You, too, may have to have a Newfoundland in your very own home before you can believe. One of our first was Ch. Little Bear's Avalon O'Lady. We felt she exhibited a rather high I. Q. Little Bear Kennels then was situated on our Vermont farm, high up in the Waitsfield Pass of the Northfield Mountains. The telephone was, of necessity, on a party line including nine more farm houses each with its own ring. The signal for our kennels was two long rings. Avalon, who at the time had only been in the house for the duration of a whelping and nursing her puppies, without any training learned to distinguish our ring from the nine other combinations. Whenever she heard the two long rings, Avalon would hasten to find one of the staff and to make certain that her intentions were understood, she would pull her charge by the jeans toward the ringing phone.

Race, a big Newfoundland pup of ours, had been mysteriously getting out of his six foot, link-chain fenced pen. "He must jump clear of the top," decided Red, our dog-loving fire chief. But my husband, Vadim, protested, "Over a six foot fence? I doubt it. He's not yet grown."

But if not over the fence, how *did* he get out? Over, through, or under—it would have to be. And never would the rascal let us see him making the escape. We doubted it could be *over*. We had never seen

Seeing your dog finish to championship is always a special thrill. Here Mrs. Isabel Kurth (at right) watches Edenglen's Sovereign of the Sea, handled by Jo-Ann Lancaster, finish under judge Willis Linn. Sovereign sired many champions.

And on the West Coast, Peppertree's Sand Piper—an important Specialty winner—is pictured finishing for title in puppy coat at San Gabriel, 1970, under judge Vincent Perry. Owned by Penelope Freeman, and handled by William Buell.

Ch. Little Bear's Gemini, owned by Little Bear Kennels.

Am. & Berm. Ch. Little Bear's Blockade Runner, sire of Group winners. Owned by Mrs. Wallace Jordan, of Arizona.

Ch. Little Bear's Tim of Tuckamore, the 100th champion bred by Little Bear, finished in 1973. Owned by Barbara and George G. Finch, Tuckamore Kennels, West Chester, Pa.

him jump so high. *Through* a new link-chain fence was impossible. *Under?* The base of the pen was thoroughly examined and nothing found amiss. No signs of burrowing.

We did find that Race's waistcoat was wet. There is a tiny brook running through one end of the pen, providing a splashing pool for our water-loving Newfoundlands. Its entrance and its exit from the pen were the first places we had checked. It comes in by way of a submerged clay pipe, definitely not large enough for a Newfoundland to squeeze through. Where it flows out we had barricaded the opening with criss-crossed sticks. A few days after Christmas these sticks were removed and our Christmas tree stuffed into the opening as a temporary measure until we could devise something better. But the Christmas tree was always found to be securely in place, filling the gap.

The gate to the pen had a dog-proof catch that really worked although we began to distrust it. Race, who was supposed to be securely lodged in his pen, had taken to making unscheduled appearances peeking through the glass-paned door facing the terrace. We would dash out and examine the gate, always finding it firmly closed and latched. We put a padlock on it. But still we'd find Race lying on the front doorstep or peeking through the window.

Once more Vadim and I made a thorough examination of the pen and we couldn't see how Houdini could get out of it. The night before New Year's Eve, the earth was blanketed in clean white snow. The dogs loved it and rolled in it and ate it and frisked together so much that it seemed that Race was going to be satisfied to remain with the rest of them and play. But just as I was sitting down to dinner I looked out toward the terrace—and there was the jolly face of Race.

I went out to the pen. The gate was locked. The Christmas tree was in place. But tell-tale prints in the snow showed that Race had pushed out the tree and then wedged it back to conceal his means of escape. I brought the clever fellow into the house so that the prints would not be destroyed before I could get a witness to the evidence.

"If he had really been smart, he would have rolled over and destroyed his tracks," said Vadim.

The stoicism of the Newfoundland as well as the breed's obedience under stress are unsurpassed by any other breed of dogs. These qualities are demonstrated by two incidents, the first of which involved Race.

True to his name, Race loved to race in the woods, much to our consternation, for we well remembered his last bout with a porcupine, when he came out endowed in pincushion fashion with a hundred or more quills. Vadim with Race and Race's sister, Bonnavista, were returning from a hike to Bald Mountain, some four miles north of Little Bear Farms. They were still some distance from the kennels and were following a steep, abandoned lumber road cutting through a dense cover of spruce and balsam. Both Newfoundlands were off lead.

Bonnavista darted under a huge red spruce. There was a sharp bark, swift commotion, a pitiful cry of pain. Broken boughs and spruce needles showered down and Bonnavista scooted out with a dozen porcupine quills in her muzzle. Before my husband could restrain him, Race, gallant gentleman that he was, rushed to the defense of his sister. There was more commotion under the spruce tree, more broken boughs showered down. An angry growl, a shrill, painful cry, and Race staggered into the open — bleeding and literally covered with porcupine quills.

Race must have tackled his hedgehog adversary with a frontal attack, for his bleeding tongue and mouth were infested with literally hundreds of quills. The dog was in horrible pain. His eyes were bloodshot and bloody foam dripped from his mouth. Out of his head with agony, he made for the woods — but even at this point, obedient to his master's command, he hesitated long enough for my husband to get hold of his choke collar. The dog could not close his mouth and every effort to do so just drove the quills more firmly through his chops and palate.

Vadim tried to pull the quills out by hand, as he had no knife or pliers. This was futile. The pain was driving Race mad, and he struggled to dart out for the woods, which Vadim knew he had to prevent or lose the dog. The quills in Race's mouth were most critical and had to be removed before the dog went stark mad with pain.

Race allowed Vadim to open his jaws wide and insert his left thumb in between to keep them from closing. Then, necessity being the mother of invention, Vadim tried pulling a quill out with his teeth. This worked. One by one he pulled them from inside Race's mouth, first out of his tongue and gums, finally working up to the dog's palate, which was most difficult. At times, Race, agonized with pain, would press on Vadim's thumb, which began to bleed. The whole ordeal took some two hours, Vadim removed some one hundred quills to enable Race to reach the farm house. The local veterinarian then completed the extractions.

The second incident starred our Little Bear's Ocean Bride, and also involved a serious bout with the wild life in our Vermont woods. With her it was her curiosity which led her to poke her head into a mother bear's winter quarters. From the hollow tree Bridie came running to us for help. Nearly blinded with blood she had had her forehead clawed to the skull in three long gashes.

We rushed her down to the farmhouse and phoned two veterinari-

Am. & Can. Ch. Halirock's Boulder, owned by Dr. and Mrs. Roger S. Foster, Jr., Halirock Kennels, Vermont.

Ch. Black Mischief's Christopher, a late '60s standout, owned by Alice Weaver, Black Mischief Kennels, Kansas.

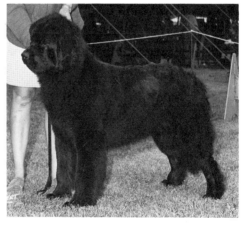

Ch. Koki de Nashua-Auke, sire of champions. Koki finished at 15 months with 5 majors in 1970. He is owned by Jane and Ronald Thibault.

ans: one down the road a few miles, the other our good friend Dr. George Brightenbach, then in Montpelier some 18 miles away. The nearby veterinarian still has not arrived.

But, as if with wings, George Brightenbach was there with needle and suturing thread. He had come so fast, knowing that the bitch would probably bleed to death if he could not reach her in time, that he had not brought any kind of anaesthetic, general or local. But the pain was no factor with Bridie. No one needed to hold her. She sat upright, staring straight ahead through tear-filled eyes while 13 stitches were taken in her forehead.

Sensitivity and ability to understand the more subtle aspects of their masters' speech seem to distinguish this breed. The following episode appears to bear this out.

A Scottish family was faced with the necessity of leaving their spacious country house and settling in Edinburgh in very close quarters. Mr. Simpson, the father, was visited by a family friend to whom he remarked, "Our new house in Edinburgh will be very small. We may have to part with our dog, for he is too large for such a small place." The family Newfoundland was present during this conversation and must have understood every word of it. That evening he left the house and was never heard of again.

In the *Standard Horse and Stock Book* by D. Magner, published around the turn of the century, we find:

> A lady was once recounting to a friend the virtues of her Newfoundland dog, Lion, which lay on the carpet at her feet; and when she told how he watched the baby, played with the children, and how high a price she set on him, Lion's tail would go up and down in delight at the praises bestowed upon him.
>
> "But Lion has one serious fault," said his mistress after a while. The tail ceased to thump the floor, and Lion's face wore an expression of great concern. The lady continued: "He will come in with his dirty feet and lie down on the carpet, when I have told him time and again that he mustn't do it." Lion, with a dejected and humiliated air, arose and slunk out of the room, his tail hanging down, and completely crestfallen.

Lifesaving is a basic characteristic of the Newfoundland. In expression of this he follows a strict sense of priority. First he will rescue the youngest baby, children, women, then men. His family takes precedence over others. But even a stranger will get his excellent services if all of his family is safe.

A man was crossing the Seventeenth Street bridge in Wheeling. He

Ch. Shipshape's Spinnaker Mast, C.D.X. owned by Bob and Wilma Lister.

Ch. Kwasind Johnnie Cake Jennie, winning bitch owned by Dr. John D. Thomson.

Ch. Little Bear's Tao of Kwasind, BOS at the 1970 National Specialty, owned by Dr. Thomson.

stopped, looked over the ballustrade, lost his balance, and fell into the deep creek below. He could not swim and sank twice. It looked as though he were going to disappear for good when a big Newfoundland dog leaped to his rescue. Grasping the man by his coat, the dog pulled him ashore.

The man recovered his senses and walked off. The Newfoundland shook himself amid the cheers of the crowd of people that had gathered, and departed in the opposite direction. It was obvious that the dog was a stranger to the one he had saved.

The Newfoundland's devotion to those he loves is demonstrated in many ways and in many instances has been known to continue after his master's death as well as to be manifested during his lifetime.

On the occasion of opening a family vault at Ravenfield, England, after the death of Mrs. Bosville, a Newfoundland belonging to Colonel Bosville, who had been interred several weeks before, had found his way to the mistress' coffin. He placed himself upon it and remained there until the funeral of Mrs. Bosville took place, and then could only be removed by force. Although there were several coffins in the vault, the dog had proceeded directly to that of his mistress.

A grim example of the Newfoundland's devotion to his master came to light in a newspaper account of a suicide in Salem, Massachusetts. A bachelor hung himself and the police came to remove the body. The dead man's Newfoundland was found on guard, trying to revive his master by licking his feet.

The dog allowed the policemen to cut the body from the rope by which it was suspended, but the minute they tried to carry it down the stairs, attacked them with fury. The officers dropped the body and retreated in haste, and the Newfoundland was seen caressing the dead master's face, whining pitifully all the while.

Each time the police tried to approach the body, the dog snarled, showing his teeth, growling threateningly. This continued for an hour. Then a policeman fired two shots, wounding the faithful guard. The Newfoundland plunged down the stairs, but still blocked the approach to his dead master, snapping at those who tried to reach him.

Fourteen bullets fired at close range ripped fist-sized holes in his body and every sign of life was gone from the huge, sprawling heap of blood and fur that once was a Newfoundland, before the body of the suicide could be carried out over that of his faithful pet.

Pride is a trait of character more often associated with humans than with animals, but should never be excluded from the list of characteristics manifested in the Newfoundland. An old clipping from the *New*

Ch. Little Bear's Sealed Cargo, pictured in 1971 win under judge Haworth Hoch. Handled by Jane Forsyth. Owned by Ken Aretsky.

Ch. Knickerbocker, winner of Group placements and many breeds at the ripe age of over 7 years. Owned by Newton-Ark Kennels, and handled by Alan Levine.

Ch. Black Molly of Warren, lovely bitch, BOS winner at the 1973 Specialty. Here winning under judge Kenneth Tiffin. Owned by Jean Goodrich, Warren, Vt.

Ch. Jeggy de Nashua-Auke scoring under judge Mrs. Nicholas A. Demidoff. Bred by Mr. and Mrs. Ronald Thibault, owned by Dr. and Prof. George Hotte, and handled by Gerlinde Hockla.

York World tells of a Newfoundland who committed suicide because he could not bear the humiliation of a beating for some transgression.

All New Durham knows that Nero did commit suicide, for everyone in that town would vouch for what a serious and sensitive dog he was.

Not an engineer on the West Shore Railroad, familiar with the daily sight of a magnificent Newfoundland racing beside a train or giving it a lordly greeting as it passed by, would dispute the popular contention.

"Why that dog knew as much about a train as the best man alive," said the trainman. "Suicide?" said the engineer of the 4:15 why it was a plain case — as you ever heard of. I felt just as bad as if I had struck a man, it took all the nerve out of me.

"There he was across the track, his head resting on the rail. Never had he done such a thing before.

"His tail never quivered as the engine approached. He was steeled for the death stroke. His eyes were sad and he licked his lips. As I saw him going under the pilot I shut my eyes and groaned. I could feel the pilot wheel cutting off that noble head."

Nero had been whipped for tearing the dress of a little girl with whom he played. From that point on he had avoided the company of his juvenile friends. He had refused to eat, remaining brooding and unhappy, and eventually his damaged pride had caused him to seek his own death.

Another *New York Times* story concerns a large Newfoundland who was too sensitive to be a burden to his family. He used to draw his little master to school in a cart each morning and go after him at the close of the day. One evening the dog was home playing with the little boy. The boy's father said to the child, "Johnny, we must get rid of your dog. We cannot afford to feed him." Whereupon the Newfoundland walked to the door and begged to go out. That was the last the family saw of him, for he never returned. Later it was learned that the dog had gone to a neighborhood store where he was well liked and often petted. There he insisted upon staying. At his new home he spent most of his time carrying parcels to the customers. If disturbed by the neighborhood dogs while on his errands, he would first deliver the parcel, then return and punish the offenders.

Again from an old clipping from the *New York Times* comes a story of devotion to a master which illustrates the Newfoundland's homing instinct. Neptune belonged to Captain Stephen Lemist, and like many of his kind, the dog was loved by all hands on board the captain's ship.

The Newfoundland had full liberty of the quarterdeck and sometimes reached it by way of the taffrail. The ship, bound for New Orleans, was being towed up the Mississippi River. Neptune, true to his

167

custom, was walking the taffrail when the ship lurched, the dog lost his balance and fell overboard.

It was impossible to stop the ship without disarranging the tow, which the captain of the tug refused to do. Captain Lemist had no alternative but to leave Neptune to his fate. For a while he was seen swimming after the ship, but finding that it was drawing away, Neptune finally struck out for the western bank of the river. The captain and the dog's shipmates were heartbroken. With his head against the binnacle, the captain sobbed like a child.

The ship was fifty miles below New Orleans when Neptune fell overboard. Three days later, while berthed to a tier of vessels taking a cargo of cotton and tabacco on board, the crew again welcomed Neptune on deck. To reach the ship, the dog had had to travel fifty miles up the river, cross it to New Orleans, and then find his way to Lafayette and walk two tiers of other vessels. Their faithful companion thus returned, the joy of the ship's crew knew no bounds.

Late one evening in the fall of 1963, Sylvia and Winthrop Wadleigh's 180-pound bundle of Newfoundland kindness and devotion was taking his evening constitutional only a few yards from his beautiful home in Manchester, N.H. Sylvia heard a heavy truck stop by their driveway, then a muffled sound of Moxie barking. She rushed out of her house calling Moxie — but Moxie was gone. There was a strong scent of ether in the air. The slim clue to his disappearance was a beaten-up truck loaded with dogs that had stopped by the local dog pound, inquiring for large dogs.

For five gruelling months a search for Moxie went on throughout the United States and Canada. A sizeable reward was offered with no questions asked and the Wadleighs were flooded with telephone calls that continuously buoyed their hopes only to have them broken.

It so happened that one evening Joy Adamson, of the lioness Elsa and *Born Free* fame, was with the Wadleighs. The main topic of conversation was Moxie's kidnapping.

The next morning Mrs. Wadleigh found Moxie on the terrace back of the house. He must have been there the night before while they were talking of him. His pads were worn from the miles and miles he had traveled. Goodness only knows how far or from where he had escaped. His coat matted and covered with burrs, thin almost to the point of not looking himself, the dog was in terrible condition. Moxie had accomplished a final goal in life. He lay quiet and in a seemingly exhaustive sleep. Moxie had come home — but only to die.

Important filming of the Lewis and Clark documentary took place at the Bud Basolas' 66,000-acre *B Bar B Buffalo Ranch* in Wyoming

Am. & Can. Ch. Edenglen's Falstaff, winner of 1970 National Specialty. Falstaff finished for American championship within one month, and for Canadian championship within one week. Owned by Jerrald B. and Lois M. Potts of Ithaca, N.Y.

Ch. Dryad's Compass Rose, an outstanding Newton daughter, owned by Shipshape Kennels.

Ch. Indigo's Bozo The Clown, outstanding winner and sire, owned by Mr. and Mrs. Myron O'Neil, Indigo Kennels.

where the largest herd of buffaloes roam. While there, on location, Hard Tack, who played the part of Scannon, became a close friend of Bud Basola and his wife, Georgia. Mrs. Basola wrote of Hard Tack: "He kept us so entertained. We loved him so very much and when he left the ranch to go on to another location he was really sad just as if he knew he had to go. That was the only time he didn't want to get into the back of the pickup. He seemed to sense this was goodbye. We always said he just never really became a dog."

Later Ted Yates sent a Newfoundland puppy to the Basolas, which was appropriately named Little Bear's Sacajawea. Saki, as she is called, became a close friend of the Basolas' 9-year old retriever, who taught her all the refinements of retrieving.

From Georgia Basola: "Saki retrieves doves with a very soft mouth and will jump into the back of the pickup with the dove in her mouth without harming the bird. She was taken wild turkey and pheasant hunting last Sunday and worked beautifully. She is so proud when she does things like this.

"When she was one year old she disappeared upon our ranch. She went with my husband to one of our wheat fields and being a real *nut* over water started following a small stream. The wheat was about five feet tall, and she didn't mind too well then. We searched for hours. We were all so sad that we would never see Saki again. The next morning we put a plane in the air and half an hour later she was located heading down the middle of the highway towards the ranch. She was about five miles from our main gate. Whatever made her turn in the right direction we shall never know except someone told me the sun helps to direct a dog. She had every kind of a burr, weed, grass, etc. on her and what a sorry looking sight. She must have walked all night. Saki hasn't left our sides since."

A year later Saki taught the Basola's new Pointer to retrieve.

I had felt like the child Shirley Temple's mother receiving checks from the young actor of our family. When he returned home from his dramatic career, Hard Tack rated new privileges. Instead of only taking his turn with the other kennel dogs for freedom of the house and grounds, he was made a member of that elect group, the permanent house dogs, an honor generally achieved only by seniority.

It was the kennel man's day off and Vadim was feeding the dogs. While the fresh, hot food was cooling, my husband set out four dishes of food for the little kittens. Our cat, Tommy, has the habit of bringing his offspring home after matings with back-to-nature wild queens. Every so often Tommy marches in shoving ahead of him his get, into the kennel feed room with full confidence that we will do our part in their

Ch. Edenglen's Randy of Newton-Ark, strong winner of the '70s. Owned by Newton-Ark Kennels.

Ch. Edenglen's Heidi Bear, Midwest winner of the late 1960s. Pictured at the age of 6 months and 1 week of age, upon scoring 2 points over Specials in first time shown. It was first show for owner Jill Carpenter, too.

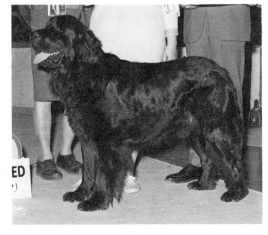

. Little Bear's Commander Tucker, e '60s winner, owned by Mrs. Helen sko.

upbringing. Tommy is a friend of all the dogs and he does his best to teach his kittens to overcome their wild woods fears.

This day as the kittens lined up beside their dishes, Hard Tack, suddenly hungry, shoved the kittens aside and quickly lapped up all of their food.

Vadim turning, saw what had happened and spoke in a very serious tone: "Hard Tack! Aren't you ashamed of yourself! Eating the poor little kittens' food! Don't we feed you enough?"

Hard Tack, looking vastly ashamed, tail between legs, walked off.

The kennel dogs were fed, their dishes picked up and put in the big sinks to soak. Vadim was just about to open a can of salmon for Tommy's babies when he suddenly saw Hard Tack trotting up the driveway, dripping with water, tail very gay. In his mouth was something about seven inches long which proved to be a catfish.

The Newfoundland threw the fish down in front of the kittens, then stepped back and proudly sat watching them eat it.

A gentleman who for many years had been commander of a ship in the West Indies trade had a fine old Newfoundland dog, which accompanied him on all of his voyages. In ports which she had previously visited, the vessel no sooner came to anchor than the dog would jump overboard and swim to the shore. Ashore he visited his friends and after staying some time would return to the side of his ship where he would howl until hoisted on board.

When the captain left the sea and returned to a little village near London, he took his dog with him. On Sunday he regularly attended church accompanied by his Newfoundland. On any occasion when the captain was unable to go, the Newfoundland, upon hearing the church bell, would set off alone and walk slowly in a dignified manner to the church where he would enter and lie down in the captain's pew. There he would remain quietly until the services were over, when he would return home to his master.

The breed's natural inclination to perform services as lifesavers is well-known, and in addition, the Newfoundland is readily trained to perform other services for his master. "Mr. Peter Macarthur informs me," wrote Captain Brown, "that in the year 1821, when opposite Falmouth, he was at breakfast with a gentleman when a large Newfoundland dog, all dripping with water, entered the room and laid a newspaper on the table. The gentleman informed the party that this dog swam regularly across the bay every morning, went to the post office, and obtained the papers of the day . . ."

Ch. Little Bear Night Train, Group winner scoring strongly on the West Coast. A son of Ch. Little Bear John Paul Jones (also a Group winner), Night Train is owned and shown by Robert and Frances Dibble.

Ch. Shipchandler's Nanook, brother of Best in Show winner Ch. Shipchandler's Sea Eagle. Owned by Dr. and Mrs. Robert Chandler.

Ch. Minowe de Nashua-Auke, son of Best in Show winner. Ch. Canoochee de Nashua-Auke.

Ch. Little Bear's Chulavista, owned by Halirock Kennels.

Ch. Little Bear's Midnight Bounty ("Cupcakes"), owned by Florence and Alfred Flessner.

Ch. Benham Knoll's Baba Au Rhum, 1974 champion, bred and owned by Mr. and Mrs. Philip B. Knowlton, Jr.

In 1960, when a Pekingese won Best-in-Show at the Westminster show, Richard Starnes, columnist for the *New York World-Telegram* and more recently writer for *Field and Stream,* put in his word for the big dogs:

Before the Peke lovers come after me with the hot tar and pullet feathers, let me quickly admit that I am a hopelessly prejudiced witness, utterly biased in favor of another breed . . . When I think about man's best friend, I think about Newfoundlands.

Now there are real dogs; honest, courageous, gentle and big as Shetland ponies. Little Bear's Petticoat, which sounds like something out of the wardrobe for a production of Goldilocks, is not only my favorite Newfoundland, she is my favorite dog of all time.

How big she is now I don't rightly know. Weighing her involves holding her, standing on a bathroom scale and then doing a complicated sum in subtraction. I can still do the sum, but I quit holding Petticoat when she got to 90 pounds. The rest of her name by the way, comes from Little Bear Kennels, which bred her.

At one time Newfoundlands were widely celebrated as rescue equipment, and few life-saving stations were without one . . . Petticoat has never had the opportunity to rescue a drowning person, but she does love to swim, preferably in Little Neck Bay on a cold winter morning. She loves to chase ducks, but let me add . . . has never caught one.

She has, however, retrieved the horned toads a couple of times, carefully removing them from their box so she could eat the dry oatmeal in which they lived. Never harmed a horn of their heads, either. Most people think a dog the size of a switch engine could eat more than an orphanage full of Armenians, but this is not true. A healthy in-law can eat a great deal more than a growing Newfoundland.

But an in-law, or a Peke for that matter, cannot sit at your feet before an open fire and wordlessly comfort you on a dark night in an age of unfathomable human *orneriness,* which is a job Newfoundlands can do wonderfully well, indeed. That's what a dog has always meant, ever since they were tamed down by cavemen, and that's what they should continue to mean.

Autice Russell, well known Boxer breeder, writes me of the Newfoundland her great-aunt had when she herself was a young child. When ladies came to call on her Aunt Ida, the Newfoundland would greet each at the carriage and when a caller stepped to the ground, would pick up, gently her long skirt and carry it inside the house as the lady walked up the walk and steps.

The eternal Newfoundland could perhaps be best appraised in the words of a "certain literary lady" who back in 1816 wrote: "His natu-

175

ral instinct approximated so nearly to human reason and his affection for people was so great that he can be no other than some benignant human being, transformed into a dog by one of those enchanters celebrated in the Arabian Nights.''

In comparison with man, we are indebted to Isabel Kurth for finding in *The Intelligence of Animals* by Ernest Menault (1871) the following:

An individual, whom, from regard to his honour, we forbear to name, had an old Newfoundland dog, which, for economy's sake, he wished to get rid of, to save the dog tax. This man, with a view of executing his cruel design, led his old servant to the banks of the Seine, tied his paws together with string, and rolled him off the barge into the current. The dog, in struggling, contrived to break his bonds, and managed, with great difficulty to climb the steep bank of the river, where he arrived almost breathless. Here his unworthy master awaited him with a stick. He repulsed the animal, and struck him violently; but, in the effort, lost his balance and fell into the river. He would have drowned most assuredly, had not his dog been more humane than himself. But the animal, faithful to the natural mission of his race, and forgetting in a moment the treatment he had just received, jumped into the water from which he had only just escaped, to rescue his would-be executioner from death. He did not accomplish this task without much difficulty; and both returned home — the one meekly rejoicing at having accomplished good deed and obtained favour, the other disarmed and, let us hope, repentant.

Water, ever appropriate for a Newfoundland, forms backdrop for this photo of Ch. Tranquilus Betty of Subira, Best of Breed winner at the 1969 National Specialty. Owned by Penelope Freeman, and handled by William E. Buell, Jr.

Am. & Can. Ch. Barbara-Allen's Newfie Nana, C.D. At 8 years of age, Nana set the female weight-hauling record for dogs—3,050 lbs.—at Northwest Newfoundland Club Working Trials in 1973. Nana, standing 29'' at the withers but weighing just 148 lbs., is pictured winning BOB at Whidbey Island KC show (Wash.) under judge Joseph Faigel with breeder-owner Barbara E. Wolman handling.

A Yukon lumber team.—*Photograph, courtesy of Samuel and Marcia Morrill, Newton Centre, Mass.*

10

The Newfoundland
As A Working Dog

In 1810, according to Scott, there were about 2,000 Newfoundlands in the town and general vicinity of St. John's Newfoundland. "They are there, by selfish and inhuman custom left during the whole summer to shift for themselves. On the return of winter season, these unfeeling two-legged animals seek with utmost eagerness their lately abandoned dogs without the assistance of which it would be absolutely impossible to go through the severe labours of a Newfoundland winter. They are constantly employed throughout the winter to draw wood cut for fuel . . . cart fish from the shore, and all kinds of merchandize from one part of the town to the other. . . . It is asserted that a single dog will by his labour support his owner throughout the winter."

In February 1815, the Grand Jurors of St. John's at the Court of Session, ordered all dogs found at large in or about the town of St. John's to be forthwith destroyed, excepting such as were employed in sheds. ". . . and in order the more effectively to promote the destroying, a reward of five shillings for every such dog destroyed" was to be paid for the body when produced at the St. John's Court House Yard. Thus "the two-legged animals," aptly so described by the early dog lover, repaid the useful services of the Newfoundland.

The modern Newfoundland often helps his master. We hear of Bruno who helped to produce about five carloads of pulpwood in four months work, netting $1,500 to his Maine farmer partner. Working as a team, man and dog mushed the pulpwood out of the woods on a sled, an eighth of a cord at a time. It was stacked about a half-mile from the woodlot. Bruno was put into harness at nine months of age to haul firewood on a child's sled. He was also employed in pulling a small plow and a light harrow in a truck garden, and later a vegetable cart.

Bruno's collar was made of oak covered with canvas and sheepskin. He pulled slightly downward with his powerful shoulders and forelegs, so that none of the strain was on his neck or throat. His master reported:

> "While the trees are being felled and cut up, Bruno sprawls on the snow at a safe distance, harnessed to the empty sled. When the tree has been cut into four-foot lengths, Bruno is called. He draws the sled to the cut logs and waits for further commands. He is then directed just like a horse but without the benefit of reins. It's 'Gee!' for a right turn, and 'Haw!' for a left, along with the familiar 'Whoa' and 'Back.' Bruno knows them all. When the sled is loaded, the sides are bound with rope. The whip is snapped when Bruno falters at a tough spot, but it is never used on him. The loaded sled is guided by its handles through the woods. Each round trip is a little less than a mile.
>
> Like any other hard-working woodsman, Bruno requires and has plenty to eat. He gets three square meals a day of dog food supplemented with generous portions of meat. He never sleeps indoors, but always on the ground or the snow, or on the back porch. In winter his long, black coat is silky with no sign of a collar mark. A person can talk to Bruno as he would to a man. Bruno wags his tail and looks at you with friendly eyes, as if to say, 'We have a job to do, let's go.' Sometimes we turn to Bruno and say: 'There is a bear around here,' whereupon he will stand up and sniff. If he detects an alien odor, his hair bristles and he growls. If not, he turns away."

Skipper Dibbon with his schooner, Jack Frost, sailed out of Burin on the West Coast of Newfoundland. He knew his rocks like the palm of his hand. As for navigational equipment, he had an old brass watch, a dry compass and a Newfoundland dog called Laddie. Skipper Dibbon was six score ten. His Newf, too, was kind of gray at the muzzle for he had sailed on the Jack Frost for ten years or more. It was about that long ago, while sailing over the squidding ground, that his sire had been swept off the schooner's deck by a great sea. Now Laddie, old as he was, still had a thunderous bark and no better lookout ever stood at a ship's bow in a peasoup night to warn of an approaching ship or the breaking shoals. Every skipper from the South Shore knew Laddie's voice, for Skipper Dibbon sailed his ship, fair weather or foul.

Coming home to Burin, Skipper Dibbon would plot his course straight for the Keys, a rock half awash at the mouth of the bay. In the dead of night, in thick fog, Dibbon would be out in the bow listening for the familiar sound of the breakers. Laddie would be right by him listening too, and the minute Jack Frost would be in the very wash of the breakers, Laddie would bark and Dibbon would bellow the order to the frightened helmsman to put the vessel about and reach for Burin.

The coming of Christmas beckoned him home from his coasting voyage to St. Johns. It was a white Christmas Eve at the out-ports and children frolicked and played in the white, flaky snow. But there was a blizzard howling at sea as Schooner Jack Frost was running for the Keys, homeward bound. It blew from the southeast with the whole Atlantic swelling up in ugly-looking seas astern. As the schooner rounded Cape Race, the double reefed foresail jibed, and Skipper Dibbon was knocked off his feet by the boom, but his tangling in the foresheet kept him from being swept away with the sea. He was carried into the cabin and there he lay, more dead than alive.

Now the young mate had to take charge, but he was as experienced as a newborn calf. It was the devil to pay and no pitch hot. Scudding before a living gale and the seas running like mountains, Jack Frost could not be put about and head back for St. Johns without losing every spar.

Laddie, the skipper's Newfoundland, was at his lookout station in the bow, solid with white snow, sniffing dutifully to leeward. Well there was nothing left to do but to trust Laddie. Laddie did it before with Skipper Dibbon at his side, so he could do it again — alone this time.

And he did. Schooner Jack Frost with her rigging and canvas a solid sheet of ice, sailed into her home port Christmas morning.

This story comes directly from the former mate of the Jack Frost. Shiver my timbers!

Today Newfoundlands are seldom given the opportunity to prove they have the capabilities they so frequently demonstrated in the past. But the Newfoundland Bing lived as late as ten or so years ago.

Bing was a fabulous worker for his master, Warren Thompson. Mr. Thompson at that time lived on a farm in a remote part of Maine. Bing had always been useful with the farm chores. The Newfoundland carried buckets of water from the brook to the cows, dragged the hay to the cows, pulled loads of firewood to the cabin, and in general did whatever might be needed.

But it was after Mr. Thompson was in a cast from a broken leg and Mrs. Thompson became ill and was hospitalized, that the Newfoundland really became indispensable. In addition to his regular chores, in the winter, Bing went alone to the village, with a sled carrying the soiled clothes, and brought back the fresh laundry, stopping to fill his list of groceries on his return trip.

One night, handicapped as he was following the broken leg, Mr. Thompson after an especially heavy working day, had fallen asleep.

The Newfoundland as fisherman.
Above, using his paw as "shiner" to
lure fish. Below, sailor raising dog
back to boat with his catch.

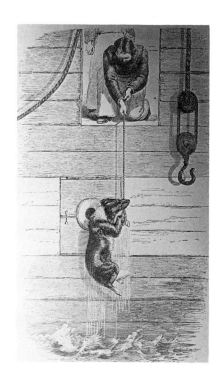

An ember from what he had thought was a well-banked fire, shot out from the fireplace and set the cabin on fire. Bing not only awakened his master but helped him carry buckets of water from the brook to put out the fire.

The Fisherman

A charming story of the Newfoundland on a fishing venture comes from J. B. Jukes, a geologist who explored the island of Newfoundland during 1839 and 1840. Mr. Jukes records: "The Newfoundland sat on a projecting rock, beneath a fish flake or stage, where the fish are laid to dry, watching the water, which had a depth of 6 or 8 feet, and a bottom which was white with fishbones. On throwing a piece of codfish into the water, three or four heavy, clumsy-looking fish, called in New-foundland sculpins, with great heads and mouths, and many spines about them, and generally about a foot long, would swim in to catch it. These he would 'set' attentively, and the moment one turned his broad-side to him, he darted down like a fish-hawk, and seldom came up with-out a fish in his mouth. As he caught them, he regularly took them to a place a few yards off, where he laid them down: and they told us that, in the summer, he would make a pile of 60 or 70 a day just in that place. He never attempted to eat them, but seemed to be fishing purely for his own amusement."

Jukes watched this dog for a couple of hours and noticed that when the fish became shy and did not come up, the dog would put his right forefoot (a white one) in the water and would paddle it about. Jukes' guide told him that the dog did this to "toll," or entice, the fish, using the principle of a shiner. It was remarkable that he consistently used his one white paw.

Perhaps it may be well to mention to the "Izaak Waltons" who are not familiar with the abundance of fish in Newfoundland waters that the fishermen jig for cod. The jigger is fashioned out of a piece of lead in the form of a fish with two sharp hooks at its end. As the jigger is pulled up and down from the side of the boat, it glistens in the water by reflecting whatever light there is, and the fish, being very curious by nature, are attracted to its vicinity and get hooked.

Should the foregoing story be difficult to believe, well-authenticated though it is, there is still another story of a white-pawed Newfoundland who lived in New England and used the same strategy in catching his fish from a stream. When the fish were running well in the spring, he kept his family well supplied. He, too, always stacked his trout neatly under a nearby tree.

Proving that work and play do mix. Reproduction from an 1858 water-color, "Winter Scene," by Frances Anne Hopkins, from the public archives of Canada.

Modern Newfoundlands proving old capabilities. Ch. Little Bear's Hardtack II and Little Bear's Chicago White Sox with antique dog cart owned by Mrs. Isabel Kurth.

It was more than 150 years ago that a law case occurred entitled "The Earl of Tankerville versus a Dog." The Newfoundland dog won against this peer of the realm. This is what happened. The dog had become so expert in fishing for salmon that he threatened to deplete the waters of a stream that ran through the property of the Earl of Tankerville. Hence the suit was brought against the dog as property of the Earl of Home.

The dog used to take position at the opening in the dam made to allow salmon to ascend, and catch them as they attempted to pass through. So skillful did he become that "he has been known to kill from twelve to twenty salmon in a morning," which he neatly placed together on one side. He never ate the salmon but left them stacked.

In Scotland we find a Newfoundland dog that on one occasion was observed to fish in the river Clyde. A codfish about eighteen inches long was leaping out of the water and thus came to the attention of the dog, which at a favorable moment plunged into the Clyde and disappeared for a short time, then reappeared fish in mouth. The Newfoundland delivered the codfish, scarcely bruised, to a servant of his master.

At Bar Harbor, on Mount Desert Island, some 40 years ago, a handsome young Newfoundland swam ashore, whether from the nearby coast of Maine or from a passing ship, no one knew. He became a member of the community, fished for his living and had his annual license paid by the town. His fishing was regular and thoughtfully pursued. Over the shoals which at very low tide show above the water, the flounder is plentiful. It was there he made his catch and always laid up a neat pile in the nearby shade for any of the townsfolk who might need provisions. And many a family larder was replenished by the grateful honorary citizen of Bar Harbor. The Newfoundland knew no individual master but visited all with friendly dignity. This is the story told me by one who knew the dog well—Ralph Hellum, long-time manager of the Ledgeland Kennels of the late Mr. and Mrs. David Wagstaff.

Our own Teddy Bear, like all good Newfoundlands, was a joyous water dog. He used to plunge into the pond at our Little Bear Farms in Northfield, Vermont, bring up a trout and lay it at my feet as a gift.

The singular behavior of the Newfoundland in storing unneeded catch and not disturbing it, or handing the fish to the master or servant, has often aroused curiosity as to the dog's motive. Some naturalists have felt that perhaps the dogs do it for pure sport. However, we feel that the Newfoundland's action should be viewed in the light of ancestral behavior.

The Indians depended primarily on their spear and their dog to obtain fish. In fact, they seemed to have had less luck with fish than with game, due to the inadequacy of their fishing tackle. Consequently, their big fishing and retrieving dog must have been bred and trained to fetch fish and game unmarked and unmolested.

The Newfoundland's natural ability to catch fish apparently was too startling to accept at face value, hence the overpublicized pulling of fish nets. Granted that a Newfoundland would lend his teeth and strength to pull along with his master. As a fisherman he can outdo man.

The Benevolent Guard

More than a watch dog, the Newfoundland is a natural, instinctive guard, able to perceive the difference between a potential friend or enemy. No training is necessary for this protection. We, ourselves, have never had one fail us when help was needed.

In 1820, Scott wrote in *The Sportsman's Repository:*

> No risk is incurred by pronouncing this dog the most useful of the whole canine race, as far as hitherto known, upon the face of the earth. His powers, both of body and of intellect, are unequalled, and he seems to have been created with an unconquerable disposition to make the most benevolent use of those powers. His services are voluntary, ardent, incessant, and his attachment and obedience to man, natural and without bounds. The benignity of his countenance is a true index of his disposition, and nature has been so partial to this paragon of dogs, that while he seems to be free from their usual enmities and quarrelsomeness, he is endowed with most heroic degree of courage, whether to resent an insult, or to defend, to his last gasp, his master or companion when in danger. His sagacity likewise, surpasses belief, as do the numerous and important services rendered to society, by this invaluable race, in lives saved, persons defended, and goods recovered. The list of his qualifications is extensive indeed: he is one of the ablest, hardiest and most useful . . . as a keeper or defender of the house, he is far more intelligent, more powerful, and more depended upon than any other . . . .
> The dog Jowler, after many hard-fought battles, and when he had attained his full growth, soon established his character for superiority. He was not quarrelsome, but treated the smaller species of dogs with patience and forbearance; but when attacked by a dog of equal size, or engaged in restoring peace among other dogs, he would set to, most vigorously, and continue the struggle until submission was obtained, or peace completely re-established. He would then leave the field of battle with a haughty look, and a warning growl, and be afterwards as quiet as a lamb. His master was perfectly secure in his company; for the least appearance

The Newfoundland—guard dog.

of an attack on his person, raised at once the dog's attention, and produced a most tremendous growl as the signal of action, in his master's defense. The sagacity of this animal was astonishing, and on all occasions he seemed to want only the faculty of speech to place his intellect on a level with the human.

A Newfoundland named Sultan had a most distinguished career in France as a guard dog. He counted among his exploits the arrest of a thief, the capture of an assassin, the rescue of a child from drowning in the Marne and of an attempted suicide from the Seine. The Society for the Protection of Animals presented him with a collar of honor. Prior to his death, he belonged to the Countess Foucher de Carrell and guarded her castle at Perdy. Here he is credited with routing robbers. He paid with his life for his devotion to duty.

A very old story of a Newfoundland written by Mrs. P. W. Latham, relates the facts as given her by a then very old man:

> Neptune became mine when I was a very little boy. His first master was a great brute of a fellow: he used to starve and beat him most cruelly. I saw and pitied him, and I persuaded my father to buy him. I am sure Neptune understood all, for from that day he seemed to love me, nay, worship me. He never willingly lost sight of me, and I think would have endured the most lingering torment for my sake. At one time I was sick, and Neptune never left me for the long weeks of my confinement to my room, unless he was forced away, and he would come and lay his great shaggy head on the bed close by me, and look so lovingly and so pityingly into my face, I could not bear him to be driven away.
>
> With returning health Neptune shared all my pastimes; and as if he really knew my feeble strength, he would after a little time lie down on the grass and entice me to rest. Many were the sweet hours of sleep I have enjoyed with my dog for a pillow. One day, and I could not have been more than six or seven years old, I went to play on the river bank, with nurse and Neptune, as usual. After running about some time, I spied a tiny boat lodged among some aquatic plants growing near the shore. With the thoughtlessness of childhood I slid down the bank and endeavored to reach it, and fell into the water, which was deep in that place. I should probably have been drowned before the nurse could rescue me had not Neptune, quick as thought, plunged in and brought me to the shore. You may well suppose, after this, he became a sort of hero in my father's family, and that in all my boyish rambles my parents thought me quite safe with Neptune.

More than twelve years later, with Neptune trotting beside the young master on horseback, the two went for a visit to what was then considered the Far West. Continuing with the old man's account:

> One day I had wandered far away from the little clearing occupied by

my friends into the still depths of a grand old forest, now attracted by the gay plumage of a bird, then by some new and singular form of vegetation. At length I espied a little, playful animal, almost like a kitten; it came caressingly around me, and I was delighted with it, and stooping, took it in my arms. A moment's reflection would have shown me I was in a dangerous proximity, and I should have made a speedy retreat. No sooner had I taken the little creature in my arms than a terrible shriek rung in my ears. I was conscious of a severe blow, like a heavy object falling on my shoulders, and the teeth and claws of some animal were buried deep in my flesh. The next moment I fell to the ground, my head struck some hard substance, and I became insensible. How long I lay I know not; but when I awoke to consciousness, Cato was pouring water in my face from his hat, and the shadows were all in another direction. Neptune was not there, but the leaves and soil were torn up all around me, as if in mortal combat. We followed the signs of battle till we reached a projecting ledge of rock, beyond which was a frightful precipice; looking down deep in the ravine below lay the body of poor Neptune, and not far off, the form of a huge panther. Both were terribly lacerated and bloody. They had drawn nearer and nearer the abyss, and the fall had ended the contest, in the death of both. Need I tell you, hurt as I was, I forgot my own injury in my grief for my poor friend, who a second time had saved my life, though at the expense of his own.

Two Newfoundlands from the very first litter of Lila and Chuck Visich's new Thunderoc Kennels have proven to be excellent rescue dogs. Thunderoc's Morgan, owned by the Fischers, saved the life of a Beagle-type dog. The little one hit by a car, hurt and frightened had run into the woods. The entire neighborhood was enlisted to search the woods for the little dog. The search went on until dark, the owners of the small dog even continuing with flash lights. The next morning when the Newfoundland, Morgan, was let out for his morning constitutional, he ran directly into the woods, sought out the little dog and brought him back in his soft mouth. The little one had had his leg broken by the car but fortunately had no other injury.

Thunderoc's Mermaid, called "Panda," is the heroine of two rescues. A letter to Lila Visich from Paul Katzoff relates:

> I was traveling west from New York City to my home in Aspen, Colorado. It was mid-summer. Panda, my traveling companion on the trip was at my side watching the road, interested in everything that passed by. Once in a while her eyes would follow something until her neck was turned over her shoulder.
>
> One night, somewhere in the middle of Kansas, I stopped at the side of the road to sleep for awhile. It was hot, so I left the windows open for Panda. The night air was still. I dozed and fell off to sleep.
>
> In an instant I found myself awake and being dragged out of the car. I was on my back on the ground. I felt fists hit my face. I smelled death

and my own terror. It wasn't real until Panda came into my view. She was biting one man on the thigh; he yelled in panic. Panda jumped up, and down went a second man. They all ran, more panicked than I. Panda came over and lay down next to me and panted from exhaustion, more mental than physical, I'm certain. She only took about ten seconds to save my life.

I can imagine those poor fellows sitting around some local bar telling their buddies that they missed the robbery because they picked on a dude who had a pet bear in the back seat.

The second exploit of the 15-month-old Panda:

It was late afternoon, and I was standing about fifty yards downhill from the dirt road that passed by our cabin. I was watching Richie, my five-year-old son, climb the hill up to the road. Panda was standing at my side. Together we watched the boy quietly wandering through the scrub oak to the road.

Suddenly a truck came into my view, coming down the road out of Richie's view. He was now at the road but on the far side of a curve so neither the driver nor he could see each other. I yelled to Richie but he didn't know what I was yelling at. And there was no time to do anything.

Panda saw it all happening. She covered the fifty yards in time to push Richie down the hill, much to his surprise. The truck passed by — the driver never knew what had happened, but Panda knew.

Dr. Isabel Bittinger, who at one time was living alone with four young daughters, has a trophy room for her Newfoundland Vicki's mementos of victory. Not silver bowls and ribbons (Vicki has won those too) but the Newfoundland's greatest prizes are knives, blackjacks, revolvers and whatever she has taken, disarming intruders. There is even the seat of the pants of one prowler who departed through the nearest window without opening it.

Dave Brubeck, world-famous jazz pianist, lives with his lovely family in a spectacularly modern Connecticut home. One night they suffered the harrowing experience of being awakened by an intruder. The man who had broken in turned out to be a mental defective, not a thief, but the danger was none the less real.

The next morning Mr. Brubeck phoned me and came to get a Newfoundland to be a protector of the family. He chose a yearling, appropriately enough named Lifeguard. He did not want to wait for a puppy to grow up. The dog was to be an all-purpose dog: companion for young Matt and the older children, lifeguard on the Brubecks' lake and night watchman for the entire family.

The very presence of a large black dog will generally deter prowlers. In any event, the Brubecks were able to sleep securely and had no more uninvited night guests.

Another popular pianist, Carlos Cortez, had a Newfoundland, Little Bear's Boatswain, that was his constant companion. When Mr. Cortez played late at night clubs, Boatswain waited in his master's parked car. The night club parking lot was filled one night and the dog and car were left, locked, five blocks away in downtown Detroit. It was four in the morning when Mr. Cortez walking back to his auto was beset by a large gang of boys with knives.

Providentially, the car was a convertible. The dog hearing the scuffle some blocks away, tore through the canvas top and in minutes was with his master dispelling the attackers. Mr. Cortez suffered only superficial cuts and bruises. Although he is a strong man, unarmed he could not have held off his many assailants long. He said that at the moment the dog arrived, he was at the end of his strength and thought his life endangered.

James Thurber, often called Gentleman Jim, was the friendliest of Newfoundlands. So we always admired and loved him for his outgoing personality but frankly never thought of him as being any kind of a guard dog. He just insisted on loving everybody.

Yet, he went after an armed hold-up man who had a gun on us one early morning in a motel room while we were on a return trip from the Detroit show.

James heard the robber tampering with the window and awakened my husband and me without making a sound. On being let out, James confronted the man who was still on a step-ladder beneath one of our windows. The man made a hasty retreat by jumping into his steamed-up car and drove off. James received a hero's award from the Journal American to add to his Best-in-Show achievements.

In late December 1947 a deep snowfall marooned North Westchester families and their food had to be brought in by state troopers on snowshoes. Butch of Camayer, a Newfoundland belonging to Abraham Samuelson, rescued both his master and a neighbor. On two successive days, Mr. Samuelson and the neighbor had each collapsed from exhaustion while struggling through the snowdrifts. Butch was awarded a medal by the A.S.P.C.A.

Edna Travinek, *Rocky Mountain News* dog columnist, tells the story of the Newf, Pluto. Pluto was combat trained by the Czechoslovakian army to kill if necessary. At the time of the incident he was attached to the local police department which also employed as a translator a girl named Judy.

It was a night in 1943 in Presrov, a small town near the Soviet border.

Writes Mrs. Travinek:

On this dark night, Judy received a phone call from a German major. He wanted her to come over to his office and translate a story from a Russian that they had picked up.

The 9 p.m. curfew was in effect and all the town activities had ceased. Knowing Judy would have to pass through the ghetto, the major told her to wait for a jeep that he was sending over. But Judy enjoyed walking and she refused this escort service.

Pluto watched Judy getting ready to leave the police station and he began dancing around as dogs do when they think that they are to be included in any human endeavor.

Judy told him to stay in the police station where he belonged, but Pluto kept circling around her as she walked through the doorway. She couldn't understand what had gotten into this otherwise obedient dog, who always responded to commands without fuss or ado. She became impatient with Pluto and scolded him back to his usual place by her desk with a much sharper command to stay. Then she hurried on out into the deserted street.

Judy had walked a few blocks, passing tiny shops, old and asleep in the silent night. Her thoughts were quiet, too, as she mused over that lovable Newfoundland who tried so hard to go along on this urgent errand.

She was brought to a sudden halt when two men jumped out from a doorway. They grabbed her arms and pushed her against a wall. She froze with fear, sensing that her assailants were Russian underground men intent on stopping her from reaching the German military office. She also realized that the telephone line had been tapped.

Her service pistol was useless in this violent situation with a man's hands gripped around her throat. Judy quickly glanced down the empty street, but all she saw was the moon glowing brightly. In the path of its illumination she thought she saw the silhouette of Pluto galloping down the street.

In hopeful relief, she found enough breath to scream, "Pluto, kill!" and then passed out.

Later, Judy regained consciousness in the German major's office; quite surprised, indeed to find herself lying on a cot with a doctor standing by. Her reassurance returned when she discovered Pluto sitting by the cot.

She reached out to pet her only friend among strangers in this bleak room. Her fingers told her that Pluto's muzzle and neck were sticky-wet and, when she looked at her hand, Judy was sickened to see it was streaked with blood.

192

The German major came into the room and checked with the doctor on her condition. Except for neck bruises and a sore throat, Judy was well enough to talk about her shocking experience.

The major told Judy that Pluto had killed the man who nearly succeeded in strangling her. The other assailant was captured and hospitalized, as part of his body was ripped away.

Following this encounter with the enemy, Pluto was formally assigned as Judy's official escort at all times in all places.

John Rendel in a feature article in the *New York Times* "*A Newfoundland in Heroic Role,*" writes about Little Bear's Horatio Hornblower's saving the life of his owner:

The Blumenstocks of New Canaan, Conn., Bob and Joy, are convinced that their 3-year-old 175-pound Newfoundland, Horatio, is gifted with extrasensory perception. As evidence, they point to a time in Newport when the dog saved Mrs. Blumenstock from being run down by an errant automobile. Blumenstock would be a stumper for the panel of *What's My Line?;* he earns a living by measuring racing yachts, mostly for long distance events, but last summer for the American defense candidates and the Australian challenger for the America's Cup competition. That's why he and Mrs. Blumenstock were in Newport.

"We were staying at the Hotel Viking and Joy was standing in front of a car parked alongside the swimming pool," Blumenstock said. "Suddenly the automobile began rolling down a slight grade. There was nothing to indicate it would start, but Horatio barked and barked. He pinned Joy against the wooden fence that encloses the pool and would not let her move. We don't know how he knew, but he undoubtedly saved Joy's life. The car drove two other automobiles to the opposite sidewalk."

"Mrs. Blumenstock says Horatio is highly protective, sometimes to the point of embarrassment.

"Once when our daughter Betsy (she will be 16 next month) went swimming, Horatio nudged her to shore because he thought she was in trouble," Mrs. Blumenstock said. "Betsy swam out again and this time began playing under water. When she came up, Horatio took her by the hair and towed her back to the beach."

The couple has owned dogs before, but Horatio is what Blumenstock calls their first 'dog dog.' He was bought as a puppy from Little Bear Kennels of New Milford, Conn.

Blumenstock sports a blond walrus mustache and it curls upward in pleasure when the dog is even mentioned. Mrs. Blumenstock smiles joyously. To them there never has been a dog like him.

"He has a great sense of humor," Mrs. Blumenstock said. "When chickadees come to our feeding station, they sit on his head cracking sunflower seeds while he waits happily until they are through. Then he goes to the kitchen door. He protects the birds from cats. He brings us moles and field mice and there's never a mark on them."

THE NEW FOUNDLAND DOG

A DESCRIPTIVE BALLAD

Sung with enthusiastic applause.

by

MR. H. RUSSELL.

The Words by

F. W. N. BAILEY ESQR.

The Newfoundland has been celebrated as a lifesaver over many years and in many forms. This cover sheet for "A descriptive ballad", *The Newfoundland Dog*, dates from 1845. The music was by Henry Russell, the words by F. W. N. Bailey, Esq., and it was published by Firth & Hall in New York City. The sheet also notes that it was "sung with enthusiastic applause" by Mr. Russell. —*Courtesy, Samuel R. Morrill, Edward Morrill and Son Inc. Rare Books & Prints, Boston, Mass.*

11

Sea Rescues

As FABULOUS as his deeds, the Newfoundland's character offers nothing that could be interpreted as ordinary. His acts very often border on the fantastic, but his character is incredible unless you know him. The dog's world-wide fame rests strongly on his life-saving prowess. It came to a test in Kent, England, when a vessel was driven on the beach at Lydd. The surf was rolling furiously. Eight poor fellows were crying for help, but not a boat could be got off to their assistance.

At length a gentleman came on the beach accompanied by his Newfoundland. He directed the attention of the dog to the vessel and put a short stick into his mouth. The intelligent and courageous fellow at once understood his meaning, sprang into the sea, and fought his way through the waves. He could not, however, get close enough to the vessel to deliver that with which he was charged. But the crew understood what was meant, and they made fast a rope to another piece of wood and threw it toward the dog. The Newfoundland dropped his own piece of wood and immediately seized that which had been cast to him, and then, with a degree of strength and determination scarcely credible — for he was again and again lost under the waves — dragged it through the surf and delivered it to his master. A line of communication was thus formed, and every man on board was rescued.

Another saga of the Newfoundland's appreciation of human life and his desire to save comes from the annals of the *William and Ann* on a whaling voyage to Greenland in the 1830s:

> Seven men were on an iceberg. It gave way. Six of them got hold of the bow-ropes, but the seventh sank. The waters closed over him, and

his comrades concluded he was lost. Mr. Smith, master of the whaler, was in bed at the time, but hearing the noise, he promptly sprang on deck, and, in obedience to his signal, boats from the other vessels immediately came to assistance. His faithful Newfoundland dog was at his feet, and gazing intently, he observed the head of the sailor above the water. He pointed it out — gave the word — the dog leaped from the bow of the vessel, and while swimming towards the man, he barked, either with anxiety, or with a view to cheer the perishing sailor with the prospect of assistance. When the dog was within a few feet of his objective, the drowning man was picked up in a state of utter insensibility by a boat from the *Rambler of Kirkaldy*. Observing the rescue, the dog returned to his own ship, and when taken on board, his gambols, frisking and fawning on his master indicated that though he had not saved the man, he was aware that he had gone to his aid and the sailor was safe.

There are times when not even a courageous and powerful Newfoundland could carry a man alive through the boiling surf. This evidently was one of such instances. During a severe winter storm near Yarmouth in 1799, a Newcastle ship was lost. The only survivor was a Newfoundland dog. All that was in his power to do was to carry tidings of the death of his master. He swam ashore, bringing in his mouth the captain's pocketbook. Landing amidst people who had gathered on the beach, he avoided some and singled out a man against whose chest he leapt and to whom he relinquished his prize possession, the captain's pocketbook. His duty done, the dog returned to the spot on the beach opposite the wreck and watched with great attention for anything that the surf might bring from the foundered ship. He tried to bring ashore a piece of wreckage that came off his vessel. For days after, he refused to leave the beach and kept vigil. Finally, Lord Granville, an ancestor of Sir Wilfred Grenfell, persuaded the dog to leave, took him home and kept him for many years until his death, at which time Lord Granville wrote a eulogy in Latin for the marble monument on the grave at Dropmore of the Newfoundland he called Tippo.

Another incident which comes to our attention concerns a German traveler in Holland who was accompanied by his Newfoundland dog. The two were walking on the side of a dyke when the man's foot slipped and he fell into the water. Unable to swim, after thrashing about for a few moments, he sank. His next recollection was of being in a cottage surrounded by peasants who were working vigorously to revive him. He was told by one of them that the big dog was seen in the water dragging or pushing along something which he had difficulty in supporting, but which he at length succeeded in propelling into a small creek on the opposite side. The peasants discovered the object to be the body of a man whose face and hands the dog was licking very industriously.

"To The Rescue," from a Currier and Ives print. A copy of this print hangs in a bedroom of the home of late President Calvin Coolidge in Vermont.

Sailor saved by a Newfoundland. From a print out of an early 18th century book on life-saving devices.

The Hollanders took the stranger to a cottage where he soon regained consciousness. The Newfoundland had left two bruises of considerable size with marks of teeth, one on the man's shoulder and one on the back of his neck. Presumably, he had tried to keep his master's head above water, first by holding him by the shoulder, then finding that failed, had resorted to holding his head out of water by the neck. In this fashion, the dog had swum, pushing the man for a quarter of a mile in order to find a bank low enough for safe landing.

Back to the region of the Newfoundland's origin, my husband gives me a story of the rescue of his friend, Skipper Walter Carter of Greenspond. Skipper Carter was fishing off Cape Mugford on Labrador. His schooner was anchored in the tickle, while he and two deck hands jigged from the skiff, tacking back and forth under sail. Carter's Newfoundland stood on the poop, watching his master in the skiff, which was at times barely visible.

Suddenly, a strong squall struck the tickle, blowing a living gale feather white. Carter's foot got caught in the sheet and the skiff capsized with all hands thrown into the icy water. The skipper managed to get hold of the rail and thus kept himself afloat. What happened to his companions he did not know. But suddenly he saw his dog puffing and snorting, coming right for him.

Unable to swim a stroke and thinking that his call had come, he forgot the reason the dog was kept on board the schooner. Not realizing that the Newfoundland had swum all the way from the vessel, he was so confused he imagined that the dog was trying to save himself by seeking support. By this time scared out of his wits, Carter lost his grip on the skiff rail and sank. He stayed down as long as his breath would permit, then came up to the surface.

The sea, still lashed by squalls, was nothing but boiling foam and spray. Carter could see the schooner anchored over a mile to windward, but there was no one on deck. He prayed that his strength would last until help could come and thanked the Lord for getting away from the beast.

But out of sheets of spoondrift, the Newfoundland appeared again. With horror, Carter heard his heavy breath amid the sounds of breaking combers. He repeated his prayers. When the dog, laboring through the seas, swam within reach, Carter gathered his last strength and ducked. He heard the big fellow circling above him. At last all strength left him and he felt as if he had fallen into the abyss of eternity.

A little later he regained consciousness. The Newfoundland, with strong teeth holding Carter's shirt in a tight grip, was pushing his numb body irresistibly against the wind and sea. Carter lost his senses again and remembered nothing until he was hauled on deck and the Newfoundland was licking his hands, while the boys were rubbing his limp body and pouring rum into his throat.

The dog, watching his master from the vessel, had seen the skiff capsize and on his own had gone to the rescue. None of the crew had seen what happened. The two men fishing with the skipper went down and the sculpins of Mugford tickle finished what was left of them.

A French brigantine named *Marie* was dismasted in an equinoxial gale. She was water-logged and sinking when sighted by the *S. S. Muldeau*. The French crew abandoned their vessel and the men were dropping into their dories while the steamship laid to windward, ready to pick up the survivors. The sea was running high and one of the crew was swept overboard while waiting to be picked up. In an instant, the vessel's Newfoundland leaped overboard and kept the man afloat, holding him firmly by his blouse, until his shipmates pulled both of them into the dory. The dog was elated over his good deed and kept his huge tail wagging, while the crew hugged and kissed him in an outburst of Gallic enthusiasm.

An earlier account speaks of a sea rescue off Newfoundland:

> About twelve o'clock the mainmast gave way. At that time there were on the main-top and shrouds about thirty persons. By the fall of the mast the whole of these unhappy wretches were plunged into the water and ten only regained the top-mast which rested on the mainyard and the whole remained fast to the foundering ship by some of the rigging. Of the ten who thus reached the top-mast, four only were alive when morning appeared. Nine were at that time alive on the mizzen, but three were so exhausted and so helpless that they were washed away before any relief arrived; two others perished, and thus only four were at last left alive on the mizzen.
>
> At the place where the ship went down was barely a hundred fathoms to the east of the entrance to Pigeon Cove. Some fishermen came down in the night to the point opposite to which the ship foundered, kept up large fires on the shore, and were so near that their shouts could be heard by the crew on board the wreck. The first exertion that was made for their relief was by a powerful Newfoundland dog from Pigeon Cove who ventured out to the wreck bearing a line in his teeth. This dog with great labor and great risk to himself boldly approached the wreck and maneuvered amid the breaking seas so close to the mizzen top as to pass the line to the two men who could not with safety hold on any more.

Every Christmas season brings to memory the heroic rescue of the 90 passengers and crew of the S.S. Ethie by a stalwart Newfoundland. *For the number of people saved, it is believed to be the record for any dog of any breed.* It was more than 50 years ago, during a blizzard, that the Ethie was wrecked off the coast of Bonne Bay, Newfoundland. No boat could be launched on that stony shore during such a raging storm. There were more than 100 souls utterly helpless within sight of land.

All of them would have been lost and many would have been the mourning families that Christmas, had not a Newfoundland and its owner appeared on the nearby shore. The dog went to the rescue upon an order from its master. The Newfoundland swam out through a sea in which no man could possibly have survived. The powerful dog made it to the ship and carried a lifeline back to the shore. With this a buoy was rigged and all hands saved. Among the rescued passengers from the Ethie was an infant in a mail bag.

In 1897 a New London, Connecticut man, A. A. Martin was hunting with his Newfoundland, Colored Boy, on the James River above Richmond, Virginia. Hearing the cry of a man in distress the Newfoundland jumped over the side of the boat, swam to the drowning man and towed him ashore. When consciousness was restored, Mr. Jenkins, the rescued man, tried to buy the dog which had saved his life. But his owner would not listen to any offer then or on the many subsequent times Mr. Jenkins tried to buy him.

Two years later, Mr. Jenkins died and left $2,000 in cash and other property to Mr. Martin in gratitude to the Newfoundland. Colored Boy went with his master to receive the bequest.

The Newfoundland's adaptability to water poses him in striking backgrounds. Here Black Mischief's Surfer rides a canoe (his owners aver "he balances himself better than many humans") in the waters of Capistrano Beach, California.

And here Little Bear's Aukai, C.D., owned by Henry and Cherri Mahi, is in the water at Blow-Hole, Oahu, Hawaii.

In 1972 the Newfoundland Club of America formally adopted Water Trial exercises designed to exhibit the breed's unique abilities as a lifesaver. The exercises are divided into two divisions, Junior and Senior. The Senior division exercises are more physically taxing—more swimming is involved and objects must be pulled through the water. Dogs are rated on a pass or fail basis and are awarded certificates and titles as follows: W.T. (Water Trial) for a passing grade in Junior, W.T.X. for passing in Senior, and W.T.X.H. for passing Senior with high honors. These two photos from the 1974 trials illustrate Senior Division exercises in (top) entering water from a dock and (below) towing a boat to shore from 100 yards out. Other Senior exercises include rescue of a person from a boat.

12

Water Trials

THE NEWFOUNDLAND is born with complete webbing between its toes and a natural water instinct. Just as any talent in humans must be used or it will atrophy, so it is with the Newfoundland. An effort should be made to introduce the puppy to water at an early age. As soon as the owner is able to stand the cold water of spring, the very young puppy can also. Care should be taken not to frighten the puppy by throwing it in water, or forcing it in. As a rule, the young Newfoundland will follow its owner into the water at any time.

For those who swim in the open ocean, breakers should be avoided until the puppy acquires some familiarity with swimming. For Newfoundlands that have missed the *magic early period* when swimming comes naturally, patience and time may be needed, but do not despair.

Water Trials

In the early days of the fancy, no Newfoundland could be considered worthy of his name unless he could prove his prowess as a lifesaver. To dramatize and preserve this outstanding trait of the breed Newfoundland fanciers are beginning to revive in part some of the old lifesaving trials. The rules drafted by C. Marshall for the conduct of water trials, adopted at Maidstone, England, in 1876, are as follows:

1. Courage displayed in jumping into the water from a height to recover an object. The effigy of a man is the most suitable thing.
2. Quickness displayed in bringing the object ashore.
3. Intelligence and speed in bringing a boat to shore. The boat must, of course, be adrift, and the painter have a piece of white wood attached to keep it afloat, mark its position and facilitate the dog's work.

4. To carry a rope from shore to a boat with a stranger, not the master, in it.

5. Swimming races, to show speed and power against stream or tide.

6. Diving. A common flag basket with a stone in the bottom of it to sink it answers well as it is white enough to be seen and soft enough to the dog's mouth.

As a means of furthering its objectives as stated in its Constitution and By-Laws, the *Newfoundland Club of America* took action February 1956 regarding the long considered establishment of water trials. A committee chaired by Lt. William D. Collins, Jr., U.S.N., Ret., went into action and came up with recommended procedures, along the lines of the old, established water trials.

It was agreed by all that trials would have to be partial at the beginning, building up, as owners and dogs learned, toward the full trials which might eventually have the sanction of the *American Kennel Club*. Hopefully, when that day comes, we may have officially recognized water trial champions.

Until recently, there have not been enough Newfoundland owners eager to do the pioneering work. For, although the *Newfoundland Club of North America*, a forerunner of the *Newfoundland Club of America*, under the leadership of Mr. E. H. Morris, put on water trials, the trials had once again become a lost art in the United States.

But now with enthusiasts springing up on both coasts and north and south, a new beginning is being made. We are still working on a *fun* basis, but significant work is being done. Georgia Arsenault came up from Florida with her big champion, obedience-titled Newf for a demonstration at the Sachem Head Yacht Club for the *Newfoundland Club of New England*. Barbara Wolman, with her husband owner of Barbara-Allen Kennels in Bothell, Washington, gave a demonstration in California in conjunction with the National Specialty held there in 1969. Mrs. Wolman is definitely the leader today in water trial work. She pursues her water trial training with her own Newfoundlands and with the Northwestern Newfoundland Club, of which she is the founding president.

G. O. Shields, in his *American Book of the Dog* (1883), in writing about the water trials, comments on a practical use of water training: "It would be well to add one of these noble animals to each of our life-saving stations, as, properly trained, they would doubtless be the means of saving many human lives. He would not only be ready to save persons from drowning, but would be of great assistance in other ways, as his keenness of sight and scent is surprising and his curiosity unlimited."

A current German writer notes the Newfoundland as one of the few breeds today retaining its original instinct. His article is accompanied

Am. & Can. Ch. Newfield's Nelson, C.D., T.D., winner of the Outstanding Dog in Trials award in 1969, 1970 and 1971. Nelson set a record for strength in dogs when he hauled 3,260 lbs. in 9 seconds, 15 feet, under International Sled Dog Association rules (Guiness Book of World Records, 1973 edition). Owner, Barbara E. Wolman.

Ch. Barbara-Allen's Great Khan established a new world record for weight hauling at the 1973 N.W.N.C. Land Trials Competition—4300 lbs. pulled 15 feet under 90 seconds (under International Sled Dog Association rules). Shown here with his young master, Daniel Wolman, who enjoys riding the travois.

by photographs of Tino, a handsome Newfoundland, being trained for lifesaving, which is a crucial part of the water trials. The first photograph shows Tino eagerly watching his trainer going under water with his arms raised in a gesture invoking help. Next, Tino races to the rescue, and the last picture shows the Newfoundland towing his trainer ashore.

Easy to train he is, if there has been no early fright to turn the web-footed dog away from his natural love of the water. But when an emotional block has occurred, it must be removed with an understanding of the Newfoundland's psychology.

The Hon. Harold MacPherson told of Billy, who at ten months of age steadfastly refused to enter the water. "We took him to the beach one time, but he couldn't be coaxed into the surf. I swam some distance out, then held up my hand and shouted for help. Billy nearly went frantic. Then he howled dismally and plunged in to rescue me. From that time on, he was perfectly at home in salt water."

James Thurber, when a puppy, became frightened and perhaps hurt by a rough surf and developed a reluctance to follow his master, Robert Dowling, in swimming. James' mother, Bonnavista, a powerful and enthusiastic swimmer, was called in to mend this regrettable situation. After following his dam for the third time into the ocean off East Hampton, the young dog lost all of his hesitancy and actually beat her to a ball thrown from shore, which each was endeavoring to retrieve.

Aside from special training for the occasional Newfoundland which must be introduced to the joys of swimming, there are basically only four phases of water *trial* training: retrieving, carrying a line, diving and racing. Being a repository of the retrieving instinct, our breed should find that phase of the work very easy. But though it is easy, it must not be slighted, for retrieving training should be thorough. Beginning first on land, one can use approved obedience training techniques for developing this faculty, always remembering that the Newfoundland make-up is such that the dog will respond best to firmness and praise, and that everything must be made a happy game. To many Newfoundlands this entire retrieving part of the work, including its transfer to water, will be so natural as to seemingly need nothing but the opportunity for the dog to display his ability. But keep in mind that obedience must be included, and that the dog must return to you promptly the article to be fetched.

After retrieving from the water has become a satisfactory accomplishment, using a dumbbell, begin by weighting it slightly with a small piece of lead fastened to it so that the dumbbell will sink a little below the surface of the water. After the dog has become accustomed to ducking his head for the slightly weighted dumbbell, gradually add more weights to it, so that the dog will have to duck deeper and deeper and finally dive well below the surface of the water to retrieve it. When his confidence is well established, throw the dumbbell from a cliff or pier, first for surface retrieving, and then for deep dive retrieving.

Racing can be developed best by making fenced lanes in a pool for competitive swimming. Give extra praise for the winning dog, but do not forget a kind word for each dog that finishes the course, or even makes a good try. Remember that Newfoundlands can understand simple sentences and they can easily learn what is expected of them. Yet, patience must be exercised by the trainer. Also, never continue with the dog's lesson long enough for it to become boring. Patience, affection, and love of play itself are qualities deeply ingrained in the New-foundland. And the trainer must also possess these qualities. If he has firmness in addition, all he will need is the Newfoundland and the water.

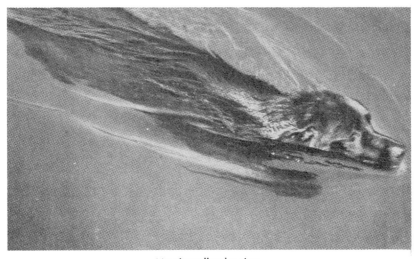

Newfoundland racing.

The monument to Boatswain at Newstead Abbey, England.

13

Friend of
The Famous

FRIENDSHIP implies affinity of spirit and in Lord Byron's words, one who "possesses Beauty without Vanity, Strength
without Insolence, Courage without Ferocity, and all Virtues of man
without his Vices" would indeed be a kindred soul in the Parthenon of
the Immortals. This was Byron's last tribute to his beloved Newfoundland friend, Boatswain.

It is not surprising that the most majestic of all the canine species, so
generously endowed with nobility of spirit, would enchant other lumi-
naries of human thought and leave a mark on their lives. Hence the
number of great ones who have loved and owned a Newfoundland is a
world-wide "Who's Who" projected into the span of two centuries.

Boatswain long has challenged curiosity, for the depth of affection
he inspired stands out even in the roster of beloved Newfoundlands.
Boatswain lived with young Byron at Newstead Abbey, the family es-
tate situated in the midst of Sherwood Forest of Robin Hood fame. He
shared his master's solitary hours amid the Gothic ruins of the crum-
bling abbey walls — haunted by the shadows of the tragic past con-
jured to live again by the magic of Byron's verse.

The poet and his Newfoundland shared the solitary delights of daily
strolls through the wooded grounds of the abbey. On rainy days, Boatswain and Byron passed their time before the ancient library fireplace
and here were born *Don Juan* and *Childe Harold*. When contemplative
moods gave way to a spirit of high revelry and the poet's merry companions invaded Newstead, Boatswain would leave for his private
haunts in Sherwood Forest. When the revelry ceased and the raucous
guests left, Boatswain returned to his master, bringing peace and tran-
quility to the poet's troubled soul.

The eternal vagabond found great joy in his reunions with Boatswain. The dog's happiness each time his master returned to England is reflected in Canto I of *Don Juan*:

> 'Tis sweet to hear the watch-dog's honest bark
> Bay deep-mouthed welcome as we draw near home;
> 'Tis sweet to know there is an eye will mark
> Our coming and look brighter when we come.

Thomas Moore, in his *Life of Byron*, sheds more light on the generosity of Boatswain's spirit. The poet's mother had a Fox Terrier, Gilpin, that waged a perpetual war with Boatswain. Hardly a day passed without a violent skirmish, and it was much feared that Gilpin would be killed. Consequently, Lady Byron decided to banish Gilpin and he was sent off to one of the Newstead tenants. Lord Byron left for Cambridge about the same time and his friend Boatswain was entrusted to the care of his house servant pending the poet's return.

Boatswain disappeared one morning and for the whole day there were no tidings of his whereabouts, much to the alarm of the servant. At last, toward evening, Boatswain returned, bringing back with him the exiled Gilpin. He led the Fox Terrier to the kitchen fire, licking him and lavishing upon him every possible demonstration of joy and affection.

It was established that Boatswain went all the way to Newstead to fetch his former foe. Having re-established Gilpin under the home roof, Boatswain lived in perfect harmony with his former enemy and loved him to the extent of protecting him against the insults of other dogs. This was no easy task for Boatswain, considering the quarrelsome nature of the little Terrier. Yet, one sound of distress from Gilpin and Boatswain would fly to his rescue.

Boatswain was black, though in Madame Tussaud's Wax Works he is represented as a Landseer. For his true color we have the authority of Stonehenge.

When Boatswain died, the poet announced that he himself, his ancient butler, and the Newfoundland would be buried together under the same great monument. The butler left Byron's service at once, explaining, "Your lordship will be buried in the Westminster Abbey. That only leaves Boatswain and myself to be buried under the monument. At Judgment Day what will they think of me On High when I rise from the same grave as a dog? No thanks. I am leaving."

Death came to Lord Byron in his beloved Greece, whose independence he sought to buy with his own blood and fortune. Lyon, the loyal Newfoundland companion of his last days was always at his side.

210

"Boatswain"

Near this Spot
are deposited the Remains of one
who possessed Beauty without Vanity,
Strength without Insolence,
Courage without Ferocity,
and all the Virtues of Man without his Vices.
This Praise, which would be unmeaning Flattery
if inscribed over human Ashes,
is but a just tribute to the Memory of
BOATSWAIN, a DOG,
who was born in Newfoundland May 1803
and died at Newstead Nov. 18th, 1808.

When some proud son of man returns to earth,
Unknown to glory, but upheld by birth,
The sculptor's art exhausts the pomp of woe
And storied urns record who rest below:
When all is done, upon the tomb is seen
Not what he was, but what he should have been:
But the poor dog, in life the firmest friend,
The first to welcome, foremost to defend,
Whose honest heart is still his master's own,
Who labours, fights, lives, breathes for him alone,
Unhonour'd falls, unnotic'd all his worth—
Denied in heaven the soul he held on earth:
While Man, vain insect! hopes to be forgiven,
And claims himself a sole exclusive Heaven.
Oh Man! thou feeble tenant of an hour,
Debas'd by slavery, or currupt by power,
Who knows thee well must quit thee with disgust,
Degraded mass of animated dust!
Thy love is lust, they friendship all a cheat,
Thy smiles hypocrisy, thy words deceit!
By nature vile, ennobled but by name,
Each kindred brute might bid thee blush for shame.
Ye! who perchance uphold this simple urn,
Pass on—it honours none you wish to mourn:
To mark a Friend's remains these stones arise;
I never knew but one—and here he lies.

Hendrik Wilhelm Van Loon, author and historian.

The Crown Prince of Morocco.

James A. Herrington and stewardess with Newfoundland being sent to the then president of Haiti, Paul E. Magloire.

"Lyon, you are a rogue," or "Thou art an honest fellow, Lyon," Byron would say. The dog's eyes sparkled and his tail swept the floor as he sat beside his master. "Thou are more faithful than men, Lyon. I trust thee more." Lyon would spring up, bark, and throw his paws around his master, as if saying, "You may trust me!" Faithful to the last, he watched over Byron's deathbed. Lyon himself ended his days in England, an honored guest at the house of Mrs. Leigh.

Sir Walter Scott, Charles Dickens, and Robert Burns were among the outstanding Newfoundland enthusiasts of their day. Richard Wagner can be credited with coining the most appropriate description of these dogs when he introduced them to his friends as "nature's own gentlemen."

George Washington, Benjamin Franklin and Samuel Adams, all owned America's own dog, and the Newfoundland tradition, regardless of fluctuations in popularity, has continued in many of the first families.

The Prince of Wales (later Edward VII) owned Nero, who took first prize at Birmingham in 1864 and at Islington in 1865. Nero was described as a rich black dog, totally free from white, powerful, good tempered, fine framed, very massive in form, and with a sagacious expression.

Among other royal devotees of the breed we find Queen Victoria, the last Queen Marie of Roumania and her son, King Michael.

King Hassan II, of Morocco, purchased three Newfoundland puppies to be his guards and companions. His Majesty is well known as a breeder of superb Arabian horses. For his horses and Newfoundlands he has a full time veterinarian, and in addition has a special attendant for the dogs. It is reported that the royal Newfoundlands are doing very well. They are much talked about in Paris where the King visits occasionally. Generally the Newfs divide their stay between the four principal castles of the realm.

Little Bear's Eben, owned by famed photographer, Mel Sokolsky, was responsible for his Majesty's enthusiasm for the breed. As a horse breeder the King appreciated the strong cannon bones, the firm back, the musculature and the proud bearing of the dog. Eben's high intelligence also impressed the King.

President Magloire of Haiti was a most enthusiastic supporter of our breed, being the proud owner of Little Bear's White Comber. Comber was presented to the President by James A. Herrington of Detroit. Comber used to swim with the President daily, either in the ocean or at the mountain palace.

Rose Burgunder, wife of the famous novelist, William Styron, in her *Summer to Summer* (The Viking Press), delights us with a penetrating and extremely sensitive study of the Styrons' Newfoundland, Little Bear's Tugwell, who together with the Styron children shared the dedication.

TUG

Big black puppy dog
    name of Tug
lies by my bed
    like a black bear rug

follows me downstairs
    follows me up
shaggy shaggy shadow
    is my brave pup

Mommy's mad at her again
    Daddy is, too,
just because she's eaten up
    another shoe

when I'm in my bath
    and smell so clean
Tug gets in beside me
    like a dainty queen

when I need a towel
    to blot my eyes
she shakes herself
    till the mirror cries

and we sneak downstairs
    for an extra snack
and I take a ride
    on Tug's wet back

big black puppy dog
    name of Tug
helps me hunt
    for my favorite bug

stays by my side
    close as she can
wonder if she ever read
    Peter Pan?

Among famous theatrical personages who have bred Newfoundlands, was Sir Henry Irving, the most renowned actor of his time, who once had a small kennel of the breed.

Bing Crosby has also bred Newfoundlands. He presented a pup of

Rock singer Roger McGuinn (of the Byrds) with wife Linda and their Newf.

The Dave Brubeck family.

his own breeding to the late President Roosevelt for a gift to the children of the Warm Springs Foundation.

The late Brace Beemer, of radio and television fame, the original Lone Ranger and Sergeant Preston of the Yukon, was the owner of Little Bear of Bonne Bay. His Newfoundland was his closest and most devoted companion, which is saying a great deal, for Beemer owned, in addition, dogs of other breeds and 18 horses, all of which competed for a favored place by his fireside. Brace Beemer, who had a way with animals, even taught his horses to retrieve. He once told me that he would not own a dog or horse that he could not take into his living room.

Bobby Kennedy's "Brumis"

Little Bear's Brumis was with Bobby Kennedy when the news of President John Kennedy's assassination reached him. The two walked into the solitude of Hickory Hill's great trees to face the unfaceable.

Brumis was *not* at his master's side, his customary place, at the time Bobby went down, struck by the murderer's bullets. Perhaps, here Brumis missed an opportunity to change the pace of history, emulating the feat of Napoleon's Newfoundland who saved the Emperor on his escape from Elba.

The most publicized, the most loved and spoiled of Newfoundlands in recent times, and by the same token — the most controversial — Brumis can boast unrivaled nationwide publicity. His real closeness to his illustrious master made him a symbol of the New Frontier and a target of political butts as exemplified by the Brumis party given by the Republicans.

A huge sign *Dog Daze Party* and a red fire hydrant labeled *Brumis Plug* decorated the front of the house at 304 Second St. S.E. in Washington in August 1962. Jolly fun was had by all as a loud speaker blared that Brumis would see that justice would prevail. F.D.R.'s Fala and Elliot's Blaze came in for the funning but the claim was that something new had now emerged from the halls of justice and that there was an old saying that the new Brumis would sweep clean.

If it was not already an old saying, it would soon become one, for one commentator after another used the phrase.

All Animals Are Equal But Some More Equal Than Others was the legend of one wall poster at the Republican ring-ding. Other banners made further references to the Newfoundland who frequented the office of his master, the Attorney General.

A song to the tune of *Let Me Call You Sweetheart* had all the Republicans singing:

A man and his dog—Bobby Kennedy and Brumis.

"Let me collie you Brumis
  I don't know what for.
We all love you Brumis
  From here to Labrador.
Keep right on a-barking
  Outside Bobby's door
A pretty girl will let you out, and
  We all know what for."

Initial limelight for Brumis had flared over a syndicated article referring to Brumis as a Labrador. A storm of indignation over the error in
breed identification swept the country from East to West. Arthur
Krock headed his two-column syndicated article of August 14, 1962
with *He's a Newfoundland — Justice for Brumis Must Sweep Clean.*

Mr. Krock called it racial injustice to miscall the Newfoundland a
Labrador. He cited numerous repetitions of the error, even referring to
an article in the *Baltimore Sun* wherein it was suggested that Brumis
was actually Teddy in disguise learning government before entering it
in the place where brother Bobby had reversed the procedure, which
Mr. Krock averred could be dismissed as improbable.

Ethel Kennedy mailed me a clipping from *Letters to the Editor* in the
New York Herald Tribune with Bobby's notation "J.F.K's favorite
newspaper." It held that Brumis doesn't object to having pretty girls
walking him but would certainly raise a howl if he knew he was being
called a Labrador.

"Both breeds," the writer said, "are smart and there might be one
among them who can read. If that is so, the word might be barked
along the canine grapevine and all offending newspapers just might find
themselves up to their city desks in panting Newfoundlands and Labrador Retrievers.

"Just thought I'd warn you."

"Brumis Refuses to Sit on Ceremony" was the headline for a United
Press release. It seems Brumis had disrupted a ceremony in the Attorney General's office when Bobby met with eight District of Columbia
school teachers. The dog disobeyed his master's command to sit and
even refused to leave the room.

Bobby then suggested that the meeting continue as if Brumis were
not there.

In an Associated Press article from Washington, August 3rd, it was
reported that Brumis had slipped out of Attorney General Kennedy's
fifth floor office and disappeared into the maze of corridors in the
block-square department building.

Continuing the Kennedy Newfoundland tradition. Court-
ney Kennedy, lovely daughter of Bobby and Ethel, with
new puppy Little Bear's Brumis II, acquired in May 1975.

For a while Bobby searched the hallways whistling for Brumis. The Newfoundland was eventually found in the FBI section of the building. One wonders if he was going to offer his services.

On the same day Brumis participated in a question and answer session on world affairs between the Attorney General and students from Brazil. The dog's contribution to the affair was loud panting under the shelter of his master's desk. Bobby reached out for an oversize glass ash tray, filled it with water and continued his discourse, while the big Newfoundland lapped away.

Evelyn Lincoln, personal secretary to the President, in her book, *My Twelve Years with John F. Kennedy,* wrote about Brumis. She said that Bobby, who attended the Security Council meetings during the presidency of J.F.K., brought Brumis with him. He would leave the dog in her office with instructions to keep the normally open door closed. As it was most unusual for her office door to be closed, it would always create quite a stir. On the first such occasion, one of the staff members after peeking curiously, asked who the visitor was — the Russian Ambassador?

Art Buchwald, in his satirical *Brumis the Great,* writes that the name Brumis in Newfoundland means a prolonged meal eaten around two a.m. He goes on to say that Brumis treated Kennedy guests picnicking on the lawn of Hickory Hill as if they were so many fire hydrants. Brumis' magnanimity was questioned by Buchwald's allegation that any Kennedy guest was in danger of losing all of his food to Brumis, who (Buchwald insists) grabbed the food off their plates.

As an example of such un-Newfoundland-like behavior Buchwald cited a meeting which took place over breakfast at Hickory Hill between Bobby, Attorney General Nicholas Katzenbach and the head of a southern university, who had come to discuss the desegregation issue. Brumis allegedly kept snatching the ham and eggs off the university president's plate. Three times in succession this happened. Apparently the southerner was thrown off base so thoroughly that he agreed to all points proposed by Bobby.

There are several reports of Brumis taking part in a swearing-in ceremony. An Associated Press release stated flatly that Brumis was back in the act again and that he had stolen the show with the lively aplomb of a big dog consuming a T-bone.

It is a fact that Brumis was not only present at the occasion of the swearing-in of N.A. Schlei as Assistant Attorney General, but also threw his weight around. One account was that while Justice John Marshall Harlan was conducting the ceremony and held out the Bible to

Mr. Schlei to swear upon, the big dog pushed Justice Harlan aside, stood up six feet high and put his great paws on Mr. Schlei's shoulders and searched his face seriously, before letting him proceed with the oath.

As the witnesses applauded, the dog was said to have romped around the room three times, vigorously wagging his tail and then settled down before the Schlei children like a great bear rug at their feet.

The Republicans threw a second Brumis party. All sang, *How Much is that Doggie in the Justice Department?* Being the breeder of Little Bear's Brumis, I am qualified to answer — $300, at seven weeks of age when my husband and I personally delivered him to Bobby at McLean, Virginia.

Whether or not that price reflects an inflationary trend in the breed may be judged against what one Newfoundland fetched at a sale in Carlisle, England, in 1832. Until 1837, when the law began taking active measures, it was not remarkable for a man to offer his wife for sale. Mary Anne Thompson, so advertised, was described by her husband as able "to read novels, milk cows, make butter, scold the maids, and is a wizard at brewing rum, gin and whisky, but of nagging disposition." At auction the wife sold for 20 shillings and a Newfoundland dog.

But it was not until the Congressional compaign of 1964 that a Newfoundland, Brumis, actually got into a political campaign, appearing on TV with Bobby in his successful bid for the U.S. Senate.

In June, 1963, after a visit with Brumis at his home, Ethel Kennedy wrote me, "We are so appreciative of your generous assessment of Brumis' character, and your comment that Brumis shares the responsibility for the country is an extremely charitable way of looking at it. He also shares our living room rug and whatever happens to be on the dinner table when he passes by."

Later, a second Little Bear named Scuffy was picked up by the *Caroline,* the President's plane, to join the Kennedy family. The third Little Bear Newfoundland was sent to Mrs. Kennedy for Christmas in 1968, already after the horrible assassination of Bobby, while she was still carrying their last child. The Kennedy children call the puppy Poochie.

Needless to say, the Little Bear prefix is all that the kennel contributed toward the names of the Kennedys' Newfoundlands. Bobby Kennedy told us that Brumis was named by the children after a bear in the London zoo.

N is for Newfoundland—
loyal and kind,
A better protector
you never could find.

Baby Chris Sagnelli (7 months) with Ch. Little Bear's Jonah Sage.

14

The Newfoundland
With Children

GOODNESS, tenderness, playfulness, and sense of responsibility are at their brightest when the Newfoundland has children entrusted to his competent care.

Neptune belonged to the master of a school and enjoyed visiting the playground, where his presence was always welcomed. He particularly liked the hoop when it came into use in the fine cold days of autumn and never tired of running and barking after it. He loved to take the hoop in his mouth, holding it by its lower edge, the upper part encircling his head, rising far above him as he marched sedately along, as proud of his toy as an African belle is of her huge nose-ring. Snowball fights in the playground became something special when Neptune appeared. Brave and good natured, he would stand against the whole school. His companions might pelt him as hard as they pleased. He never lost his temper, but stood barking at every ball, trying to catch each one in his mouth as it came, leaping from side to side to humor the stragglers.

The Newfoundland playmate sometimes is more than a playful companion. Long Island Sound sometimes freezes over the winter, but it is a treacherous place for small boy skaters. George Foster, of New Rochelle, ventured out where the ice was thin and broke through. His Newfoundland dog rushed to the rescue and held him above water until help arrived from the nearby New Rochelle Yacht Club.

Whether on the shore or far inland, it is all the same to the Newfoundland. The following comes from an old clipping of the *Topeka State Journal:*

Sam Dodge, a ranchman living southeast of Caney, went to Vinita, Indian Territory, on business and shortly after he had gone, Bessie, his five-year-old child, wandered away from home in an attempt to follow him. Mrs. Dodge discovered her absence about two hours after Sam's departure. She made a thorough search of the premises, and failing to find the child, notified the neighbors of her disappearance. They turned out in force, and scoured the prairies all that day and all that night and all the next day, searching for the little wanderer.

Late Saturday evening, an Indian came upon her fast asleep, just south of Post Oak Creek, in an old road known as the "Whiskey Trail." Across her body stood a Newfoundland dog, which had always been her companion about the ranch. The dog was torn and bleeding, and near his feet lay the bodies of two wolves. Although her cheeks were stained with tears and covered with dust, Bessie was unharmed. She and her protector were taken back to her home, a distance of 12 miles from where they were found, where the dog died of his wounds that night. He was given a decent burial, and yesterday Sam Dodge ordered a marble monument, which will be placed at the head of the faithful animal's grave.

It may be difficult to realize that only a relatively short number of years ago, in 1896, for instance, eagles were still plentiful enough in the Fork Mountain country of Kentucky. They not only raided the flocks but also endangered the lives of children. Willie Slone, two years old, was playing with his Newfoundland nursemaid outside of his home. A gray eagle, later measured to have a wing spread of seven feet, swooped down upon the child and buried his talons in the boy's side. The dog caught the eagle by the leg and a valiant combat ensued, the dog holding on to the eagle until the child's father arrived to assist in finishing off the giant bird.

The parents of a small girl were impressed by a boy's reasoning as to why his father should buy him a dog. His first two arguments were: when a fellow fights with his friends, they won't talk to him, but a dog never stops speaking to a boy; and when a boy is naughty and his papa and mama punish him, then they don't like him, but a dog always likes a boy.

On reading these reasons, two worried parents decided a dog would be the solution to the problem of their daughter, too precocious in school, unable to adjust to her schoolmates, high strung, sensitive, imaginative, shy. With everything that loving parents give her, she was still unhappy.

So they went to the Westminster Show, each going his separate way in search of the ideal dog that would give the little girl the most comfort and confidence. Independently, each gravitated toward the benches of the big, black, benevolent Newfoundland, a breed they had never

Throughout the years, the Newfoundland has been treasured as the protector and life-saver of children. These prints are from the collection of Mrs. Isabel Kurth.

known. And this was the dog they chose, a dog whose size would give the child the needed feeling of security, whose docility would reassure her, and whose tender devotion finally made her a very happy little girl.

Some years ago, Willis Hoyt, of Aurora, Illinois, had a fine New-foundland who always accompanied his young master to school, carrying the boy's lunch basket. It was necessary to cross a bridge over a small river, and in warm weather the dog would leave his basket on the bridge while he cooled himself off with a bath. One morning, one of the other lads took the basket and hid it to annoy the dog and see what he would do. The dog hunted around for some time until finally the lad gave the basket back to him. The next morning, when the dog arrived at the bridge, he plunged into the water with the basket still in his mouth, thereby wetting it and its contents. His young master said to him, "Now, you take that basket home and get me another dinner." The dog took the basket home, but did not return, for his people at home could not make out why the dinner was wet, or what the dog wanted. Undoubtedly, if they had been a little brighter, he would have completed his mission.

Here is another faithful nursemaid story. Some years ago, a child, playing with a dog on Roach's Wharf in Yorkshire, accidently fell into the water. The Newfoundland immediately sprang in after the child and, seizing the waist of his frock, brought him in to the dock where there was a stage. The child, who was only six years old, held on but was unable to get to the top. Finding himself unable to pull the little fellow out of the water, the dog ran to an adjoining yard where a nine-year-old girl was hanging out clothes. He caught her skirt in his mouth and notwithstanding her efforts to get away, he succeeded in dragging her to the spot where the child was still hanging by his hands to the stage. When the girl took hold of the child, the dog assisted her in the rescue. Then, after licking the face of the little boy, he leaped off the stage, swam around to the end of the wharf and ultimately reappeared bearing the child's hat in his mouth.

The Best Friend Polka, a spirited and charming song by J.H. McNaughton enjoyed some popularity at the time it was published, 1860, in New York. The cover picture for the song was of a Newfoundland, a child with a hoop leaning against the dog. Both picture and song made a cover for *American Heritage* about a century later.

Practically the same picture was previously printed and distributed throughout English, French and German speaking countries over the title *The Faithful Companion.*

From a Parisian lithograph of the 1800s.

The Newfoundland as rescuer, from an 18th century book illustration.

In those days it seemed the thing to bodily lift pictures of an earlier artist, change a minor detail or two and call it one's own. Currier and Ives borrowed freely from Landseer. We have better copyright protection today. This custom prevailed with Sir Augustus John in lifting the head from Sir Edwin Landseer's *A Member of the Humane Society.* With no credit to either artist, the same head was later used on the earliest postage stamp with a Newfoundland, issued in 1887.

After the first edition of *The Complete Newfoundland,* I received many letters asking for further doings of Tarby, who was sometimes referred to as the "Lemon Drop Kid." Mary Lyons wrote (Tarby was about 11 years old at the time): "If I am busy and Johnny starts to cry upstairs I simply say, 'Tarby, go up and check on baby.' Upstairs he goes, into the baby's room, nudges John a little, then lies down beside the crib until I get up there. Johnny simply adores him and, when walking, steps all over him, usually falling on top of him at some point. Tarby doesn't object at all."

Bruce Terriberry tells me that when he was a child his favorite Newfoundland, a big male, Ch. Far Horizon's Stormalong (his parents had Far Horizons Kennels) was the best football player in the neighborhood. Stormy could tackle, carry the ball or run guard and his desire to win was second to that of no player.

Another football player belonged to the Gunthers who lived in Greenwich, Connecticut. In this case it was a Newfoundland bitch named Searescue of Perryhow. She was also a capable player and equally enthusiastic until the baby, after his nap, was wheeled onto the terrace. Then Searescue was no longer tomboy, but all nursemaid. She took her post by the baby and nothing would entice her away, although now and then her glance would wander to the playing field.

Newfoundlands are enchanted by children and at the same time they weave a spell of fantasy around children, so great is their storybook charm. In 1956 my husband and I were in Detroit to see the Progressive Dog Club show. A pretty waitress, long-time admirer of Newfoundlands, told us that she had taken a small friend to the show. It was Ch. Little Bear's James Thurber who won Best-in-Show that day, his sixth all breed Best-in-Show. The waitress told us that the child rushed back to her from the arena in great excitement and confided: "You know, the dog that won the show! He looks like a dog! He walks like a dog! People think he's a dog! But honest and truly they are mistaken — he is really a bear!"

No wonder that in the early times the Newfoundland was known as the Bear Dog.

J. M. Barrie, in the first published edition of the story which preceeded the play, tells how the characters in *Peter Pan* evolved from reminiscence of childhood adventures recorded in his *The Boy Castaways.* "The loyal Newfoundland who . . . applied, so to say, for the part by bringing hedgehogs to the hut in his mouth as offerings for our evening repasts . . . was the model for Nana."

Peter Pan owes much of its charm to Nana, the Newfoundland nursemaid:

> Mrs. Darling loved to have everything just so, and Mr. Darling had a passion for being exactly like his neighbours; so, of course, they had a nurse. As they were poor . . . this nurse was a prim Newfoundland dog, called Nana, who had belonged to no one in particular until the Darlings engaged her. She had always thought children important, however, and the Darlings had become acquainted with her in Kensington Gardens, where she spent most of her spare time peeping into perambulators, and was much hated by careless nursemaids, whom she followed to their homes and complained of to their mistresses. She proved to be quite a treasure of a nurse. How thorough she was at bath-time; and up any moment of the night if one of her charges made the slightest cry. Of course, her kennel was in the nursery. She had a genius for knowing when a cough is a thing to have no patience with and when it needs a stocking around your throat. She believed to her last day in old-fashioned remedies like rhubarb leaf, and made sounds of contempt over all this new-fangled talk about germs, and so on. It was a lesson in propriety to see her escorting the children to school, walking sedately by their side when they were well behaved, and butting them back into the line if they strayed. On John's soccer days she never once forgot his sweater, and she usually carried an umbrella in her mouth in case of rain. There is a room in the basement of Miss Fulson's school where the nurses wait. They sat on forms, while Nana lay on the floor, but that was the only difference. They affected to ignore her as of an inferior social status to themselves, and she despised their light talk. She resented visits to the nursery from Mrs. Darling's friends, but if they did come she first whipped off Michael's pinafore and put him into the one with the blue braiding, and smoothed out Wendy and made a dash at John's hair.

Karen and Her Newfoundlands

Karen through her mother's best sellers, *Karen* and its sequel, *With Love from Karen,* is one of the best known true-life, young heroines today. And through the girl, Karen, her Newfoundlands are nearly as well-known. The Dell paper edition of the second book shows on the

229

cover the lovely smiling Karen with her Little Bear's Perigee Tide. Perigee, a litter sister of Hard Tack, was as devoted, thoughtful and resourceful as her Newfoundland brother and an unceasing joy to her young mistress.

The books are a Cinderella story of a lovely, serene personality coming through against impossible odds. From the near tragedy of being born with severe cerebral palsy, victory is snatched, not easily, but with unfailing determination and a light heart.

The Killilea family is an animal-loving family (and a people-loving family) in the extreme. But their reason for getting a Newfoundland had more purpose than just adding another to their menagerie.

As a child, Karen had been able to hold her own with her peers. There were many games in which she could join, and with her delightful high spirits and fresh imagination, being a cripple did not set her apart. But it was in adolescence, when social life changed character, that a problem arose. Dancing and sailing became the order of life for her childhood companions. Some activity was desperately needed which would afford the girl in a wheel chair a chance to compete with the unhandicapped on equal footing.

It was here that loving, ever-resourceful parents displayed their never-failing ingenuity. Dog showing was the answer they came up with. Granted, Karen would not be able to take her dog into the ring. But there is nothing odd about having a good professional handler.

It was at the Saw Mill River Show in White Plains that the parents, Marie and Jim Killilea, along with a dog man friend, Ralph Hellum, and of course Karen, went to choose the breed Karen would like to show.

Karen in her wheel chair was being pushed down the aisles by a young girl friend, past the various breeds benched in their dark red, yellow-floored stalls. Their parents had struck out on their own.

We had three Newfoundlands at the show that year. I well remember seeing the bright eyed girl in the wheel chair stop by our bench. Our Newfoundlands fell in love with her at first sight. In a minute Karen, now laughing, was swung by her friend, Nina, out of her wheel chair into the center of our bench with the dogs.

Her mother later told me she was truly frightened, when missing Karen and looking for her, she suddenly saw her empty wheel chair. Marie came running to find Karen snuggled among the big Newfoundlands, hugging them and being kissed by them in return.

"Mother!" exclaimed the girl. "I've found my breed!"

The success of Karen's Newfoundlands in and out of the show rings was more than her parents had dared hope for. In the enthusiasm of grooming her dog for show she found herself automatically using her hands in fine motion handling the comb. With the long sweep of the

Karen with her Newfoundland, Little Bear's Perigree Tide. From the cover of the best seller "With Love from Karen," Marie Killilea's true story of a triumphant child and her family.

Karen Killilea looks on as her Ch. Little Bear's Bonnavista II is shown to a Best of Breed win.

brush down the dog's back Karen was straightening out unconsciously the right arm which previous therapy had failed to correct.

I recall one sunny day a few years back at the Westchester show seeing Karen in her wheel chair being pulled to the ring by her Newf, which went on to win. Most of all, the ring competition gave a new dimension of enthusiasm to a life which might have become withdrawn. And the new friends met at the shows, sharing love for all dogs, opened new vistas which have built and continue to build.

Today Karen is an Honorary Member of the Newfoundland Club of America and of the Newfoundland Club of New England. Since the latter was formed as a family club, the entire Killilea family has honorary membership.

The boy Rory, who explained to non-dog friends about being in season, is now grown, married, in the army, and father of an infant. "It's the hunting season," the ten-year old Rory had said, "when the boy dogs hunt the girl dogs."

The beautiful Marie, Jr. (Mrs. Ron Smiley) a mother, is as exquisite as ever. The always lovely Gloria is married to Russell Lea. They have children and a Newfoundland they call Sweetheart. Karen through the years has always had one or two Newfoundlands. They have had outstandingly good show careers. Kristen, the youngest of the Killileas is a talented handler — a slim fifteen year old who has often won with Karen's Ch. Little Bear's Bonnavista. Kristen is beautiful too. As a *matter* of fact the whole family is beautiful and none more handsome than mother and father.

Karen gave a dog obedience demonstration with hand signals from her wheel chair at the two-day all Newfoundland specialty held at the Yale Motor Inn in Wallingford, Connecticut, in May 1971.

Heidi Chandler, 10 years old, with 10-months-old Ship Chandler's Thunderoc Fluf, co-owned by Sandra Chandler and Lila Visich. Fluf finished with four majors in six shows, at age of 18 months.

Baby sitter. Ch. Black Mischief's Christopher shows how Newfoundlands serve added purpose at the dog shows.

Ursa and Owloisius, pets of Mr. and Mrs. Willim E. Olsen.

Nana and Tommy.

15

The Newfoundland
With Other Animals

SHIPWRECKED on a voyage from America, a British general, always a lover of Newfoundlands, owed his life and that of his companions to his devoted Newfoundland bitch. The ship was wrecked off a desolate island and for six weeks the general and his shipmates depended for their sustenance solely upon salt pork which was adrift from their ill-fated vessel and was fetched ashore by the Newfoundland.

In 1798, the same general was quartered not far from Niagara Falls. His soldiers kept a tame fox as a pet. The animal's kennel was an old cask to which she was attached by a long line and swivel. A Newfoundland named Neptune accompanied the general to his new post. Upon arrival, the dog and the soldiers' fox soon scraped acquaintance, which in due course ripened into friendship. One day the general took a walk over to the barracks, and not seeing anything of the fox, he gave the barrel a kick, saying to his man standing by "Your fox is gone!" The general's knock at the back door of the kennel had so alarmed the vixen, which was sleeping inside, that she bolted forth with such violence that she snapped the light cord.

The soldiers were heartbroken, fearing their pet fox would never return. But not the general. He watched the fleeing fox and observed that she made a beeline for the woods. Then he dispatched Neptune after his friend. The soldiers set about wagering whether or not the two pals would return amiably together. Neptune returned indeed, dragging the fox by the rope around her neck. The fox was struggling fruitlessly against reinduction into His Majesty's services.

Neptune was properly lauded and caressed for his sagacity, and the general was so pleased that the next day he purposely had the fox re-

Newfoundland bringing in the fox—illustration of story told in the accompanying text, from an 18th century book.

Mrs. Virginia Roberts' Mohonk Amah of Windy Hill and Poodle puppy.

leased, and again Neptune brought back his friend in triumph. A new kind of fox hunt was enjoyed daily thereafter, the officers hallooing the dog to the utmost. Neptune enjoyed the game thoroughly, and it is hoped the fox finally entered into the fun of the occasion, too. At least she had a daily chance to stretch her legs.

A number of years ago in Rochester, a man had a fine Newfoundland and a Toy Poodle. It was the owner's custom to put the Poodle in a small basket every morning, and give the basket to the Newfoundland to take the small dog for an airing. In the neighborhood there was a black cur that used to nip the Newfoundland's hind legs as he was passing. One morning, the Newfoundland put his basket down on the ground, went for the cur, gave him an unmerciful shaking up, and after that he could perform his duties as nurse without being annoyed by that cur. This same Newfoundland went to the post office each day, and, placing his front paws on the window shelf, waited for the family mail. After getting it, he trotted home, and he was never known to lose any of it.

In the early part of the nineteenth century, there was a Newfoundland who won fame for his resourcefulness and was immortalized in a pair of handsome parian ware figures. His is the story of a Newfoundland who meted out retribution effectively. It was his regular duty to take a grocery list in a basket to market. On the way, with his empty basket, he proceeded unmolested. But it was the habit of several small mongrels to attack the Newfoundland on the return trip. They would nip at his heels when the basket was full and the dog had to suffer the indignity of being nipped by the little dogs or put down his basket.

He always held duty above comfort, put up with the nuisance, and brought home the family supplies intact. One day, however, he went to the market with his basket and after a suitable time returned on the route toward home. But he had not gone to the market and had nothing in the basket. So when the little curs beset him, he put down the empty basket and gave each a good going over. The lesson taught, the Newfoundland then went to market and got the family provisions. He had no further annoyance then or any other time.

There is an old account of a Newfoundland and a Mastiff. They detested each other. Every day produced fresh battles between them. But it happened that, in one of these terrible prolonged combats on the jetty of Donaghadee, they both fell into the sea. The jetty was long and steep; they had no other means of escape but that of swimming, and the distance was considerable. The Newfoundland, being a good swimmer, managed to reach the shore without much difficulty. He landed dripping wet, and began shaking himself. A moment after, he saw that his late antagonist was exhausting himself in struggling against the waves and was just on the point of sinking. The Newfoundland, moved with a feeling of generosity, flung himself again into the water, seized the Mastiff by the collar, and holding his head above the water, brought him safe and sound to land. This happy deliverance was followed by a scene between the two animals which was truly touching. They never fought again and were always seen together.

Years later, the Mastiff was killed in an accident. The Newfoundland was inconsolable.

Youatt gives a touching example of this wonderful animal's tender heart. A lame puppy was lying close to a gate through which the Newfoundland desired to pass, but he could not push the gate open without causing the animal pain. To his surprise, his Newfoundland dog put out a strong paw and gently rolled the invalid out of the way and drew back to allow the gate to open. Idestone relates having frequently seen a dog push a hare through a gate when he could not conveniently jump it, and then take it from the other side.

Another gentleman had a Pointer and a Newfoundland that were great friends. The former broke his leg and was confined to a kennel. During his convalescence, the Newfoundland repeatedly brought bones and other food to the Pointer and would sit for hours by the side of his suffering friend.

During a period of very hot weather, the mayor of Plymouth gave orders that all dogs found wandering in the public streets should be secured by the police and removed to the prison yard. Among them was a Newfoundland belonging to a shipowner of the port, which, with several others, was tied up in the yard. The Newfoundland soon gnawed the rope which confined him, and then hearing the cries of his companions, he set to work to gnaw the ropes which confined them and had succeeded in three of four instances when he was interrupted by the entrance of the jailer.

A somewhat similar incident frequently occurred in the Cumberland Gardens, Windsor Great Park. Two dogs of the Newfoundland breed were confined in kennels there. When one of them was let loose, he was frequently seen to set his companion free.

Dr. Coburn shares with us some touching incidents from the life of his beloved Salty (Ch. Midway Sea Raider, son of Ch. Midway Black Ledge Sea Raider):

We have a Miniature Poodle from Puttencove, Noodles we call him, who is seldom out of the house except on leash. However, on several occasions last year, when he was out on his own, he would run full speed toward the street, down the driveway. Salty, with no command or comment, would take off and chase him back to the front door.

When we were in Minnesota escaping hay fever, on two vacations Salty was with us. I could never lure him into the water behind any type of craft I was in. However, when my girl and boy would go out in a rowboat to paddle about in a small bay, Salty always was swimming along, powerfully and easily, a short distance behind their boat. It mattered not how long they were afloat, Salty was always convoying them. At those times, the children were ten and seven, and eleven and eight years old respectively. As soon as they docked, he would go ashore not far off, but watch them until they were away from the dock.

We know not whether the Almighty has a special kennel for our canine friends, but be it so, God rest their souls and with them our beloved Salty.

Mildred Aiken told us of her dog's love for other creatures.

Our first Newfoundland here was a dog whose sire and dam were brought in as puppies for pets from Newfoundland. She was a very large female, gentle as could be. After a very bad storm she brought home to me a Philadelphia verio blown from the nest — so young it had no feathers. We kept it indoors and out until ready to fly, the mother feeding it frequently every day, much to the joy of the Newfoundland Dinah, our own son, and all the neighborhood children. All lined up on the porch daily to see the feedings. Neither the baby bird nor its mother had any fear of people or the dog. Dinah wanted no one to handle the bird but myself.

She was the same about every litter of kittens we had. I could handle them, Rich and his father could look at them, but Dinah never allowed others to get nearer to them than outside of her own area. Any baby that was brought here and put down was ours, and could not be picked up by anyone but me. If a hand was reached toward kittens or baby, Dinah took it in her mouth and pulled it away.

A marked characteristic of all our Newfoundlands has been courtesy and gentleness to small creatures or baby things. Even as our present "Mr. Aiken" lets the baby puppy pull his tail, take his food, or chew him, and much as all three play together, it is he who the puppy sleeps on, tags everywhere and sticks closer to than Linda Lou, her mother.

Peter Boggs wrote in his *New Haven Register* column of a Newfoundland which became foster mother of lambs. The Newfoundland, who belonged to a Colorado sheep rancher, had lost her first litter. Whereupon she went straight to a pen where orphaned lambs were kept, made her way in and took upon herself the duties of a mother, feeding, cleaning and keeping the lambs warm. Having brought the lambs up, she went to the pasture with her adopted children, where she caught rabbits for them and could not understand why they would not eat them.

The John Gibbons family of Tennessee, have a Newfoundland, Little Bear's Silver Flute, who in turn has her own pets. She is fascinated with tropical fish. She spends hours every day watching them and becomes quite excited over any population changes. She tugs members of the family to the aquarium to make sure they see newly hatched fish and never fails to lead visitors to see her pets. People who call frequently are usually taken only once. After a long lapse between visits, friends are proudly escorted by Silver Flute to view any population variations among her aquatic pets.

In connection with the Eastern Dog Club show in Boston, a few years ago, Ahtuckta C.D.X., T.D. (Companion Dog Excellent, Tracking Dog obedience titles holder) was interviewed by Jim Fansulo on WHDH-TV. Peter Marden, Ahtuckta's master, who by the way took Ahtuckta through a leg on his Utility Dog title at the Boston show, was not on the TV with his dog. Ahtuckta was interviewed alone, directly, by the TV newscaster. Throughout the entire TV performance, Ahtuckta watched Mr. Fansulo intently and wagged his tail non-stop. When asked to get up and sit on a folding chair, the dog did so with alacrity.

Mr. Fansulo mentioned that Ahtuckta was the hero of the Logan Airport incident of the previous year, when a Dachshund puppy had been lost for two days. After the available Bloodhounds had failed to locate the little fellow, Ahtuckta was called in and succeeded in locating the missing puppy. The big Newfoundland brought back the tiny Dachshund unhurt, in his soft mouth.

Johnny, a young Newfoundland, spent his first summer vacationing in Branford on Long Island Sound. His favorite pastime was to spend most of the day on the beach, swimming, diving and playing with the neighbor children. He delighted in swimming out to the raft a hundred yards offshore and use it as a lifeguard's tower for keeping an eye on his young playmates. Whenever any poor swimmer ventured beyond his depth, quick as lightning Johnny would dive from the raft, swim to the child and tow him ashore.

Of evenings, when Johnny's master would walk in the country, the Newfoundland would be given a lighted flashlight which he would take in his soft mouth and light the way for him as long as he was out-of-doors. This habit of Johnny carrying the torch for his master is reminiscent of another Newfoundland of the distant past, the lantern carrying dog of Harbour Grace and is evidence of our present-day Newfoundlands retaining the original intelligence of the breed.

When winter came and Johnny moved back to New York City, an old blind Afghan, called Rufus, became his charge. It seems that Rufus was taken advantage of and molested by neighborhood dogs whenever his owner took him for his daily constitutional around Gramercy Park. It was discovered, however, that with the 150-pound Johnny walking side by side with Rufus, the malicious dogs gave the old, blind dog a wide berth.

Johnny became very fond of Rufus. One day he took the Afghan's lead from his master's hand and holding it tight in his teeth, walked Rufus completely around the park enclosure. His master was delighted. The next day, on leaving home, Johnny was given Rufus' lead. He walked him to the intersection, waited for the green light to cross the street, and carefully led the Afghan around the park. From that day Johnny took complete charge of exercising the blind Rufus.

Newfoundlands are clannish. They love all creatures but show preference for their own breed and especially favor their relatives. In our early days of breeding, our second and third litters were whelped eight days apart. Our Ch. Stubbart's Greetings O'Lady was dam of one and granddam of the other litter. We had kept two of O'Lady's own and were holding three of her grandchildren from which we were going to choose some to keep for breeding. As well, we had bought another puppy of about the age, totally unrelated.

The puppies had been separated from their mothers at a little over six weeks of age and at that time O'Lady had gone up to our Vermont farm and the puppies were with us in Connecticut. O'Lady came down for a visit when the puppies were about four months old. They were all in a paddock and having a jolly time together.

O'Lady had not the slightest hesitation in recognizing her own which she had not seen in more than two months. She went directly to Chance and Avalon, washed their faces and clucked over them like a mother hen. She then gave a swift greeting to each of her grandchildren — James Thurber and his brother and sister. These last she had never before seen. The little stranger, which we had named King's Bargain, came up for his kiss.

You could almost hear O'Lady say, "Hmph!" as she turned her back on him and resumed lavishing attention on her own.

King's Bargain kept presenting himself for O'Lady's acceptance. More and more she made evident her disregard for him. When she left the paddock, all the other puppies ostracized Bargain. He became so dejected that the next day we sold him to a loving family who could give full time to restoring his self esteem.

241

When we bought Can. Ch. Eskimo's Grey Mug from Veronica and Bill Payne of Canada, he was already a Working Group Winner and Specialty Best of Breed. My husband, with his strong instinct for hospitality, tried to make Mug feel at home with us. He may have given the new dog too much attention in the eyes of our Little Bears, for they quite evidently resented him. We were careful to keep him separate from our males for fear of their jealousy leading to a fight.

Something, uncommon among Newfoundlands, occurred to Mug. He had a heart attack. Our veterinarian advised us that we should not show Mug any more. He needed only one point for his American championship, having made his wins at Westminster and two Specialties. We loved Mug, and although we would miss seeing his light-footed flying-trot in the ring, we arranged a way of life for him which we thought might keep him with us for a long time.

Months passed. All seemed well with Mug. Then one day, just as Vadim and I were driving off on our way to New York, our kennel man, Walter, called us back. Mug had just had another heart attack. Vadim and Walter carried the dog to our sun porch where I had hastily brought a mattress. After first aid the dog had regained some strength, but almost all the time lay quietly on his mattress.

It was moderate weather and we left the sun porch door open so that the fastidious Mug could go down the two steps to take care of his needs. He would then lie down by the steps waiting for us to lift him back to his mattress. During this time we carefully kept all of our own dogs in their pens so that Mug would not be disturbed.

One day our Ch. Little Bear's Broadside was brought to our kitchen for a visit. He had been lying there by the television for several hours. Someone must have forgotten that he was there and left the doors to the pantry and dining room open.

Like a flash Broadside took off through the house toward the sun porch.

We were frightened. Any unpleasant encounter might prove the end of Mug. Vadim and Walter and I went three ways at once, they around each side of the house and I straight through, to meet simultaneously and hope to forestall a fateful fight.

To our complete amazement, we found Mug peacefully lying on his mattress, Broadside lying behind him and hovering over him, one paw on the ailing dog's shoulder. He was tenderly *licking* Mug's face.

Broadside stayed on as Mug's male nurse. They ate their meals side by each. Slept side by side. When Mug needed to go out, Broadside escorted him and then barked until we came to carry Mug back to his mattress.

One day Mug was markedly losing strength. The veterinarian did what he could. He held no hope. That night we stayed very late with Mug, until he seemed to sink into a coma. Broadside stayed on.

Early in the morning we went down to find Broadside hugging and trying to warm the cold, stiff body of Mug.

Broadside never recovered from the loss of his patient. Although young and never sick a day in his life, he never regained his gay and happy nature. Three weeks later, walking across the lawn, he dropped dead by the great maple tree. Broadside is buried in our rose garden alongside Mug.

Mrs. S. J. Navin's Can. Ch. Nanahboozoo of Stevens was a tremendous dog, 34 inches high at the shoulder and 35 inches long, of massive head and with everything his name implies. Nanahboozoo, an Indian name, means sleeping giant, and a giant he was, with the strength of a giant and the soul of a gentle poet. He was a fabulous dog who often pulled a mule team of carts loaded with seven children. He swam in the coldest waters, even dived under ice.

His love for other animals knew no bounds. Up in the Canadian bush where he was raised, he even made friends with dogs' greatest enemy, the porcupine. A porcupine there would come out to meet him at a regular hour every day and the two would take a walk down a path together, the porcupine ahead, the Newfoundland following, sometimes gently nudging his small barbed friend. One day Nanahboozoo was late and some hunter was there to meet the porcupine and shot him. When Nanahboozoo arrived and found his friend dead in the path, lying in a pool of his own blood, the big Newfoundland sat down and cried. Mrs. Navin witnessed it.

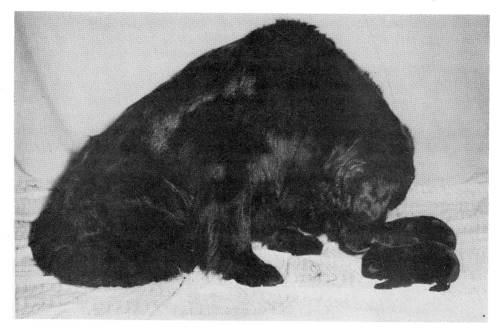

Puppies at 3 days.

Puppies at 5 weeks.

16

Breeding
The Newfoundland

W$_{}$HEN CHOOSING your stock for breeding Newfoundlands, it is most important to bear in mind the purpose of the
breed, that of a land and sea dog, a born lifesaver capable of great
physical exertion and stamina, a dog of the highest intelligence and
benevolence.

The early Newfoundland male was generally about 24 inches at the
shoulder, the female generally somewhat less. Greater size was developed for English demands, in several instances through planned infusion, more than 100 years ago, of Tibetan Mastiffs. The Leonberg dog
may have been similarly used. Unusual size was too frequently
achieved at the cost of soundness. With the Tibetan came the great
size, 30 to 34 inches in height, a monumental rise in a relatively short
time. Such forced increase in size tends to be at the cost of stamina,
longevity and even physical soundness. There are exceptions to this
rule but generally, a Newfoundland specimen closer to the breed
standard average is apt to be more sound physically than the quickly
achieved giant.

In speaking out for the Newfoundland approaching the average
height indicated by the official Newfoundland breed standard, I am not
recommending the puny, small-boned, skimpy, unsubstantial specimen
but the hard muscled, well-boned, beautifully balanced dog. In choosing your stock for breeding, do not be ensnared by extremes, but keep
to the middle of the road.

Good running gear is of primary consideration. Do not breed from
any dog or bitch faulty in this respect. You will be breeding on sand.

Likewise avoid like the plague the notion of a breeding aim of head,
size or profuse coat, etc. It is the dog — the whole dog — that is important and not any particular part.

In striving to achieve a perfect physical specimen, one cannot overlook temperament. Intelligence and benevolence are responsible for the world-wide fame of the breed. The only way to preserve character is to breed physically and mentally sound dogs. Never take the chance of breeding a Newfoundland showing the slightest fault in temperament.

Consider pedigrees, but do not rely on them beyond the dogs you know. Championships are some indication of merit but do not always mean what they should. There are dogs which have achieved the title and those which have missed, neither through merit nor fault of their own. A dog in an uncommon breed, like the Newfoundland, may win through the accident of less than average quality in competition. And the contrary is true, that an excellent dog may not have had proper exposure. Therefore counting titles may be misleading. There is no substitute for *knowing*. You must have the basic *eye for a dog* and then develop it with study of the Standard and by observation at dog shows. Learn what you can from others. Read McDowell Lyon's *The Dog in Action*, a bible for the understanding of gait. And study the dogs themselves. Three generations will suffice to begin. Then if you have the opportunity, a post-graduate course in earlier generations can be added.

Anyone who cannot see faults in his own dogs simply should not attempt to breed. An eye for a dog is something with which one is born. One must have it to be either a breeder or judge. Of course the eye must be developed, but there must be something basic to develop.

To test oneself on this very important point, dispatch yourself to a show ring when a breed related to yours is being judged, say Goldens, or Labradors, by a really knowledgeable judge. See how closely your choices agree with his. Do this with many of the best judges with large and giant Working breeds.

Inbreeding and *line breeding* produce the best possible results *if* you start with the best possible dogs and *if* you know what you are doing. Close breeding should not be attempted unless one is using genetically clean stock, a good eye and knowledge of the faults and virtues of the stock for three generations. The process of cleaning the stock is so strict that few have the necessary detachment.

Sagacious, placid Newfs bred to sagacious, placid Newfs will produce offspring of stable character no matter how closely bred. In fact, all virtues and faults will be magnified tenfold. So it is a road of greatest possible returns and at the same time greatest possible hazards.

Family breeding is the safest road to take for the average breeder and comprises the mainstream of good breeding. One must still be highly selective in cleaning the line but an error would not necessarily be lethal.

246

Outcrossing or mating of unrelated individuals, with a purpose, is advisable now and then. It can be a good corrective measure for eliminating a fault that has crept into a family, but should not be followed routinely. If pursued without purpose you will acquire a genetic grab-bag with all results accidental.

From the standpoint of the breeder, the all-black Newfoundland seems in general, in its best examples, to be genetically the repository of best Newfoundland type and soundness. It is highly advisable that Newfoundland breeders who are interested in producing other than blacks, keep in mind always, and know how to breed with best blacks to improve and maintain true Newfoundland type.

Due to dominance in Newfoundlands of all black coat color (including those with minimal white markings) there should be no difficulty for the breeder, if he so wishes, to keep his stock free of colors and parti-colors.

In our breed, coat color in general follows the simple genetic breeding pattern set forth in the Mendelian theory. By breeding Newfoundlands homozygous for black to Newfoundlands homozygous for black, all offspring *therefrom* will be black and in turn should never throw other than all black offspring.

A simple formula can be provided for anyone wishing to clear his stock of other than black, through determining those animals carrying the heterozygous gene and eventually establishing all homozygous stock. Establishing good quality color breeding is more difficult, but scientific formula is available to those interested.

Let us consider, as an example, breeding blues. Genes are paired as placed on the chromosome and when they may affect in different ways they are said to be allelic to each other. There may be more than two alleles of the same gene but only two of an allelic series. When the blue is dilute blue produced from the agouti series there are no special factors to consider which would concern normality beyond that which we must consider when breeding blacks. But when breeding blue merles, which are from an albino allele, one must use certain precautions to avoid albinism, blindness and deafness.

Inasmuch as, to the best of my knowledge, all blues recorded within the Newfoundland breed are dilute blue (from the agouti series), it is most unlikely that there will be a special problem in our blues. The dilute blue is a bluish gray, truly solid color. The blue merle is a mixture of blue, gray and black. For anyone breeding Newfoundlands for any colors of the albino allelic series, certain breeding formulas must be followed to protect from abnormalities.

This special problem is mentioned both to clear our Newfoundland blues from any confusion with well-known blue merle problems and to

Bathing beauty.

point out that breeding for color, although complicated, need never endanger the quality of the breed.

Blacks will always be easiest to breed. There is no possible problem in retaining the blacks. With literally thousands of years of black Newfoundlands in the background, it will not be possible in the lifetime of one breeder, or many, to change the dominant black to recessive black.

Other colors are protected by our Standard, but it clearly states that blacks and Landseers are to be favored. Landseer breeding follows the general Mendelian formula plus another genetic factor for amount of white. Like all other than blacks, Landseers must be frequently bred to the very best blacks to attain and maintain black quality. At no time should rarity or beauty of color be favored for itself alone over an all black Newfoundland. The dog is the thing; it should be judged on all other factors before color.

Mating

A Newfoundland bitch comes into her first season about ten to twelve months of age. The first, is usually not a very strong season and may even pass unnoticed if there are no dogs around.

If the bitch is not to be bred any specific heat, from the first sign, such as show of blood or unusual interest from the opposite sex, it is highly advisable to give her four Nullo tablets each morning and at night for the duration. Each tablet contains 100 mgms. of chlorophyllins. Nullo kills body odor completely, hence discourages serenaders. It is made by the De Pree Co. of Holland, Michigan, and can be purchased at drug stores.

The second estrum should come six months after the first and at that time the bitch is most probably breedable. In slow maturing specimens it is best to wait until the bitch is two years old before she is bred.

When you decide you would like to mate your Newfoundland bitch, have a pelvic X-ray made. This should be done after she is a year old and well before the onset of the season during which you would like to breed her.

In the event the pelvic X-ray is less than perfect, the degree of imperfection should be taken into consideration in deciding whether the bitch is suitable for breeding. If the X-ray indicates actual bone changes or hip dysplasia, *do not breed the bitch.*

By the same token the bitch should only be bred to a stud with excellent hips. Certification by the Orthopedic Foundation for Animals or other highly reliable authority is desirable.

The degree of inheritance or predisposition factor toward hip dysplasia has not yet been precisely determined. Due to the complexity of the factors involved it may be a long time before this is really known. Some authorities presently believe that less than 42% is due to inheritance or predisposition, and that the remaining 58% plus is environmental. Chemical adulterants in the feed, such as stibesterol, may be a major cause.

Whatever the percentages may be, we find through many generations of breeding, that you can breed only from stock radiologically normal to reduce to the minimum incidence of hip dysplasia. Dysplastic parents may produce some normal puppies with radiological imperfections, even sometimes with clinical cases of hip dysplasia. This factor has led some breeders to the extreme of disregarding the pelvic X-ray and breeding from stock showing serious radiological imperfections.

Since it may take years before the true nature of hip dysplasia is thoroughly understood and both environmental and genetic factors properly evaluated, a sincere breeder can only afford to breed from radiologically sound stock. Given stibesterol-free food, the odds for normal puppies are overwhelmingly in favor of those from normal parents, and especially if those normal parents are in turn from normal parents and grandparents.

Also *prior* to breeding, the bitch and the stud should be checked for worms. Fecal examination under a microscope should be made and, we hope with use of a centrifuge, to determine if there are internal parasites. Include a test for heartworms, and in no case breed a bitch with heartworms until she has been treated and pronounced cured by your veterinarian. Presence of heartworms might mean her death.

As to hook and whip worms, they should be eradicated before breeding, certainly before whelping, so that the matron does not pass them on to her puppies, as well as for her own sake. Round worms are difficult to avoid in puppies but you can greatly reduce them by having the dam clean of them. The bitch should be free of all worms before breeding.

Tapeworm treatment is necessary if cucumber seed-like segments of the worm are observed either in the stool of the bitch or under her tail.

Obviously the stud should also be worm free before service.

First indication of the bitch coming into season is swelling of the vulva. There is a flow of blood, quite light in color at first. Some bitches may keep themselves so clean that the beginning of the season may pass unnoticed. Hence there may be a question as to the exact day when the season actually began.

If you suspect, due to unusual interest of dogs, that your bitch is coming into season, insert into her vulva a piece of sterile cotton. The first secretion is light rose color which will brighten into blood red as the season progresses. The vulva continues to swell and becomes noticeably large on the twelfth day. The discharge fades and becomes straw-colored.

Now the bitch should be ready to breed and remain breedable for about five days. If you touch her hindquarters, she will swing her tail to right or left. She may back into the fence and sing. Males will respond from afar. The mating call is more dependable than other signs.

Contradictions:

Not all bitches follow the classical pattern described above. Some will not accept a male after the secretion from the vulva changes to straw-color. In such a case one can be guided by the appearance of the vulva — largeness and softness.

There are also matrons who are breedable for a day or two at the most. A few have to be bred earlier in their season.

Under no circumstances should a reluctant bitch be forced. If a bitch does not accept a dog at the full height of her season, there is usually a clinical reason. Thorough internal examination by a veterinarian is in order.

Never breed a bitch when there is a sickly sweet, odorous, green discharge. It is a sign of metritis and the bitch should be treated by a veterinarian. The malucidin treatment developed by Drs. Leon and George Whitney of Orange, Connecticut, has proven successful. In the past twenty years we have had several bitches which would have been faced with the usual alternatives, hysterectomy or death. All of ours that have been treated by malucidin have produced healthy litters six to twelve months after the treatment. Some uterine infections have been known to respond successfully to other antibiotics.

The best time for mating a Newfoundland is in her second or third estrum. She is then sufficiently mature.

Mate whenever she flags and howls for the male — this is the height of the season. Get a long tie, usually five to thirty minutes. Skip a day and try to breed her the second time. If the second service is refused, it is a good sign. Probably the first breeding took and the bitch has gone out of season.

At Little Bear Farms we make a practice of breeding only from naturally good studs. During our first few years of breeding we resorted to breeding contraptions for holding the bitch and used assistance to accomplish a tie. With increased skill and growing confidence after more than twenty years, which we in turn conveyed to the Newfoundlands —the stud now does the job unaided.

Consider the advantages of the sire being a natural stud. Never use the dog for artificial insemination and then expect him to perform well in natural breeding. Choose for stud a dog with strong masculine traits, muscular and well coordinated.

By the same token, very feminine bitches make the best brood matrons and are actually easier to breed.

Break the stud in at about eighteen months of age, with an older, experienced bitch. It is more difficult if both parties of the *mating* are without experience. The breeding pen should afford privacy. Some Newfoundlands are reluctant to mate in public.

There is also an occasional stud who happens to be a strong exponent of monogamy and is willing to mate only with one bitch. We had one such in our early days of breeding. His name was Ch. Midway Black Ace. His favored spouse was Little Bear's Abundance O'Lady. We built him and his family a pen by a running mountain brook. There he raised his family. Black Ace taught his puppies to wipe their feet and not carry snow or mud into their dog house.

Whenever we came to visit them, my husband would ask, "Are you really a good husband, Buzz?" The big dog would wag his luxurious tail in affirmation and proceed to pantomime the prerogatives of a husband.

A young stud should not be used more than two to three times per week. Generally a dog should not be used for stud service before a year of age. If you should use him before one year of age, positively do not repeat until he is more than a year.

Avoid great disparity of size between the stud and the bitch.

A good Newfoundland stud seldom welcomes assistance except when being broken in for the first time. If your dog is not a natural stud, and unless you have an expert, your dog may require the assistance of three people: one holding the bitch by the collar, one keeping the tail out of the way and one keeping a knee under the bitch's belly to prevent her from sitting under the weight of the stud. A fourth may be required to manipulate the actual insertion and take care that the knotting does not occur outside the bitch. It is sometimes necessary to use full strength to keep the dog and bitch joined until knotting inside occurs.

Once a tie is accomplished it is sometimes advisable to hold the bitch so that the stud does not get dragged around during the tie. This could injure the stud seriously.

Do not feed the stud for at least six hours previous to service. Normal ties last from five to twenty minutes or more. Conception is possible when the stud ejaculates within the bitch even when there is no tie. In such a case keep the bitch from urinating and hold up her hindquarters for a minute or two to retain the sperm.

Use of hormones is *not* recommended. Vitamin E in natural form, wheat germ or wheat germ oil, plus a diet free of preservatives and with plenty of fresh, raw, red muscle meat and fresh, raw beef liver are in order.

It is obvious to anyone that the bitch must be in top condition at mating time or she should not be bred. Carrying the puppies, nurturing them prenatally and after whelping, requires that she be in excellent health and able to give without overdrawing from her own resources.

Also there is a theory, which is gaining credence, that both parents must be in top condition at mating for genetic reasons. The claim is that the parents throw their dominant genes when in excellent condition and their recessives when in poor condition. Inasmuch as generations of selective breeding, by design of man or nature, tends to make the most typical, hence desirable, characteristics dominant, we should go along with nature and only breed from the dogs and bitches in good health and muscle tone which can impart their best.

In Whelp

Try to breed the bitch in the morning. If you do, so the theory is, she will, likewise, start whelping in the morning.

Gestation period in Newfoundlands as in all dogs, and wolves is sixty-three days. Occasionally there is one who whelps in sixty-four, even sixty-five days. If the matron's temperature stays under 101.8 and there is no black or brown discharge from the vulva, do not be alarmed. However, anything over the normal period should be taken up with your veterinarian. You count your days from the first and from the last tie. All ties should be recorded and the count could be from any.

During the first four weeks of pregnancy the Newfoundland bitch can remain with her pen mates, play with children, and pursue normal activities with the exception of swimming. She should not sit in water, nor wade in water above her knees.

Immediately after the breeding, an ounce or two or raw beef liver should be added to her regular diet. Her daily meat should be at least three to five pounds of *raw* beef, plus an abundance of milk, whole raw if possible. Carotene, brewer's yeast and wheat germ should be maintained in her diet.

In the event the bitch was not successfully wormed prior to mating, it can be done safely at three weeks in whelp.

From the fifth week on, the bitch in whelp should be separated from her companions. She should be encouraged to have plenty of exercise, but care should be taken that she does not try to squeeze through narrow openings. This is the time of prodigious digging and the bitch may try to tunnel under her dog house or perform some similar action. If the tunnelling is too successful, level it at once.

The bitch in whelp should retain her muscle tone. Take her for long walks but keep her away from her kennel mates and small children.

During the last two weeks, introduce the bitch to her whelping room and her whelping box. Let her sleep in the box.

Location of the whelping room is of importance. It should be in a quiet spot, away from other animals and strangers. The matron must feel completely secure. In the winter it is very important that the bitch be transferred to indoor facilities, two to three weeks prior to due date. This points up the necessity of keeping your records of matings. Carelessness, especially for a winter whelping, may cause the loss of part of even all of the litter.

Remember that the puppies will be coming out of body heat temperature environment of more than 100 degrees. The first two weeks after they are whelped they will be developing ability to adapt to a lower temperature. See that the change in temperature does not present too much shock. Give the puppies time to adjust.

Be prepared, with heating pads to be put inside the grocery store cartons which will be their basinettes. If it is not a summer whelping, have an electric heating tape running under the floor around the perimeter of the whelping box. Thus the area under the shelter of the ledge will be warm for the puppies without overheating the mother. Plan on keeping your whelping room at about 80 degrees, plus installing an infra red lamp for higher heat for a limited puppy area.

Most important: During the last four weeks the bitch is in whelp she will require tremendous amounts of fresh water. Use a 12-quart stainless steel milking pail and have the water changed three to four times a day — *changed, not just added to.* The bucket must be washed thoroughly in between waterings. Avoid all detergents. Ivory Snow is safest, but even it must always be well rinsed away.

Prior to whelping, the coat should be cut from around the vulva under the tail. Equally important, expose all the nipples by trimming the fine undercoat which surrounds them right down to the skin. This will keep hair out of the puppies' mouths.

The basic list for supplies needed for whelping should be checked and everything should be ready for the happy event:

1. Clock and calendar
2. Record sheets (with previous records and sheets prepared for whelping data and individual puppy records)
3. Baby scales

4. Electric heating pads (two, each with three heat levels)
5. Cardboard cartons (two, large, fresh clean, not previously used for detergents, cleaning materials, or anything possibly toxic)
6. Scissors, dull
7. Iodine (tincture of, double strength)
8. Ear syringes (2)
9. Nail brush
10. Surgeon's glove
11. Sterile lubricant
12. Thread (linen carpet thread, sail thread or 10 cotton thread *never colored*)
13. Hypodermic syringes and needles (disposable)
14. Oxygen and mask
15. Oxytocin (20 USP strength)
16. Cambiotic
17. Glucose (5% in saline solution)
18. Malted milk tablets
19. Honey
20. Raw ground chuck
21. Raw beef liver
22. Hypodermic syringe (10 c.c.)
23. Baby feeding tube
24. Turkish towels or soft rags (12)
25. Large stack of newspapers (black and white newsprint only)
26. Alcohol
27. Infra red lamp for whelping box
28. Heating element electric tape under whelping box.

Whelping

A Newfoundland will rarely touch her food for about twelve hours prior to whelping, but will drink increasingly greater amonts of cool, clean water. Sometimes she will drink milk during this period and if she can drink it without altering her stool consistency, milk should be encouraged. Once in a rare while there will be a bitch whose appetite does not flag. She will eat, up until whelping begins.

A better indication of impending whelping is the breaking of water. This varies in time, but when it happens you know that the whelping time is drawing close and the bitch bears continuous watching.

Whether or not it is the first whelping for the bitch, she becomes restless and nervous. Presence of a competent person is highly desirable. If inexperienced, a visit from your veterinarian at this point is to be considered.

If the 63rd day has arrived and labor has not started, you sometimes can facilitate the birth by taking the bitch for a walk. Be sure to carry a towel and scissors in case she should drop a puppy while on the promenade.

Usually her temperature will drop to near 98° F. and begin to come back up within 24 hours of birth, normal temperature being 100.2 to 101.8.

Lack of fever, when overdue, is unfortunately not a reliable sign that all is well. There could be a dead puppy which might throw off the whelping schedule. A dead puppy causes a black discharge from the vulva. Clean discharge with odor of iodine is favorable sign.

Over the last twenty years or so, my husband and I have whelped more than two hundred litters at Little Bear. Yet I can say that each mother was an individual. Generally speaking, a young dam with good muscle tone can push the puppies out with the greatest of ease. Injudicious over-use of pituitrin in its various forms such as Oxytocin or P.O.P., will render the uterus flabby and in an extreme case may make it necessary to resort to a Caesarean in later whelpings.

When labor starts there may be just a ripple of abdominal muscles and muffled grunts. The straining will cease and resume at greater intensity. Some bitches will squat for a final push, others will achieve the same results lying down.

The puppy arrives completely encased in a membranous bag filled with fluid. The dam may rip the bag open and sever the umbilical cord with her teeth.

If the bitch is too young, or gets tired or flustered, you may have to do this yourself and should always be prepared. If you are helping, do not tear open the bag until you have pulled out the placenta, or afterbirth, which is on the other end of the umbilical. Quite a stream of fluid will shoot out when the bag is broken and the puppy is not a live separate entity until it is out of its watery environment and draws its first breath.

If the dam is squatting, the shock of being dropped usually gets the puppy's heart going and produces the first breath. Sometimes it is necessary to jolt the puppy by swinging it, holding it by its rear legs, head down, to get the heart to beat and the lungs to operate. Paradoxically, it is the increase of carbon monoxide which triggers the breathing cycle. Consequently we have had situations where a puppy given up for dead began to breathe minutes later.

In normal birth the head of the puppy appears first, and the body will follow after a few moments of straining on the part of the dam.

With a breech presentation, unless it comes easily, it is best to have veterinarian assistance. If unavailable, place the bitch at an approximate 40° angle, with her forelegs on top of the whelping box and her rear on the floor. Have an asisistant hold her in this position.

Newborn puppy.

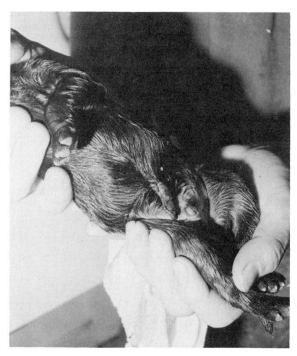

Wet puppy, just from dam.

Drying the puppy.

Using two fingers (for this you wear the surgeon's glove well lubricated with the sterile jelly) try to grab hold of the puppy's hindquarters now evident in the canal and pull gently but firmly, synchronizing the pull with the mother's labor. Be sure not to lose hold once your fingers have clamped on the puppy's hindquarters. If you should lose hold, the puppy will move out of your reach, back up the canal and it will take ever so much more effort on the part of the mother to push it back to the position where your fingers can again clamp around its limbs.

It is necessary to emphasize the importance of pulling out the afterbirth, as it too has a tendency to go back up the birth canal if let go. Frequently the mother will instinctively pull out the afterbirth and eat it. This is a perfectly normal thing to do and is essential for the mother's ability to make antibodies. There is one exception. Following a dead and decomposed puppy, the dam should be prevented from eating the afterbirth. The decomposing placenta should be removed at once and destroyed.

Since there are two horns of the uterus, after the first puppy is born, the second usually follows in a matter of minutes.

The room temperature during whelping must be maintained at 80° F. When born, the puppy is taken immediately away from the mother, the umbilical dipped in iodine and tied with a string if bleeding continues. The string, or thread, ought be linen carpet thread or whichever substitute you may have chosen. It is knotted about 1/16 inch from the naval.

If the dam has cut the umbilical cord too short and intestines start coming out, rush the puppy to the nearest veterinarian. He can push the intestines back in and stitch up the opening. Chances are if you get help within an hour, you will not lose the puppy.

If the umbilical cord was cut by the bitch but is too long, cut it closer with dull scissors, but do not cut it shorter than two or two and a half inches long. As soon as the puppy's umbilical cord is under control (or — in some cases — before if the cord is not severely bleeding), holding the head down, liquid must be drawn from mouth and nose with the ear syringe. Some puppies do not need this, others need it urgently. Next, the puppy must be thoroughly dried with the turkish towels or rags. These should have been washed in nothing stronger than Ivory Snow — *no* detergents.

Now the puppy should be put on the mother to suck until signs of the next labor appear. The first milk, or colostrum, carries the globulin and is high in A and D vitamins, both extremely important for the health of the newborn puppy.

Once it is definite that the bitch is through whelping, 6 c.c.s of cambiotic is routinely injected intramuscularly and this procedure is followed each day for four days.

The dam will seldom touch food during whelping. If she will take warm milk with honey, she may gain the immediate strength to postpone the oxytocin. Should calcium be somewhat low in her system, the milk will be especially effective.

Often labor can be induced by merely walking the bitch. If this will work, it is another means of postponing the oxytocin.

Toward the very end of the whelping, the bitch should be offered *plain lean raw hamburger* or raw beef liver. The raw meat will prevent any possible cannibalism. Cannibalism is very rare, but do not blame the bitch if it occurs for you can prevent it.

Injection of oxytocin will not only induce labor but also brings down the milk.

When the bitch is through whelping, take a bucket of lukewarm water with Ivory Snow and immerse her whole tail in the suds. Wash off her pantaloons. Remove all the soap with several lukewarm rinsings. Dry with turkish towels and hair drier. Then, and only then, when the mother is thoroughly dry, let her handle all of her newborn puppies.

The bitch is replaced in her whelping box which has been cleaned and covered with several thick layers of newspapers (black and white only — none with color).

When the new mother is relaxed in her box, place the puppies one by one on her nipples, being sure that each one sucks. This is usually a woman's job. It requires gentle patience. Sometimes it is necessary to hold the puppies on and squirt a little from mother's nipple to baby's mouth to get it started.

The mother will with her tongue nearly always wash each puppy under its tail and on its belly. In this way the puppy is stimulated to defecate and urinate. If the dam fails in this respect the puppies must be cleaned with cotton dipped in lukewarm olive oil. You simulate mother's tongue by rubbing cotton very gently under each puppy's tail and over its abdomen.

Once the whelping is over, a Newfoundland mother should be given a hearty meal. This may be easier said than done. Some new mothers reject their accustomed foods and must be tempted with something new. Start with two to three pounds of fresh, raw, lean hamburger. Do not add or mix anything with it. If this is not acceptable, try two to three pounds of plain cottage cheese.

The secret in feeding a choosy new mother is to abstain from mixing too many different ingredients in one dish. She distrusts hash. Keep to one ingredient at one time. This usually works. Although I recall one, a number of years ago, that we found would not eat anything but well-seasoned stewed chicken and corn bread for one week after each whelping.

Cutting the umbilical cord.

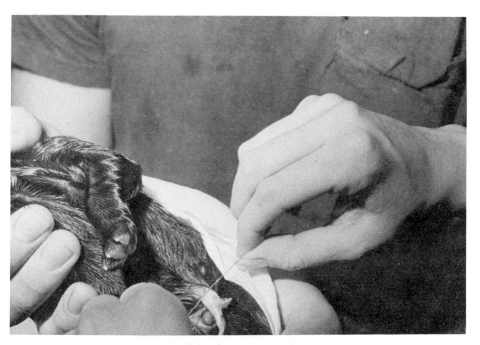

Tying the puppy's cord.

So, if she refuses both meat and dairy products, try chicken. Boiled chicken with all bones (excepting neck bones) removed will most likely work when everything else has failed. Raw beef liver should be provided routinely after the whelping. The new mother has remarkable tolerance for quantities of raw beef liver, up to five to ten pounds per day, while feeding a litter and still maintaining good consistency of stool.

As previously stated it is not safe to use oxytocin till the end or near the end of whelping. It is given when the uterus becomes tired and the bitch is too exhausted to push the puppy out. It may likewise be necessary when there is a dead puppy blocking the way. In this case, consult your veterinarian.

It has been our experience with the Newfoundland bitch that 5/8 of one c.c., 20 USP strength oxytocin, intramuscularly injected, is the correct amount for the first injection, either to help expel a lagging puppy toward the end of whelping or to expel an afterbirth.

Prior to this, it is necessary to ascertain that the birth canal is clear. Time of injection is written down and no further injection given for two hours. The second injection is automatically increased to 1 c.c. If further injections are necessary, the dose is increased by 1/2 c.c. each time. The gap of two hours between injections is always maintained.

The injections are continued until the retained puppy or afterbirth comes forth. Two hours later a final injection is given.

The average litter contains six puppies, but there may be only one. If it should be a litter of one, you may have extra trouble, for the puppy could then be too large for natural whelping and it may be necessary to resort to a Caesarean. The largest litter of Newfoundlands of which I have actual knowledge is twenty-four. Our largest litter was sixteen.

Since palpation may be somewhat misleading to an amateur, the veterinarian should check the bitch for being finished. Retained afterbirths or a dead puppy may cause serious trouble.

Eclampsia. As with anything else undesirable, the best cure for eclampsia is prevention. When the diet of the in-whelp birth is high in fresh raw milk, fresh raw meat including liver, cottage cheese, and with minimal (preferably no) chemical additives and of course, a daily (or at least every second day) carotene capsule and cooked buckwheat groats, a healthy Newfoundland matron is most unlikely to have eclampsia. With the between two and three hundred Newfoundland litters that we have whelped, we have never experienced a true case of eclampsia. With but one exception, warm milk with honey was all that was ever necessary to refresh a tired dam.

And even the one exception was not true eclampsia. In that case the bitch still seemed exhausted after the warm milk. She had had a very long and trying problem whelping. We had a veterinarian give her an intravenous calcium injection, which did the trick.

I personally do not believe that eclampsia is a frequent problem with Newfoundlands of any breeding line. But if during or after whelping, there should be signs of general weakness, twitching or clamping of the jaws, get veterinarian assistance.

Lactation

The greatest threat to the mother's ability to feed the newborn is fever. Fever may be caused either by retention of an afterbirth or a dead puppy. That is why I have tried to emphasize avoiding these possibilities.

Routine injection of cambiotic as suggested in the previous chapter, will help. A plentiful supply of fresh water, changed four to five times a day is a must.

Ample supply of milk-producing food is also necessary. Quantity of food should not be overlooked. *A Newfoundland mother nursing a litter of twelve would easily consume twelve to fourteen pounds per day!*

One of the best milk producers is corn bread, which the mothers usually eat eagerly. Next best to corn bread is corn meal mush, if the matron will eat it. For this, boil corn meal in a double boiler. Add fresh suet with liver or ground beef, chicken or any other available fresh animal protein. If glandular meat such as tripe, lungs and kidneys are to be used, make sure to add a generous supply of calcium lactate to maintain the proper calcium/phosphorous balance.

The new mother should be fed three to four times a day with milk in between. Further to increase milk, mix Horlick's malted milk with goats or cows milk, or feed malted milk tablets. Do not give malted milk prior to a regular meal as the appetite would be impaired. *Feed as dessert only.*

Use buckwheat groats cooked with ample fat and milk, as a substitute for, or change from, corn meal. To the buckwheat add boiled eggs and meat. Or in any case get about a dozen boiled eggs into one of the meals, perhaps with cottage cheese. The lactating bitch may need variety but the foods we have listed will prove best for producing milk. Moreover, the buckwheat provides essential vitamins and minerals. Of course it is necessary to maintain the natural supplements as outlined in the puppy feeding sheet and carried up to increases for adults. Double the amounts for an adult for a lactating dam.

A whelping box of proper design will save puppies from being rolled on and squashed against the side when the dam falls asleep.

However the greatest dangers to the survival of the new litter are strange noises and strangers in the vicinity of the whelping room. The new mother is most protective and in her effort to guard the puppies

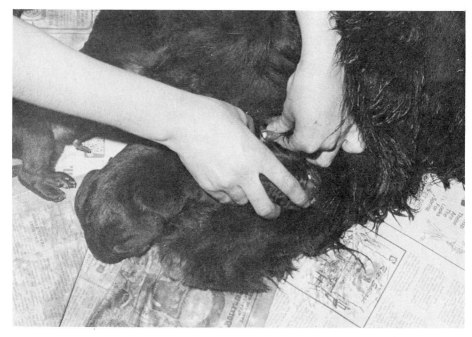

Squeezing nipple to get milk flowing, and to show puppy there is milk.

A 2-hour puppy.

can easily squash one. Do not make newly born puppies a social exploitation.

Count the number of nipples and if the litter is greater, divide into crews. Change the puppies every two hours with one hour for the mother to rest in between shifts. Those not nursing should be kept on their low heat electric pads within their cardboard cartons.

Should a puppy get chilled away from its mother during the night and lose its ability to suck, give saline glucose injections subcutaneously up to 20 to 25 c.c.s for a new born puppy. This is suggested as an emergency treatment. However it would be best to get your veterinarian for this. The injection should be followed with tube feeding to bring the puppy up to ability to suckle its mother. The best formula for tube feeding is simply raw goat's milk at body temperature. Next best is whole raw cow's milk. If neither is available use Esbilac, following instructions on the can.

A newborn Newfoundland puppy will take 10 c.c.s of milk per tube feeding. This should be done every two hours during day and night. At night if the crisis is past and milk from mother is available for the puppy which has suffered a set-back, time between tube feedings may be four hours.

For the technique of tube feeding, get help from your veterinarian.

When not on the mother, puppies should be kept on an electric heating pad inside a spacious carton, half covered on top with cloth secured with clothes pins. Keep the pad on low heat and cover it with a layer of cloth that can be removed and washed with Ivory Snow.

The whelping box should be kept clean and washed with Ivory Snow, nothing stronger. A low temperature heater should be kept under the whelping box floor, preferably one of the corners, unless an electric heating tape has been fastened under the floor of the whelping box. The new litter will gravitate naturally to the warm spot and the other will get accustomed to their position.

In the winter, an infra-red lamp can be used overhead as well, directly over the area being heated from underneath the whelping box floor.

Above all, the room temperature must be maintained at an even level of at least 75° F. until the puppies are four weeks old, preferably 80° for the first two weeks. Their enclosure must be free of drafts and dampness. Cellars and garages are most undesirable for whelping.

If there are no regular whelping facilities available at home, do not assume that a veterinarian will have facilities for whelping a Newfoundland. The multiple activities constantly going on in a veterinary hospital and the size of the cages are generally not suitable. You will do much better at home although you may have to convert your dining room to house the whelping box. We did just that with our first litter!

Weaning

Weaning begins as the mother's milk reduces. Adequate feeding with correct food can postpone the inevitable. But the puppies' teeth become sharp and the dam can no longer stand the punishment of the needle-like jabs, mother love notwithstanding.

In weaning, proper food consistency is essential. Food must be at body temperature and not too sloppy lest it get into the puppy's nostrils. It is important to wean each puppy individually. Take a cupful of cottage cheese, thoroughly mixed with a little honey and milk, and spoon feed the puppy until it gets the idea of eating from an individual dish without burying its nose in the food. This may take two to three days.

Weaning overlaps with nursing the mother. As the mother's milk reduces, the number of cottage cheese feedings increases from two a day to six or eight a day. By the time the dam has little or no milk, twenty minutes after the solid food the puppy is given milk to lap up out of a saucer — only a very little at first, increasing to a cupful each time.

Raw lean beef is first ground, then put through a blender, mixed with well cooked buckwheat groats or mixed baby cereal—two parts meat to one of cereal. This meat mixture replaces one of the cottage cheese meals. The quantity of the meals increases and the number of meals reduces to four a day. This takes place at about four to five weeks of age according to the progress of the puppies.

By the time the puppy is five weeks old it is usually weaned or nearly weaned. We usually separate the puppies from the mother part of the day, increasing the separation until at six to seven weeks the mother is only with the puppies at night, and final separation takes place at seven weeks.

Worming

Before the puppies graduate to lean meat, they should be wormed. This we do at three to four weeks. The puppy is given honey and milk the night before worming. Then 20 to 30 minutes prior to worming, the puppies are again fed honey and milk, a quarter cupful. The puppies are weighed and recorded and put in an individual stall.

Puppies are never wormed at their full weight. That is, if the puppy weighs six and a half pounds, it is wormed as if it were five pounds. At all points underworm them by ten to twenty percent of their actual weight.

A worming pill (we use Task) is inserted in the puppy's throat and one makes sure that the puppy swallows it. Then the puppy is given a mixture of baby cereal, milk and honey, rather thin in consistency.

Now this is most important: Each puppy must be kept in an individual stall for at least four hours after worming. After four hours the puppies can be put back with their mother and again fed milk and honey.

By this time you will be ready to pick up piles of roundworms unless the mother beats you to it. Be alert and save her from such an unpleasant chore.

Be extremely careful to follow religiously directions for worming in relation to pesticides, other medications, etc., as given on the container.

Puppies may receive measles vaccination earlier or, at about six weeks, tissue cultured live virus vaccine for protection from canine distemper along with vaccine for protection from canine hepatitis and leptospirosis. Whichever is used first, at between three and four months of age, the tissue cultured live virus vaccine must be repeated (or given for the first time) and given each following fall as a booster.

The greatest threat to survival of the newborn is inability of the mother to produce milk or weakness of the newborn and consequent inability to suck. There is always the chance, remote as it may be, that you could lose the mother. Should this happen, a wet nurse would be best, but may not be easy to come by.

High fever, if it should develop in the dam, would dry up her milk supply. Likewise inadequate calcium intake or assimilation of it, extreme youth of the mother or extreme infestation of worms could affect her milk supply.

Bearing in mind that the mother devotes full time to feeding and cleaning, it is next to impossible to equal the results of her efforts without going into almost continuous around the clock attendance of the newborn. Then it becomes a test of one's endurance, especially if the litter is large.

Bottle feeding is not only slow, but dangerous. It is too easy for the formula to be sucked into the air passages and cause mechanical pneumonia. Many a good Newfoundland puppy never matured to be weaned just through this very thing.

Fortunately tube feeding, judiciously handled, preferably by two people, can save the litter without too great a strain. One person holds the puppy upright with left hand using fingers of the right hand for gently prying the puppy's mouth open and holding it open.

The second person, using a 10 c.c. hypodermic syringe and baby feeding tube or a 18 rubber catheter tube, measures the distance from the puppy's mouth to the puppy's stomach which is situated immediately below the rib cage. The number two person will draw the lukewarm formula up into the syringe, insert the tube down the esophagus, pinching the tube with one hand to preclude milk escaping before the tube reaches the stomach. Then very slowly, the plunger is pressed and the formula squirted gently into the puppy's stomach.

With a newborn Newfoundland puppy we start with 5 c.c.s, gradually increasing to 10 c.c.s each feeding for the first week. The puppy is fed every two hours. It takes no more than a minute to feed each puppy.

Simple as the procedure is, it may be advisable to have your veterinarian demonstrate this method to you before you attempt it.

The danger of getting the milk into the lungs is still there, of course, but to a far lesser degree than with bottle feeding. Therefore, once one person in the family acquires this skill do not change your "syringe engineer" or the puppy holder.

Basic formula for tube feeding should not be changed unless you can move up higher on the preference scale.

1. Raw, whole goat's milk.
2. Raw, whole cow's milk blended with beaten raw egg yolk and honey.
3. Esbilac.

We use one egg yolk, one teaspoonful of honey to one cup of whole, raw milk.

Winter in northern climates is a difficult time to bring up a litter. Bear in mind that while enjoying its mother's womb, the puppy is accustomed to an even body temperature of more than 100°. That is why the change must be gradual, and maintaining the whelping room at an even 80° is in order day and night for the first two weeks. Even so, during the night, the puppy may get pushed away from the mother and get accidently chilled. Checking frequently during the night, especially the first week or two, is a great preventative.

Once the puppy is chilled you are in trouble. Chances are it will have diarrhea. You can detect diarrhea by a strong odor and wetness under the tail. You can detect dehydration, which usually follows diarrhea in puppies, by puckering of the skin and general weakness, resulting in ability to stay on the mother's nipple and suck.

At this point you need a veterinarian. And he may not be able to come to your aid. Yet time is critical.

To restore the body fluid in a Newfoundland puppy, newborn to one week old, we usually inject 15 to 20 c.c.'s of saline solution (5% dextrose in isotonic solution) subcutaneously, using sterile technique, not giving more than 10 c.c. in one location.

To stop diarrhea we use honey mixed with water, about one tablespoonful, and *entromycin* (a Pitman-Moore product).

In diarrhea caused by bacteria, we also find *entromycin* the most effective remedy, far superior to anything else we have tried. Again we mix it with honey and a little water and feed it with an eye dropper, not directly in the throat but inside the mouth to the back of the puppy's cheek. One tablespoonful of the mixture usually does the job.

It sounds like a lot of work, doesn't it? You should not put yourself through the long and intensive chore unless you have a firm desire to breed ever better Newfoundlands.

But there are compensations, too. You may see the nimbus of light over the heads of the baby Newfoundlands with which all are crowned at birth. The glow surrounding all new life is regenerating. And if you love them, and talk with them, some of the angel dust they bring with them just may rub off on you.

Feeding time for puppies just hours old. Note that umbilical cord of front puppy has not yet dried off.

Home.

Welcome—with love.

17

Care of
The Newfoundland

___

THE NEWFOUNDLAND is a traditional breed and Newfoundland love often runs in a family. It is very simple for a member of such a family to make his breed choice, as the deeds of nature's own gentleman are usually well ingrained in the fondest memories of childhood.

But there is also the newcomer — someone who may have been fascinated by the Newfoundland's majesty in the ring, or have seen evidence of his heroism, or have been captivated by his whimsical charm.

**First — Are *You* Right
For the Newfoundland?**

Once the Newfoundland takes possession of one's heart, the new love is a proverbial hope chest of fascinating discoveries which ultimately lead to the stark realization that one's life will never be complete without a Newfoundland puppy. Then arises the crucial question as to whether one can own a Newfoundland. The answer, you feel, depends on the climate of the area in which you live, the amount of space at your disposal, and the care required for this relatively long-coated dog.

Fortunately, the Newfoundland's marvelous adaptability to extremes of temperature can only be matched by his general hardiness. The breed is thriving in the kaleidoscopic varieties of climate from the arctic regions to the islands of Hawaii and Haiti, in Spain, Portugal, Italy and Morocco, not to mention our own Southern states. The Newfoundland adapts itself to climatic extremes by growing a thick undercoat in the North and an outer coat only in the hot South. High altitude or proximity for swimming will add to the Newfoundland's comfort in the tropics.

It must be borne in mind, however, that the South if humid is a hotbed of fungus; consequently, the matter of daily brushing and combing becomes of paramount importance for keeping the dog's skin in healthy condition. There are preparations which can be added to the rinsing water following a bath which will protect against fungus. Most of these preparations are toxic and may be dangerous to puppies. Read the small print on the label. Rotenone which is a root, and pine tar are safe.

We find Hilo, a commercial dip, safe and effective for this. This is the way we use it: First, with an eye dropper, drop one drop of castor oil in the corner of each eye to protect the eye. Then, shampoo the puppy using lukewarm water and lanolin shampoo. Rinse the puppy thoroughly in luke warm water, but do not dry it. While wet, immerse the puppy in a solution of the dip (three tablespoonsful of dip to each gallon of water). The solution should stay on for at least four or five minutes. Then dry the puppy, using towels or a hair drier. (The same procedure is used against ticks, only use a tick dip.)

You can raise a Newfoundland puppy as a family pet in a Manhattan apartment, provided you have the time and inclination to exercise the dog in a city park. We would not recommend the metropolitan way of life for a promising show prospect, although we know one city-raised Newfoundland that became an all breed Best-in-Show winner. It was Melvin Sokolsky's Little Bear's Eben, which he took to New York City at six weeks of age.

An acre or more of land in the country, a place on the bank of a river or lake, or an ocean beach is ideal. To raise a show prospect successfully it is best to have enough room to provide a hundred foot long run—a shorter run is a handicap. Preferably, the run should be adjoined by an equally long run for a Newfoundland companion to fence-run and exercise your show dog.

Selecting the Right Puppy

In selecting your first Newfoundland puppy, you will most likely want *just a pet*. You may fear that a show is a great ordeal for a dog and the idea that you would not want *your dog* to be confronted with such unpleasantness will influence your selection.

But curious as it may seem to you, the Newfoundland *loves* to show. Its gregarious nature is stimulated by crowds of friendly admirers at the show ring and at the bench. Nothing is more misplaced than sympathy for those poor suffering show dogs. They certainly are not straining at the bars of their gilded cages. To the Newfoundlands, a show is truly

At 3 weeks. At 4 weeks.

At left, 4 weeks old; at right, 12 weeks old. Elongation of muzzle begins to take place at 8 weeks, and one can no longer determine final shape of head until dog is mature. Head is last thing to mature in the Newfoundland.

a gala occasion. The dogs make new friends, big and little. And they are proud of their ribbons, and especially rosettes. One of our Little Bears, usually most social and outgoing toward people, once turned his back on throngs of admirers and sat transfixed, enjoying the sight of his first rosette tacked under his name on the back bench partition.

The most successful Newfoundland breeders never cease trying to preserve the best in Newfoundland character and virility as the very essence of best Newfoundland show type. And, this is what you want in a pet, too.

From the standpoint of price it pays to get the best you can afford, as it costs as much to feed a poor specimen as a champion. By going to a reputable kennel with a reputation to uphold, you're pretty much assured that you'll get what you pay for — and very often more.

As to price, the truth is that the show breeder can never hope to fully realize the actual out-of-pocket expenses incurred in producing an individual puppy. To the show breeder, however, breeding is not business and the kennels that breed the best usually do it as a sport and sell off the surplus not immediately needed for their breeding programs. Consequently when you do buy a puppy from a serious breeder carrying on a long-range breeding program, you may receive a one- or two-hundred dollar gift whether you know it or not. This is a clear case of getting something for nothing, but it is done for the good of the breed. That is how it is possible today to buy a good seven-week Newfoundland puppy for only $300.

If your basic selection of a reputable kennel was correct, you can put yourself entirely in the hands of the breeder and merely tell him which dogs of his breeding stock you admire the most and want the puppy to resemble physically and in personality. If you happen to have hit on a real breeder who understands genetics, he can foretell with some degree of probability what that lovely ball of fluff will be like when he reaches maturity. If, on the other hand, you are considering the purchase of a puppy from a breeder who possesses no sound knowledge of genetics, your guess may be every bit as good as his and this may be the proverbial potluck approach.

Should this be the case, the following are the points to analyze painstakingly:

1. Be sure that both the sire and dam are healthy. Look for good sheen of coat, clear eyes, pink gums, and plenty of spirit.

2. Be sure that the kennel runs are spacious, free of old stools, and that the puppies are clean and pleasant to smell.

3. Make certain that there are no loose stools in evidence. Examine the belly of the puppy for possible breaking out which would be a symptom of worms, unsanitary kennel conditions, or something worse.

6-weeks-old puppies.

3-months-old Landseer. Note lack of ticking at this age.

3-months-old black puppy.

4. Check the eyes to be certain they are clear.

5. The nose may be moist from excitement but avoid like the plague any sign of actual mucus.

6. Do not give undue importance to the largest puppy but give more consideration to the one that shows good coordination and moves most gracefully, has heavy bone and is in good proportion throughout. Be sure that the puppy moves and stands true.

7. Watch for well-developed occipital bone and prominent chest bone.

8. Avoid a puppy with a hollow or sway-back. He may grow out of it or he may not. Do not be beglamored by a puppy with an over-massive head — he may still grow up to be a cowhocked wonder.

Generally speaking, all other things being equal, the puppy exhibiting the most spirit, the most initiative at an early stage, is most likely to succeed both as a companion and as a show dog. Do not choose a puppy simply because he looks soulfully at you or runs toward you. This *could* result in the best choice, but not necessarily.

Dark eyes, of course, are desirable in a Newfoundland, but depth of color of the eyes at maturity is impossible to determine when the puppy is six or eight weeks of age. If both parents have light eyes you can be sure that the puppies will all have light eyes, otherwise chances are in favor of dark eyes.

Last but not least, you may be confronted with a great deal of talk about "typey dogs." Good type is, of course, desirable. But type is, to some extent, fashion, and within the broad limits of the Standard, it varies with the times. Current type is influenced by the dogs winning consistently in strong breed competition at the current shows. The Newfoundland is a working dog and by nature of its functions has to be a sound dog. Consequently, in order to be of good type he must be sound, sturdy, alert, well-coordinated, brave, and beneficent appearing. Arguments of type versus soundness should be discounted in the Newfoundland breed. *Soundness is inseparable from type.*

Back in the days when Alexander Wolcott was the voice of wisdom in the American theatre, a young dramatic aspirant asked him what was the best way to achieve theatrical success. He answered, "Choose your grandmother."

The same advice might be given those who want success in choosing the best puppy. A young man may be wise in observing a girl's mother before gambling on lifelong marital bliss with her. And you will have better fortune in selecting from all the engaging bits of fluff that may wag their tails as they run to you, a puppy whose dam, sire, grandsires and dams have the quality you seek.

The choice between male and female for companion is purely personal. The female, of course, has the mother instinct and in families with babies or very small children nothing could be sweeter than the Newfoundland nursemaid as exemplified by Nana, immortalized in Peter Pan. The female Newfoundland has a strong attachment to home, abounds in affection, and is unsurpassed for gentleness with both children and adults. The male is always ready to get children out of trouble after they are in it. The female worries more over children and tries to prevent trouble. They are equal in devotion and valor for protection.

Care of the Newfoundland Puppy

A Newfoundland puppy is usually weaned at four to six weeks of age and by the time it is seven weeks old should be ready to join its new family. It is important to introduce changes in the puppy diet gradually. Usually the kennel will supply the new owner with instructions for preparing the diet on which the puppy was weaned.

This is the way we feed at Little Bear:

NEWFOUNDLAND FEEDING SHEET

Do not at any age give synthetic vitamins or mineral compounds, or special vitamin pills, etc. — only the natural vitamins and minerals as listed below under daily supplements.

First year: no glandular meat, no meat by-products. Exception: liver up to 2 ozs. daily.

6 weeks to 10 weeks: 3 meals daily (lukewarm)

Basic meal: 1 cup finely ground, very lean, raw beef. NO FAT. Mix with hot water to take off chill. Add Gerber's mixed baby cereal to consistency of hamburger. Basic meals morning and dinner time.

Noon meal is of cottage cheese (1 lb.). Until 3 mos. of age, add warm milk to cottage cheese to take off chill and add mixed baby cereal to consistency of hamburger.

10-weeks-old bitch.

3-months-old bitch.

Bitch and male at 12 weeks.

To one of the basic meat meals add the following supplements (which may be purchased at health food stores) daily:

¼ tsp. sea kelp
¼ tsp. wheat germ
1 tsp. bone meal*
carotene
1 pinch brewer's yeast
½ tsp. calcium lactate

About 20 minutes after meals give lukewarm milk (about 1 cup). Goat milk is best, next raw, whole cow milk. Increase amount gradually.

All amounts increase, meat to 2 lbs. per day at 4 months.
Supplements also increase gradually:

Sea kelp to 1 tsp. at 6 mos.
Bone meal probably to ¼ cup at 3 mos.
Cod liver oil to 1 tsp. at 3 mos., 2 tsps. at 4 mos., 1 T. at 6 mos.
Wheat germ to 1 tsp. at 3 mos.
Brewer's yeast increases very gradually to 1 tsp. at 6 mos.
Calcium lactate to 1 ½ T. at 6 mos.
(These supplements need no further increase.)

10 weeks to 3 months: Continue with 3 meals, lukewarm. Also remember NO FAT. Fat cannot be digested before puppy is 6 mos. of age. Cooked whole grain cereal (such as quick oats or whole wheat cereal) can replace baby cereal. Cooked buckwheat groats (kasha) is an excellent cereal. The objection we find to kibble is in the chemical preservatives, artificial flavorings, artificial colorings, anti-oxidents, etc. Some kibbles are better than others. The purer and the less chemical additives the better.

*Bone meal must be edible, not fertilizer. Neither bone meal nor calcium lactate can be assimilated without Vitamin A—in this diet supplied by carotene.)

3 months: Increase meat to 1 ½ lbs. per day, cottage cheese to 1 ½ lbs.

4 months: Increase meat to 2 lbs. per day, cottage cheese to 2 lbs.

6 months: Two meals a day.
Begin to add fat to diet — very gradually. Never more than 20% suet by volume and *very* less in concentrated form (2 T. lard, 1 T. corn oil). Fat must be limited strictly in relation to stool. Fat is loosening. Cotton seed oil is not desirable.

1 year: Combine solid meals into one — about 4 qts. Drop calcium lactate. Other supplements can be continued but other than carotene and sea kelp, not so critical. If cooked cereal is too much nuisance, substitute milk bone, crumbled, or a good kibble, such as Old Mother Hubbard, which has less chemical additives than most. After puppy is 10 weeks old, give plenty of fresh water between meals. If hot summer weather, water must be provided from 6 weeks of age.

Correct feeding the first year, is essential for longevity, normal bones, and full development, with fewer trips to the veterinarian. With the giant breeds, growth of bone structure is so great during the first year that the daily feeding must include balanced nutrients for the bones themselves. For the young puppy, the most complete food is milk before tampering. Nothing equals raw milk for the young puppy.

Tests show that milk can be rated: first, raw goat milk second, raw whole cow's milk. At Little Bear we use raw milk exclusively. From our good friend, neighbor and Newfoundland fancier, Helen Hunt, we are often able to get milk from her prize herd of Toggenburgs. At other times, we fall back upon raw cow's milk. For the first six months, it is worth the extra expense of raw milk from a health food store, if no dairy is available.

Sea kelp provides the trace minerals, as well as organic iodine. Edible bone meal should be a regular part of the diet. Calcium lactate should balance the phosphorous in the meat. The meat is very important for the growing puppy. We rely heavily on raw, lean, muscle meat, no meat by-products the first year because they are much too high in phosphorous, and no meat fat before six months of age because fat is indigestible by young puppies.

In order to avoid chemical additives, we feed cooked cereals in place of kibble to a great extent, but find some kibble useful for emergencies, and to help reach the right consistency in the food. The kibble that we use must have the least possible amount of chemical additives. It is wise to avoid artificial flavoring, coloring, preservatives and anti-oxidants.

In this world of pollution, we avoid most pesticides and all chlorinated hydrocarbons, such as DDT, chlordane, etc. Protect your puppy from detergents, lead or mercury paint, sponges and plastic toys.

Some time ago a man was introduced as a very witty man. The one to whom he was presented exclaimed, "Say something funny." It is from such a vacuum that once in a while a new owner will expect his new puppy to scintillate. The Newfoundland puppy will go at least half way in showing charm. But let the new owner be reminded that he must talk with the new puppy, give attention and even something of himself to make the puppy bloom.

The best Newfoundland puppies are made of love, good genes, love, correct prenatal and early postnatal feeding, love, and correct environment. It is up to the new owner to continue with these important elements of puppy-raising.

Love is not just mush. Results are of tangible, measurable value. Love helps the glands to perform well. Love and security help to build a more stable nervous system, true Newfoundland character as well as rapport with you.

At ten weeks.

Yearling.

First swim—puppy being trained to water.

Being taught to retrieve.

Puppy Training

One summer, a few years ago at Little Bear, we did some experimental training with four-week-old puppies and older puppies of varying ages. The trainer began by taking one puppy out of sight of all other dogs and people. For a few moments he would pet the puppy, then take a hard rubber ball (too large for the puppy to swallow) and gently roll it a few feet. The puppy invariably ran after the ball and when asked to bring it back, would do as asked. The exercise was repeated several times, stopping when the trainer thought the puppy's interest might be about to lag. Each time the ball was fetched, the puppy was praised. The trainer always used a soft voice, gentle motions and strongly willed the puppy to comply with instructions.

Training continued for one week. After two months with no interim training, we found that puppies that had had basic fetch training at even four to five weeks of age, had lost none of their enthusiasm for retrieving. Tossing the ball a very short distance was the next step in fetching exercises. Distance of toss was gradually increased and dumbbell and sticks were introduced. The utmost patience is needed by the trainer and progress must be geared to the aptitude of a puppy. Lead training should follow fetch training.

Swimming in a little wading pool was made available for the four-week-olds. Here we found that, like many children, the puppies cheated a little and while "swimming" with their front legs, their rear feet were on the floor of the pool. All of the older puppies, six weeks and more, followed trainers into the deep pond; swimming was group training at this point.

I feel strongly that early retrieving for Newfoundlands is the best possible way for developing the desire to cooperate. The dog will always bring you something, itself and its love. New owners of young puppies, older puppies, or grown Newfoundlands could probably do nothing better for their special relationship with the Newfoundland than to repeat or initiate retrieving exercises, starting as we did with our four-week-old ones with their head start program—gently, patiently and lovingly.

To accustom the puppy to walking on lead, a few minutes a day for a week or so is all at the most that should be needed. Use a slip (or choke) collar, very lightweight for the young puppy. Length should be two inches more than distance around neck. Remove collar when the lesson is finished. Never leave a slip collar on an unattended dog. The dog could get caught and injury might ensue. If the collar is not readily accepted, stop the first lesson there. Usually gentle flattery will take care of any reluctance.

When the collar is accepted, snap on a lightweight leash. If the puppy rejects the lead, drop your end of it and let the puppy play with the lead dragging (only under observation). After a few minutes you may be able to take your end of lead and walk off with the puppy. If not, snap off the lead, remove the collar, and repeat the lesson next day.

When puppy ceases to reject the lead, it is time for a short walk. At first, keep the leash loose and walk with puppy rather than puppy with you. Later the slip collar is used for control, a quick jerk and quick release makes you the master and does not disturb the dog. But always make the lesson a happy game. The collar and leash must be loved objects to the puppy, signs of fun to come.

Newfs are very proud. Praise for anything done right will get better results than scolding for an error. Praise is better reward than tid-bits for the Newfoundland. The power of your own thinking cannot be overemphasized. You should be able to con a recalcitrant Newf into being well behaved. Basic in controlling a Newf is a firm intention and a loving heart.

Housebreaking is very easy with Newfoundlands. If the puppy is kept indoors, as may be necessary if it comes to you in the winter, let it out first thing in the morning, last thing at night and after each meal. A pen is best for training. Newfoundlands do not like to take care of their needs on lead. When the puppy has done what it should, invite it back in the house.

If it should be deep cold and your puppy is young it may be necessary to keep the puppy indoors altogether. In that case, the floor of the room where the puppy is to be kept should be well covered with a thick, woven layer of black and white newspaper (not colored, the dye is harmful, even lethal, to very young puppies). Keep dirty papers well-picked-up and replaced. Newfoundlands are naturally fastidious and if you recognize this you can encourage a trait you will find nice to live with. When you discover the area the puppy likes to use, it will not be necessary to cover the entire floor. Gradually recede the papers to the area used.

Do not give a puppy access to the entire house until thoroughly housebroken.

A few days of careful watching may be all that is necessary to train a Newfoundland. Observe its behavior and try to get the message when the puppy needs to go out. It is far easier to prevent the first errors than to correct bad habits.

Of course, if the season is warm, your puppy can be kept in a pen until well housebroken, bringing it in only while it can be under surveillance and gradually increase the time that it is inside.

Never chain a Newfoundland. Anyone well acquainted with the breed knows fully well two of the underlying traits of the Newfoundland — his profound dignity and his love of freedom. I find now and then that an owner will occasionally chain a Newfoundland. The importance of abstaining from such practice cannot be overemphasized. Chaining can do irreparable damage to the Newfoundland's personality. Even if the chain is on a long line, this type of restriction is most harmful.

Quite another reason for not tying the family guard is that by so doing one may accidentally deprive himself of the dog's protection when most needed. Here is a case where a life might have been saved had the family Newfoundland been free. Of course, the young puppy is not going to be immediately able to act as a lifesaver. But its personality is vulnerable, and it does grow up rather fast.

This is the story of the Barrows family of Rahway, New Jersey, their child Annie and their Newfoundland, Dinah, from a clipping dated 1889:

> Ten-year-old Annie was generally entrusted to the tender care of the Newfoundland. They played together on the banks of the Rahway River which ran past the Barrows home, the dog always keeping the child away from the treacherous stream. One day, however, Mrs. Barrows chained Dinah to her kennel and leaving the child just for a few minutes, hurried to the front gate to buy some vegetables from the passing huckster. As Mrs. Barrows approached the gate she heard Dinah's frantic howl. She turned back and saw her dragging the whole kennel toward the river's edge. The Newfoundland was almost choking as she strained against her chain, striving to get to the river. It did not occur to Mrs. Barrows that her daughter Annie was in trouble. When suddenly realizing that something was critically wrong, she ran toward the river and saw her child going under for the last time with the chained Newfoundland helpless to save her.

Some Suggestions on Care
Applicable to All Age Dogs

If you buy an older puppy or even a grown Newfoundland to become a member of your family, most of the foregoing will apply. The feeding information is graduated for all ages.

Newfoundlands are unusually adaptable. Without forgetting previous loyalties, they can make new family alliances. One can buy one at any age. But just as the young puppy must be received with love so must the older Newfoundland.

In one instance a tragedy was barely averted when a yearling Newfoundland was brought to its new home in the owner's absence. This account points up the necessity of a real welcome with affection, food and water for the new dog member of the family. In this case the new owner, with day and night searching, helped by numerous Newfoundland friends, found the lost dog which for nine days had been wandering in the woods. The Newfoundland had escaped during her first night at the new home, obviously perplexed by strange surroundings and no real welcome. When either a puppy or grown dog arrives, it must be met with warm hospitality.

Summer eczema, or hot spots, can easily ruin the dog's coat overnight. If detected immediately the coat may be saved for the next day's show.

Wash the spot thoroughly with hydrogen peroxide and dry with sterile cotton. Separate gently the matted gummy hair.

Use solution (which can be put up at any drug store): 5% tannic acid and 5% salicylic acid in solution of grain alcohol. With a toothbrush, rub the solution into the infected area. Rub very hard. Be sure to break up the crust. Rub not only the affected area but also around the edges, covering the outer edges first and working toward the center.

In the summer it may be a good idea to give the dog a laxative dose of milk of magnesia.

Summer eczema is caused by fungus and is most prevalent in humid weather. However the diet of the dog may also be a contributor. Rancid fat, certain commercial dog foods with high content of BKA or BHT and other chemical additives may cause this condition or contribute to it.

Should the "hot spots" occur, take the dog off commercial kibble and feed fresh meat and cooked cereal, plus dairy products. Keep up the corrective diet until all symptoms are gone.

When the "hot spot" is healed completely shampoo the dog with lanolin shampoo. While still wet apply Sargeant's Sarcoptic Mange Medicine. Keep it on the dog for fifteen minutes. Then shampoo it off with the lanolin shampoo.

Another medical bath which is inhospitable to fungus is Hilo. When "hot spots" are caused by parasites such as fleas or lice, we recommend use of Hilo Dip as the specific. Fleas usually come from house cats or a sandy beach. Lice are usually carried by birds.

Before any bath, comb the dog thoroughly. Before any medicinal bath, first shampoo the dog with lanolin shampoo, making sure that the dog is wet through. Rinse thoroughly. Make about nine gallons of Hilo solution, four tablespoons of the Hilo to each gallon of water. Use as a rinse, making sure that it soaks into every inch of the body surface. Let the dog shake. Use a hair drier in the winter or sunshine in the summer to dry your dog.

Never let a Newfoundland lie on cement.

Never chain a Newfoundland. No trollies.

Groom daily if you like. Once a week is sufficient.

Use stainless steel 12-quart milk pails for water, thoroughly cleaned daily. Newfoundlands will not drink water from dirty pails. Always have plenty of clean water available. Avoid galvanized buckets.

Feed in stainless steel mixing bowls, four to five quart size. Remove and wash after each meal.

Mrs. Chern with her favorite puppy, Little Bear's James Thurber.

BIBLIOGRAPHY

ALL OWNERS of pure-bred dogs will benefit themselves and their dogs by enriching the knowledge of breeds and of canine care, training, breeding, psychology and other important aspec of dog management. The following list of books covers further reading recommended by judge veterinarians, breeders, trainers and other authorities. Books may be obtained at the finer boc stores and pet shops, or through Howell Book House Inc., publishers, New York.

Breed Books

AFGHAN HOUND, Complete — Miller & Gilbert
AIREDALE, New Complete — Edwards
ALASKAN MALAMUTE, Complete — Riddle & Seeley
BASSET HOUND, Complete — Braun
BEAGLE, Complete — Noted Authorities
BLOODHOUND, Complete — Brey & Reed
BOXER, Complete — Denlinger
BRITTANY SPANIEL, Complete — Riddle
BULLDOG, New Complete — Hanes
BULL TERRIER, New Complete — Eberhard
CAIRN TERRIER, Complete — Marvin
CHESAPEAKE BAY RETRIEVER, Complete — Cherry
CHIHUAHUA, Complete — Noted Authorities
COCKER SPANIEL, New — Kraeuchi
COLLIE, Complete — Official Publication of the Collie Club of America
DACHSHUND, The New — Meistrell
DALMATIAN, The — Treen
DOBERMAN PINSCHER, New — Walker
ENGLISH SETTER, New Complete — Tuck & Howell
ENGLISH SPRINGER SPANIEL, New — Goodall & Gasow
FOX TERRIER, New Complete — Silvernail
GERMAN SHEPHERD DOG, Complete — Bennett
GERMAN SHORTHAIRED POINTER, New — Maxwell
GOLDEN RETRIEVER, Complete — Fischer
GREAT DANE, New Complete — Noted Authorities
GREAT PYRENEES, Complete — Strang & Giffin
IRISH SETTER, New — Thompson
IRISH WOLFHOUND, Complete — Starbuck
KEESHOND, Complete — Peterson
LABRADOR RETRIEVER, Complete — Warwick
LHASA APSO, Complete — Herbel
MINIATURE SCHNAUZER, Complete — Eskrigge
NEWFOUNDLAND, New Complete — Chern
NORWEGIAN ELKHOUND, New Complete — Wallo
OLD ENGLISH SHEEPDOG, Complete — Mandeville
PEKINGESE, Quigley Book of — Quigley
PEMBROKE WELSH CORGI, Complete — Sargent & Harper
POMERANIAN, New Complete — Ricketts
POODLE, New Complete — Hopkins & Irick
POODLE CLIPPING AND GROOMING BOOK, Complete — Kalstone
PUG, Complete — Trullinger
PULI, Complete — Owen
ST. BERNARD, New Complete — Noted Authorities, rev. Raulston
SAMOYED, Complete — Ward
SCHIPPERKE, Official Book of — Root, Martin, Kent
SCOTTISH TERRIER, Complete — Marvin
SHETLAND SHEEPDOG, The New — Riddle
SHIH TZU, The (English) — Dadds
SIBERIAN HUSKY, Complete — Demidoff
TERRIERS, The Book of All — Marvin
WEST HIGHLAND WHITE TERRIER, Complete — Marvin
WHIPPET, Complete — Pegram
YORKSHIRE TERRIER, Complete — Gordon & Bennett

Breeding

ART OF BREEDING BETTER DOGS, New — Onso
BREEDING YOUR SHOW DOG, Joy of — Serann
HOW TO BREED DOGS — Whitne
HOW PUPPIES ARE BORN — Prir
INHERITANCE OF COAT COLOR IN DOGS — Litt

Care and Training

DOG OBEDIENCE, Complete Book of — Saunde
NOVICE, OPEN AND UTILITY COURSES — Saunde
DOG CARE AND TRAINING FOR BOYS AND GIRLS — Saunde
DOG NUTRITION, Collins Guide to — Collir
DOG TRAINING FOR KIDS — Benjam
DOG TRAINING, Koehler Method of — Koehl
GO FIND! Training Your Dog to Track — Dav
GUARD DOG TRAINING, Koehler Method of — Koehl
OPEN OBEDIENCE FOR RING, HOME AND FIELD, Koehler Method of — Koehl
SPANIELS FOR SPORT (English) — Radclif
SUCCESSFUL DOG TRAINING, The Pearsall Guide to — Pearsa
TOY DOGS, Kalstone Guide to Grooming All — Kalstor
TRAINING THE RETRIEVER — Kersle
TRAINING YOUR DOG TO WIN OBEDIENCE TITLES, — Morse
TRAIN YOUR OWN GUN DOG, How to — Gooda
UTILITY DOG TRAINING, Koehler Method of — Koehl
VETERINARY HANDBOOK, Dog Owner's Home — Carlson & Giff

General

COMPLETE DOG BOOK, The — Official Publicatic of American Kennel Clu
DISNEY ANIMALS, World of — Koehl
DOG IN ACTION, The — Lyc
DOG BEHAVIOR, New Knowledge of — Pfaffenberg
DOG JUDGE'S HANDBOOK — Tietje
DOG JUDGING, Nicholas Guide to — Nichola
DOG PEOPLE ARE CRAZY — Ridd
DOG PSYCHOLOGY — Whitne
DOG STANDARDS ILLUSTRATED
DOGSTEPS, Illustrated Gait at a Glance — Ellio
ENCYCLOPEDIA OF DOGS, International — Dangerfield, Howell & Ridd
JUNIOR SHOWMANSHIP HANDBOOK — Brown & Masc
MY TIMES WITH DOGS — Fletch
OUR PUPPY'S BABY BOOK (blue or pink)
RICHES TO BITCHES — Shattuc
SUCCESSFUL DOG SHOWING, Forsyth Guide to — Forsy
TRIM, GROOM AND SHOW YOUR DOG, How to — Saunde
WHY DOES YOUR DOG DO THAT? — Bergma
WILD DOGS in Life and Legend — Ridd
WORLD OF SLED DOGS, From Siberia to Sport Racin — Coppinge